Post to Post:
MEDITATIONS ALONG
THE WAY
Book 3

By
Rayola Kelley & Jeannette Haley

Hidden Manna Publications

POST TO POST 3: MEDITATIONS ALONG THE WAY

© 2023 by Rayola Kelley & Jeannette Haley

ISBN: 978-1-7347503-4-8

Except where otherwise indicated, all Scripture quotations in this book are taken from the King James Version

Hidden Manna Publications
P.O. Box 3572
Oldtown, ID 83822
www.gentleshepherd.com

Facebook:
https://www.facebook.com/HiddenMannaPublications/

CONTENTS

Introduction

This is the third book of the posts of Rayola Kelley and the second book of Jeannette Haley. This combined work is an invitation to the reader to step aside from the busy world, sit awhile, and joyfully meditate on the beauties and gifts of life, as well as ponder the simple truths of eternity, allowing them precious time to inhale the sweetness found in the breath of creation that surrounds each of us, while entering into communion with God.

These two authors' posts on Facebook continue to touch hearts, stir emotions, and inspire souls. Their desire for this book is that their combined efforts in these daily meditations will become a means of encouragement, inspiration, and comfort to those who are struggling with the dark days we are living in.

Rayola's posts are teachings that reach the mind to challenge and transform attitudes and perceptions, while Jeannette's writings, *identified by her name after them*, touch the soul to bring inspiration and healing. Rayola points to Scriptural principles while Jeannette highlights the simplicity of God's abiding love and care through creation and discoveries. Rayola's devotions are based on topical studies or select Scriptures to bring out scriptural truths. Jeannette's, on the other hand, are often based on personal experiences and Biblical insights about life.

It is the prayer of both authors that these simple, scriptural truths of God and life will inspire the reader to come apart and sit awhile to enjoy and be refreshed by the presence of God in the garden of communion.

January

January 1

A New Year always reminds me that every day is and has been a gift from God. We don't always appreciate gifts, and as a result we can discard them because we are ungrateful, ignore them because we are indifferent, resent and mock them because they don't meet our standard, and abuse or cast them away because we fail to recognize what we have and what it cost others.

God promised Abraham and his descendants the Promised Land, but in *Genesis 15:1* He told Abraham that *He was his shield and great reward.* If I am going to start fresh for the New Year, I must understand what is the essence of my spiritual inheritance, which is Jesus Christ; and therefore, I must first consider God.

To make God first seems like is an old adage, but the Bible tells me that for any change I must begin with the One who is able to change a matter. If God created everything and can recreate that which is without form, He can do the impossible in my life. The fact is, I am needy and I need Him. Therefore, I often think about God as my Creator.

Everything must be inspired by or end with God to ensure that life does not become stagnated with the old. There will be no victory or success in the present until the old is consumed by the new that is being brought forth by the hand of the Creator. He is truly the author of all that is new, alive, glorious, and everlasting.

Prayer: God, please never let me forget that You are the only Creator, and that You alone can give me life, change the terrain of my heart, and recreate me into a creature that will have purpose in the scheme of things. Create in me a new heart that seeks only You! Amen.

January 2

One of my favorite Bible stories is about Bartimaeus in *Mark 10:46-52*. He was the blind beggar who could not be silenced by the crowd as he cried out for mercy from Jesus of Nazareth. His cry was so loud and persistent that Jesus took note of it and called for the blind beggar to come to Him. The crowd told Bartimaeus to be of good comfort and arise for the Lord called him. When the blind man got up, he cast aside his garment and went to Jesus.

Jesus hears our sincere cries and puts forth an invitation. However, are we ready to cast aside the old to receive the new? After all, the old represents the decaying rags of that which possesses no life or hope.

It is my hope that the New Year will bring in the new, but I must first recognize and cast aside the old garments of the carnal, worldly life in order to come to Jesus. It is only then that I can know the liberty of moving forward to embrace the new.

Prayer: Lord, thank You for my life. You are the source of all that enables me to function in this present world. I am so thankful that it is You who determines the quality of my life. Amen.

January 3

Any unnecessary detour is exasperating, but when it has strange and unexplainable aspects to it, then it becomes unforgettable. Such was the case many years ago when a friend (I'll call "Mrs.

B") and I set off on a road trip to hopefully evangelize in small western towns.

After spending the night in an off-the-freeway motel, we noticed several signs that pointed the way to a scenic waterfall and decided to take the time to go see this apparently awesome sight. At first, we assumed it wouldn't be too great of a distance, but after following the narrow, winding road through low-rolling sagebrush covered hills for a few miles, we began to question the signs and arrows that had initially put us on this road. Suddenly, we saw a road sign that has me wondering to this day if it was really put there by man, or if it was a warning to me from God, for it said, WRONG WAY.

What did that mean? There were no cross roads anywhere, and the road we were on was a paved, two-lane road even though we never saw any other vehicles. But even with no river in sight, much less a waterfall, we concluded that the WRONG WAY sign didn't make sense and had to be a joke or mistake, and kept going until the somewhat spooky road simply ended at the freeway which we had traveled down the day before!

Fast forward about four years when the so-called "ministry" of "Mrs. B" did end up being the "wrong way." The Lord delivered me out of it, and although I was much poorer financially, I was much richer in wisdom and experience. Truly, *"There is a way that seemeth right unto a man, but the end thereof are the ways of death" (Proverbs 14:12).* – J. Haley

Prayer: Lord, as we begin any new year or journey, we must take stock in where we are going in light of where we need to be going. It is easy to take detours and we are so thankful that You are faithful to set out warning signs that will cause us to pause and discern the right direction. Amen.

January 4

As I get older, the one thing I hate is to waste time with frivolous things, yet I have wasted my time in the past. How do you capture time that seems to flow through your fingers like running water? It is hard to bear the thought that such moments, minutes, and hours will never be regained again to truly affect eternity.

When it comes to the matters of God, wasting time is often revealed when believers hit an impasse which expresses itself in stagnation. When spiritual stagnation takes place, it is always replaced with complacency, suspicion, contempt, and judgmental attitudes and requires a tough decision on the part of leadership. Do they continue on as before by wasting time where everything ends up in a type of Dead Sea, or do they humble themselves before God and seek His face as to what He wants to do?

It seems that most people want to play at Church rather than doing business with God to ensure their spiritual well-being. The Lord showed me before the fire of the Holy Spirit can come, the sword of truth and separation must first fall to cut away blinders from the heart, soul, and mind so one can see their spiritual plight.

Prayer: Lord, let the sword fall so that the fire of revival can come! Amen.

January 5

Creation shows us God's power and care. He can grow anything regardless of the place or circumstances. I know this is true for me. God has grown me up in some unusual terrain. He has saved me out of a cult, invited me to partake of His Living Water when I was in the military, called me out of the education system, taught me during challenges and failures, and put me in the vast mission field of America.

The path that the Lord has led me has not always been pleasant, but it is has been rewarding. During the journey I struggled against giving in to doubt, and with everything in me I have chosen to trust that He knew what He was doing for my benefit and His glory. It was in such times that I had to come to a place of contentment, while I rested in the work of sanctification being done in my life by the Holy Spirit and established in my actions of obedience.

We, as believers, need to remember that we must be prepared to grow in the place God has put us, regardless of the drudgery and difficulties. We must learn contentment as *Philippians 4:11* instructs to ensure that we walk in the ways of righteousness. It is only by trusting the Lord with the details of our daily lives that we can exercise godliness in our everyday walk (*1 Timothy 6:6*).

Prayer: Lord, it is hard to grow when we allow the sourness of ingratitude to take hold in our attitude, the bitterness of disappointment to define our present life, and the foul root of selfishness to entangle our perspective into an insipid reality of vanity. Give me the grace to grow in spite of the challenging terrain of my wretched soul and the ridiculousness of the world around me. Amen.

January 6

Apostle Paul stated in *Philippians 4:4, "Rejoice in the Lord alway, and again I say, Rejoice."* We have so much to rejoice about when it comes to the Lord. However, the perverse ways of the flesh and the perverted perception of the world keep us from realizing the beauty that belongs to us as heirs of salvation.

To keep all matters in perspective, I must constantly remember that Jesus stepped out of eternity and came to make His abode among us. He not only lived and died, but He rose from the grave to bring forth the joy of salvation. He is alive, and now I must make sure He is Lord of my life.

I must never return to being a type of Herod by succumbing to my old ways, for they can only destroy. Like the wise men who first diligently sought for Jesus when He was born, I must continue to daily seek Him until I meet Him face to face (*1 John 3:2*).

Prayer: Oh Lord never let me take a detour away from finding You! Let me always see You as that glorious shining star that must daily dawn within my heart and upon my life to cause the dark night upon my soul to flee. Amen.

January 7

It was just an ordinary trip to the refrigerator—the same refrigerator we bought when we moved into our current house about nine years ago. But this time, I had an "Aha!" moment, followed by the thought, "If you tell anybody about this, they'll think you're really a dumb bunny."

On the other hand, it caused me to laugh at myself, and laughing at myself has been a great help in mentally and emotionally surviving life. You see, our refrigerator doesn't have any dials or pushbuttons inside of it to set the temperature, or control that annoying ding-ding sound it makes when the door stays open past a certain point.

Of course, that gave me an excuse to not clean it too often, because all the "dinging" drove me nuts. Therefore, you can just imagine how happy I was when the "Aha" moment came, because instead of focusing as usual on the food items, I looked up instead—and right there in front of the very top of the refrigerator were all the digitized controls—in plain sight! All I had to do was look up, not in.

What an important lesson this is for all of us who are daily wading through a world of sin, sickness, suffering and sorrow. The LORD reminds us to look up, instead of within, for He and He alone is our help. *"And when these things begin to come to pass, then look up, and lift up your heads; for your redemption draweth nigh" (Luke 21:28).* – J. Haley

Prayer: Lord we do get busy looking around, looking within and looking about, ending up focusing on nothing much, and becoming lost in some of the silliness of things. Lord, You are in none of it; rather, You are above all of it. Lift my chin up when I'm down, and cause me to look up when my focus is on the insignificant. Amen.

January 8

Today I meditated on how I first met Jesus. Initially, there was no real semblance or understanding as to who He must be to bring order to my life. I was excited and zealous about what He did for me, but love must be two-sided if it is to grow. It was when Jesus became real to my spirit, unveiled by heaven itself over a period of time, that love proved to be a springboard for spiritual growth that brought me to places of excellence (*John 16:13*).

As I looked back at the preciousness of meeting Jesus, I could not help but presently count my blessings that have come through His grace. But, when it comes to knowing Him in an intimate way, one discovers there are so many treasures and promises attached to Him, it will transform how you look at Him. Admittedly, in my initial encounter with Jesus as a sinner in need of forgiveness, I fell in love with the idea of Jesus due to His redemptive work, but I had not yet developed a love for who He is.

As believers, we need to keep in mind that the more we seek the Lord to know, love, and serve Him the more we become acquainted with the abiding power from above and develop a love for who He is and not what we imagine Him to be. After all, such imagination will always prove to be hollow and unrealistic, a self-serving idolatrous image of a god of our own making.

Prayer: Lord, You found me and I so appreciated the gift of salvation, but then in time I learned of You and the love that was a simple little bud grew into a beautiful flower that had such a sweet aroma that it brought a higher level of worship. Amen.

January 9

Healthy love will naturally grow, and the only healthy and lasting love is the love of God (*1 John 4:8*). The world's love is often aborted on the runways of selfishness and cast aside by disillusionment, fantasy, and perversion.

In every area of "love," there is an initial love that is exciting, but fickle and will emotionally fade. It is for this reason we must choose the way of love. For initial love to graduate to a state of maturity it requires the good will of faith that makes the necessary commitment to do what is right and honorable which as believers is our reasonable service to others. However, faith that endures to the end reveals that godly love, without any thought or fanfare, can become sacrificial in how it expresses itself, becoming a sweet savor to God.

Godly love is a commitment to do what is right in all matters. Initial love says nothing is too good for the one I love, but because it fades as the emotional tide recedes into reality, its passion wanes with it. This is when fickle love becomes disillusioned about the one it has been directed towards.

Each step of godly love is established by a commitment to honor or prefer the person over self regardless of feelings. Each time that commitment is reaffirmed, the life of Jesus becomes more real to the soul and His very Person sweet to the spirit. Along the way we discover that our fleshly, silly, sentimental notions about love are gone and our worldly, perverted ideas of it have dissipated like a vapor.

We need to discern what we love, our idea of God created out of ignorance or our understanding of God that has been unveiled to our spirit by the Holy Spirit through the Word of God. The latter is founded on the eternal foundation of heaven and will stand no matter what buffets it.

Prayer: Lord, my initial sentiments about love towards You were silly and as I grew, I had to shed the world's presentation of love that proved to be idolatrous and self-serving. I want Your love to be shed abroad in my heart by the Holy Spirit and OUT of good faith I want to apply it to my heart attitudes and IN good faith exercise it when it comes to others for Your glory. Amen.

January 10

I often meditate on the wrestling matches I find myself in. It seems that the waves of life constantly knock me down on the mat of reality. I am either knocked down by circumstances out of my control, confusion that shakes my understanding and throws me off guard, and blindsided by unexpected events, or just buried by the onslaught of challenges and storms.

This should not surprise me because Jesus warned in *John 16:33*, that there is much tribulation in the world but we need not fear it. The world has and always will be wrought with troubled seas on every front.

Due to technology, we are seeing much of the world in chaos and whether we like it or not we are here for such a time as this. At times I find myself feeling a bit distraught by what I see, perplexed over what I know, and overwhelmed by what I hear, but I realize that even a greater battle is going on in the unseen world.

The problem with looking around is that we can easily enough become despairing over our limitations to change a matter, sickened by the evil that seems to be successful in its bid to take souls captive, and hopeless due to the current of insanity that seems to be drowning many people. It is for this reason I take stock in what is true to remind myself that our only hope in this world is not of this world, but is of that which is unseen and eternal.

When all we see are troubled seas around us, we can only look up to find any real hope. We are reminded that Christ is in our boat of life and that the troubled seas may cast us about, but we are anchored to the Rock that can't be moved even by the worst winds of our times.

Prayer: Lord, I know I am here for the benefit of others and Your glory. I am held firm to You by the rope of redemption and no matter how high the waters reach, like Noah's ark, I will be lifted above it all by Your Spirit. However, Lord I can't help but to declare the same words as the Apostle John prayed in *Revelation 22:20, "Even so, come Lord Jesus."* Amen.

January 11

Through the years I have realized that even though Jesus set me free by His Spirit and Word, I still find myself tripping over some rotting, decaying piece from my past. Whether it is a sin that Satan wants to once again take me captive by putting me in a prison of guilt and condemnation, or some silly foolish action that loves to taunt me over my ineptness and failures, I must be ready to stand on what I know is true about the Lord, resist the devil's attempts to bring me under any condemnation, and draw near to the Lord for His perspective, knowing that past sins are under the blood, present battles have been already won at the cross, and future indictments and challenges have been settled in the courts of heaven.

It is important that our past be put in perspective so that we can presently stand on the Rock in preparation to advance into the future as an overcomer. I must remember at such times it is because of past entanglements and attachments that the Lord has to put an axe to the roots that have supplied the old life. After all, what is not of Him will not survive the holy fires that purge and purify as we are set freer to discover the great heights of His glory.

As believers we must not allow attachments from the past to pull us back like a dog to his vomit; rather, we must look back and remember that the work of the cross was complete and now I can presently stand in assurance and move forward in confidence to discover the life, calling, and gifts the Lord has for me in order to finish the course set before me.

Prayer: Lord, thank You for coming. You want to give what is beneficial and eternal to me so that my life can produce fruits that will glorify You. Prune, purge, and purify me, but O' Lord, I ask you to heal me from the deep cuts of Your axe of judgment upon the dead ways of my old life and fill them with the fullness of Your precious Spirit. Amen.

January 12

To walk with God as Enoch did and to find grace as Noah did points to being consumed by the Lord's everlasting faithfulness, while being translated into His eternal kingdom. We must remember that our days are numbered in which we can learn to walk with God and grow in the knowledge of His bountiful grace.

In following the Lord, I have learned that His grace will form an ark in which I will find refuge. I know this ark to be Jesus who is the way through this world, the truth about God's great provision of salvation, and the essence of life that I so seek (*John 16:6*). The ark reminds me that I do not have to be consumed by sin that abounds around me, and that I can truly find rest from the weary battles the world brings my way.

When I think of Enoch, I realize it is not the quantity of man's life that counts but the quality. Enoch lived a short time on the earth compared to others of his day, but he learned to walk with the Lord and that is what made him larger than life.

Prayer: Lord teach me to walk with You—to walk in Your footprints according to Your stride. I do not want to weary You with my frail humanity, instead I want to please You in fellowship and worship. Amen.

January 13

Suddenly all we could see was a big, black blank. It was if some invisible jokester timed the "No Signal" event at almost the very end of an old black and white western movie that we were watching. After patiently sitting through what seemed like more commercials than actual movie time, we were hanging on to find out who had really "dunnit."

The sheriff had awakened from his coma, and was making his way into the room where the men had gathered who either knew the truth and wouldn't talk, or who were trying to find out the truth themselves. Only the sheriff would solve the mystery. And now we would never know!

This is the type of scenario when my imagination kicks in and I try to "write" my own ending. Of course, I know that my idea isn't the "real" ending, but still, a person hates to be left dangling at the end of something with unanswered questions.

This all brought to mind how so many of us believers try to "finish" the story of someone's life who has passed on so that we can go on in peace. Let's face it, sometimes we're left with a different kind of "big, black blank" when it comes to the spiritual life of those who spent their life balancing "on the fence." We want to believe with all our hearts that they are resting in the arms of Jesus, but sometimes we just don't know.

I've discovered, in such times of uncertainty, that the Holy Spirit is able to give the "peace that passes all understanding" to my heart. (See *John 16:7; 14:18; Matthew 5:4; Psalm 94:19; 2 Corinthians 1:5.*) After all, He is our Comforter! And, in the meantime, let us who belong wholly to the LORD Jesus Christ make sure that when He calls our name, we will leave behind no doubt in the hearts of our loved ones as to how our story on this earth ended! – J. Haley

Prayer: Lord, we all want matters to turn out right for everyone, but we know that You are the only One who can assure that a life turns out right. You provided mercy to take harshness out of judgment. Meanwhile, other than sharing the Gospel, we can rest that the matters of salvation do rest in Your hands and that You will be just in the end. Amen.

January 14

I was thinking of what the heart of God reveals towards man. He called the first man, Adam, from his hiding place to confront the tragedy brought on by disobedience. He is forever calling us to receive the promised provision, miraculously brought forth through the seed of a woman. We know this provision to be a person, a man, the promised Messiah. And, what is God's heart towards us—to be reconciled back to Him in a relationship of worship and communion.

This is why the Father sent His only Begotten Son. As the promised Messiah, Jesus would overcome the death wrought by rebellion. This act and promise of redemption which points to ownership, is necessary when it comes to rooting out the enemy in our midst.

If we are to overcome, we must not only be aware of our own rebellious, treacherous hearts, but of the enemy's devices that entangle our flesh and pride into a web of thievery, death, and destruction. The truth is we will either overcome our enemies through Christ or succumb to the lies of the god of this world, Satan.

Prayer: Oh Lord it is so easy to become lost in deception and sin. Our humanity is so fragile and weak in its fallen state. We are fickle and lack wisdom to properly see You. Lord, have mercy on me. Show me my own heart and give me discernment as to where the enemy is gaining entrance into my life. Keep me from my enemy's traps and lead me from paths of destruction, as you keep me from the temptation of evil. Only You and You alone Lord, can keep me from the tentacles of my enemies and keep me within hearing distance of Your precious voice. Amen.

January 15

At times I remind myself of how temptation works. How can you recognize temptation if you don't understand the way it operates? *James 1:12-16* pretty well tells us how temptation works, but if I want to examine a good example of how it operates, I just have to travel back in time to the Garden of Eden where Eve was tempted and take note that the tree of knowledge of good and evil stood among other trees including the tree of life.

Since there was no interest in the tree until the great tempter pointed it out, I can somewhat assume that neither the tree nor the fruit of it had any real distinction to it in light of the many other trees present. However, in temptation the lusts of the flesh and eyes are stirred in order to magnify the temptation. The temptation becomes the desired prize as it begins to be magnified in the mind through the imagination which starts to fancy how something will benefit or make the person feel and look, tantalizing the pride of the self-life (*1 John 2:15-17*).

In the case of Eve, the deadly fruit of the tree promised her that she would be as God, knowing good from evil, and as she considered the benefit of eating of the tree, the fruit appeared pleasant enough and the argument made sense, bringing all three elements of the soul into agreement that partaking of the fruit was the logical thing to do and would surely bring about worthy results. It is from this point that what would be normally considered vain, common, and destructive becomes desirable.

In the seduction of temptation, the affections are taken captive by the imagination and the emotions are exalted to some euphoric state of foolishness that leaves the person swinging from limbs of possibilities of how it will all play out in the end, always bringing about satisfying results to their way of thinking. As the end result of the temptation points out, as in the case of our first parents and the Scriptures in James confirms, temptation leads to only one result—death. In temptation the consequence of death is one truth we must take hold of before being tempted by, and seduced into an altered reality based on nothing but lies and destruction.

Prayer: Lord you have assured believers that you never tempt us with evil, yes You test our faith at crossroads where we must choose the way of righteousness to be overcomers, but You want to lead us away from evil and have provided a way through such temptation. We must recognize the flesh is weak and susceptible to temptation and we must humbly recognize such weakness so we will turn towards You in need, draw near to You in desperation, take hold of what Your Word states, and know that the door of temptation will be closed behind us and the devil will flee before us. Amen.

January 16

I was meditating on the lessons our first parents in the Garden of Eden can teach us by example. To do this I must consider both words and actions. Examples are that which confirms, fulfills or lives out what level of character is present. Such character will determine the depth of conviction behind words, the authority as to our declarations, and the power available to bring forth promises that have been made. The problem with words is that our tongues can be like loose cannons that when shot, will miss the target and wound comrades, while aiding the enemy in further advancement.

Words can be zealous but void of conviction. They can sound good, but prove empty, used as a smoke screen to hide wicked ways and evil intentions, spew out innuendoes to put people in their "so-called" place without being held accountable for poor, prejudicial, slanderous judgments, or as propaganda where truth is missing so that a false narrative can be promoted to throw a wicked covering over the people so they can't hear the truth. Finally, if truth dares to pose any challenge that would awaken one who is content in delusion, it can be met with rage.

The serpent used words to deceive. Even though Eve tried to used words to reason with the devil, they opened her up to be seduced with a lie, which ended in transgression, while Adam used them to play the blame game to avoid accountability and was met with a curse. Jesus stated our words are to be yea and nay for past that comes evil (*Matthew 5:34-37*). We are also told in *Matthew 12:36-37*, that all idle words will be judged, and according to *Revelation 21:8* that all liars will end up in the Lake of Fire.

Our first parents pretty well confirmed what Jesus stated. There are only two responses to any matter and that is yea, when it comes to truth and righteousness, and nay when it comes to wickedness and evil. To step past the simple markers of truth and righteousness is to dance with the devil on his dancefloor, which allows one to reason away the truth of something in order to come into agreement with a lie that will ultimately end in death.

Prayer: Lord, I know when I fail to guard my heart, check my attitude, discern my thoughts, and carefully choose my words, my tongue will not only prove to be a loose cannon but a destructive one. Help me Lord to remember to be still before You before I open my mouth and reveal to the whole world whether my words will be backed up by appropriate actions or whether they will prove me to be a hypocrite that is merely acting a part. Shine Your light Lord. Amen.

January 17

Home Sweet Home! So, who knows why I decided to run away one day? But, decide I did; however, I had to tell my mother first, because I told her everything. Always. Without fail. Standing by the front door and looking up into her beautiful face, I announced, "I'm running away from home."

She blinked a couple of times in surprise, then said, "Ooookaaay, but where are you going?" I replied, "Up the street," to which she asked, "And, then where are you going?" I had an answer and it was, "I don't know yet." "Okay," she said again. "What are you going to eat for lunch?" "Um, I don't know," I said, hoping she would volunteer to pack me a lunch.

In response, she wisely pushed the food point further and asked, "What are you going to have for dinner?" I began to squirm at this point, and then she nailed it down when she asked, "Where are you going to sleep tonight?" At that point my grandiose plan crumbled into dust. "I think I'll stay home," I mumbled, and that was the end of that.

For those of us who know, love, and worship the Lord Jesus Christ, the Shepherd of our souls, we have a heavenly Home Sweet Home IF we "abide" in Him and His Words abide in us, and IF we keep His commandments, (see *John 15*.) Jesus said, "*LET not your heart be troubled: ye believe in God, believe also in me. In my Father's house are many mansions: If it were not so, I would have told you. I go to prepare a place for you. And if I go and prepare a place for you, I will come again, and receive you unto myself; that where I am, there ye may be also" (John 14:1-3).*

I don't know about you, but my heart longs more with each passing day to "run away" from the evils of this world to eternally live with Jesus in the peace, love and joy of my Home Sweet Home. – J. Haley

Prayer: Lord, the state of affairs in this world makes us homesick. We long for our eternal home because we know that Your peace will reign, Your light will cause all darkness to flee, and above all we will see You as You are as we come to rest in Your glorious presence. Amen.

January 18

The Bible tells us to remember—to remember who God is, to remember His covenant and Law, and to remember the many lessons in His Word. It is for this reason I meditate on and study His Word. I just don't read it; I want to understand how it applies to me, and as the Apostle Paul instructs us in *2 Timothy 2:15*, we must rightly divide it. Regardless of how many times I might have considered certain Scriptures or scriptural incidents, every time I meditate on them, I see something that refreshes my soul.

The reason the Word can be new is because it is eternal and the reason it can refresh my soul is because it is life and will bring about spiritual growth (*John 6:63*). Different experiences, reinforcement of past lessons, and learning new ones in preparation for realizing eternal promises is the work of Holy Spirit who has taken the written Word and made it living reality in the heart.

It is for this reason we learn that acceptable service to God, adoration of who He is, and communion with Him are all forms of worship. The Father seeks true worshippers, but these individuals worship Him in the Holy Spirit who illuminates the truth about Jesus Christ to our hearts, minds, and souls to magnify Him above all idols and matters of this present age (*John 4:23-24*).

Prayer: Lord, we have been given a spirit to worship You in spirit, and a soul where emotions can be lifted up by adoration towards You, a mind that can be set free by praise of You and Your ways, and bodies that can become a sacrifice, giving way to the great work You desire to do in and through us. Have Your way. Amen.

January 19

Man perceives himself as being self-sufficient, which becomes a great point of temptation. Such a perception is prideful, foolish, and it prevents him from looking upward to his only solution. It is vital to call upon the name of the Lord. We know as the great Shepherd He will hear the cries of His sheep who are lost and wandering in the wilderness, floundering in uncertain terrain, fearful of the predators, and confused by the encroaching darkness of the late hour.

However, for most of us we first must be brought low to total despair before we feel the need to cry out to God. Due to our deceptive but arrogant state of self-sufficiency, we have the initial tendency to feel sorry for ourselves. We indeed must develop the inclination to call out to Him, and then be willing to offer what is acceptable to Him.

Abel knew what was acceptable to God and it was obedient of him to offer it, while his brother Cain never wanted to be ruled by what was righteous. Ultimately, Cain was ruled by that which was inferior and doomed: his flesh (*Genesis 4*). Sadly, we all start out like Cain. We desire to rule ourselves. Granted, Cain may have built the first city, pointing to man's first government and civilization, but he had to leave the presence of God to do so.

Prayer: Lord, spare me of being influenced by lustful flesh and lawless civilization, and consume me with Your glorious presence. Let me never murder what I have with You with the self-will of self-sufficient independence! Amen.

January 20

I cannot imagine what it would be like if I did not have the Lord. There would be no hope, there would be no way out, and there would be no purpose. This is an admission that I often make to the Lord and myself to keep realistically grounded in this present world, while looking towards that which is heavenly. And, when I forget my great need for the Lord in all matters, the challenges of life will quickly remind me of my inept humanness.

I keep thinking of how God is not only Lord of my life but He is my faithful husband and protective Father. He will take care of all obstacles. At such times I am reminded of Andrew Murray's book, *Abide in Christ.* He stressed that we are in Christ; therefore, we have nothing to worry about (*Colossians 3:3*).

I know it is the 'norm' for God to walk on the scene and change the impossible. He so desires to do it because He loves us, but we humans limit Him. We limit Him because we do not believe we abide in Christ and that every aspect of our lives are in His hands.

Prayer: Oh Lord, help me to know what it means to "abide in You." Amen.

January 21

As I stood admiring Rayola's birthday bouquet, it came to mind how many ways it represents the Body of Christ. Each flower, whether it be a rose, lily, statice, mum or plain greenery to "fill it in" is an "individual" that helps make up the whole. As personalities in the Body of Christ, we all have our own special uniqueness, background, experiences, and testimony as to how Jesus became the LORD of our life, the joy of being born again of His Spirit, and of His keeping power.

The stems of the beautiful, "many-membered" bouquet, are all contained in one body of water, in one transparent glass vase just as Jesus' Body, the Church, is to be "transparent" to the world in holiness and united in Truth, in one Spirit, with one Head. *Ephesians 4:4-6* says, "*There is one body, and one Spirit, even as ye are called in one hope of your calling; One Lord, one faith, one baptism, One God and Father of all, who is above all, and through all, and in you all. with one LORD, one Gospel.*" No one "member" of the bouquet is trying to exalt itself in any way, but instead, each is faithfully glorifying God in its own place with its own beauty.

James 3:16 says, "*For where envying and strife is, there is confusion and every evil work.*" Even the "background greenery" whose purpose is to enhance the beauty of the flowers, serves to remind us that "*Whosoever therefore shall humble himself as this little child, the same is greatest in the kingdom of heaven*" *(Matthew 18:4).* – J. Haley

Prayer: Lord, You have to cultivate us before we can be placed in Your garden, but You are the field where every color graces our lives with such a variety of blessings that all we can do is rejoice in Your beauty and majesty. Amen.

January 22

God's Word possesses simple truths, as well as true life. We must live by each of them. After all, it is the light of His Word that will lead us out of darkness towards the light of the world, Jesus Christ (*Psalm 119:105*).

The problem is we often tempt the Lord to speak to us other than through His Word, or prove that He means what He says according to our selfish whims. How often is it that we, in our arrogance, attempt to humble God by insisting He first bows before our insidious, selfish demands to prove something that in our fickle, unbelieving hearts, we have already decided not to believe is true (*Matthew 4:7*). At such a stage we are looking for entertainment, not truth. At such a point, we will never have the pure heart to truly see the Lord for Who He is.

The Lord will never entertain us, but He will set us free with His unadulterated truth (*John 8:31-32*). I will, and must, choose the latter if I am to ensure that I never become barren in the knowledge of Him.

Prayer: Lord, I am thankful my meat is not of this world. Give me the inclination to seek the real bread from heaven and to see the real light of the world in the midst of temptation. Keep me from putting You to a foolish test because of pride, and help me to hear Your voice call me so that I can immediately follow wherever You are leading. Amen.

January 23

I couldn't help but meditate on the unseen currents of life. The life I speak of is not just any life, it is the life of Jesus in me (*Galatians 2:20*). Oh, what a glorious life it is! Even when such currents appear to be disrupted by the waves of uncertainty, they remain consistent underneath the surface. Their flow is never disrupted by the tumultuous events that are operating around me. Granted such events may carry the uncertain waves of life, sustain the still waters of drudgery, and flow with the winds of change, but the current remains consistent in the heavenly life that flows through the present terrain of my soul.

This is the work of the Spirit of God (*John 7:37-39*). He is the unseen current of life. In spite of circumstances, He remains constant. He is always ready to not only bring and confirm life to every aspect of the saint's being, but to bring order to the challenges of life that slam against the resolve of each of us.

The key to benefitting the most from this life is that I must ever seek the current of the Spirit and once it has been discovered, it is up to me to stay in the flow of it, knowing that it will take me through this world according to the glorious life within me.

Prayer: Lord, we always have obstacles before us which prove we need You. We need You in every way. Lord, help us to know Your authority when we need to stand, know Your power when we need to withstand, and know Your peace when we must continue to stand. Amen.

January 24

Everything around us functions according to cycles and seasons (*Ecclesiastes 3:1*). For example, we know that no matter how long winter nights seem to be that they will eventually give way to light at the dawning of a new day. We need both light and darkness to function. Together, they represent one day. To have one without the other would mean that life would cease.

Life clearly entails cycles and seasons. The very pulse of it represents a current that ensures the rhythm of all creation. It never misses a beat. It is forever walking to a drumbeat that is governed by an unseen hand of providence.

We know that the life that comes from God is the life of His Son. There are also seasons that govern His life in relationship to it being brought to full maturity in His people. However, the one thing we can be assured of is that His life is eternal, and that it is fresh in the springtime, refreshing in the heat of summer, fruitful in the fall, and enduring through the wintertime.

Prayer: Lord, You are the Creator of the world around us. Truly, it declares Your glory. Lord, I present the harvest field of my life. My heart desire is that You will be glorified. Amen.

January 25

We forget the necessity for change in our lives. We resent drudgery and eventually show contempt towards familiarity, but at the same time we fear changes we are not in control of.

We become comfortable with the present current of our lives. We do not see that even the present current will create change to the landscape of our inner beings. For example, the flow will determine what kind of attitude we adopt towards life and what kind of behavior we nurture.

The problem is we fail to realize we are in some kind of current. We assume that the tides of life are not rolling in for we do not sense what is really happening around us. It is for this reason that we must be diligent about guarding that which affects our lives (*Proverbs 4:23*). We must avoid being put to sleep by the sound of the familiar beat of the waves of life rolling in and out, and pay attention to the direction the currents are taking us and the manner in which the waves that are hitting against our resolve are affecting the shorelines of our lives.

Prayer: Lord, I will forever be learning simple life lessons about life in the classroom of the present world, but I thank You that You are faithful in teaching them to me. Thank You Lord that You are in control of my world. I choose to make You my reality. Amen.

January 26

Yesterday I was considering the currents of life. There are all kinds of tides that roll in and out of our lives. They bring different matters to the forefront. There are decisions to be made, challenges to confront, harsh realities that must not be ignored, and the ever-present tendency to succumb to such tides without realizing they are changing the shorelines of our character.

We must discern the changes that are occurring because of the tides that flow into our lives. We must never become indifferent to what is actually taking place. We must always determine what kind of character must be formed by each tide that flows into and through our inner man. It is clear, we must not let the currents of life define us; rather, we must determine what type of impact they are to make on the person we should and need to become in light of God's everlasting kingdom (*Romans 12:1-2*).

Prayer: Lord, thank You for being my source of victory over the things of this life. Although obscure in many ways, You can clearly be seen by those who are pure in heart. Give me a clean heart so I can see You. Amen.

January 27

The excitement of catching my first fish nearly dimmed as Grandma told me it was way too small and we had to put it back into the river. No doubt my face formed into an angry pucker that only a preschooler could form. Even Grandma's threats of some man called a game warden didn't thwart my stubborn determination to keep that little fish, so I shoved it into my pocket and that's where it stayed even though Grandma said we should at least put it in her woven fish basket with the trout she had caught. After all, it was my fish, and there was no way I was going to give it up.

Later that evening when my parents came to retrieve me from Grandma and Pop's dairy farm in Arlington, WA, I proudly showed them my fish while Grandma quickly explained the situation. "It will stink," my mother said, trying to persuade me to hand it over. Seeing I was outnumbered and that the situation would not end well for me with a stinky dead fish in my pocket, I finally handed my prize catch over to them.

Now, think about this: that little fish I hid in my pocket can be compared to those "little sins" in a Christian's life that he or she refuses to give up. After all, they aren't hanging out there for all to see, and they "aren't hurting anybody," and besides, they're so personal and seemingly insignificant, why bother with them? Surely God isn't concerned about small, "pocket-size" sin, or is He?

The problem is, both dead fish and sin, regardless of their "size," eventually stink to high heaven and everybody "smells" it no matter how hard you try to hide it. Maybe Jesus is waiting for you to "examine your pockets" and hand over to Him those things that are a stench to Him. *Psalm 19:12* says, *"Who can understand his errors? Cleanse thou me from secret faults."* *Psalm 90:8,*

"Thou hast set our iniquities before thee, our secret sins in the light of thy countenance." – J. Haley

Prayer: Lord, our stubbornness may be necessary for us to stand, cute at times, and even a bit comical, but if it is to hold on to that which will stink in the end, especially to You, there will be nothing funny about it. Lord, expose all sins, great and small before they begin to stink up my life, bringing a reproach to You. Amen.

January 28

I was meditating on *Deuteronomy 32:7, "Remember the days of old, consider the years of many generations: ask thy father, and he will shew thee; thy elders, and they will tell thee."* I have been thinking about how important memories are to our lives. Why must we remember that which has most impacted us?

It is true that the memories of the past sometimes leave silly sentimental notions behind that can sweep us away with waves of foolish nostalgia, or they can serve as foreboding, deep ravines that will haunt us every time we stand at the frightening precipice of remembrance. However, memories are necessary if we are going to come to terms with who we are. They are bridges that connect the past with the present, producing some semblance as to our present condition and spiritual location in regard to our lives.

I have learned that I am the one who constructs how my memories connect me to my past and define my present. I am the one who will determine how such memoirs ultimately affect the terrain of my disposition, attitude, and behavior. Therefore, I have the responsibility to consider the way in which I handle these recollections when it comes to the attitude that is being developed in me towards life itself.

Prayer: Lord, You are the One who needs to intrude into my present reality and change the rugged terrain of my soul, but often it is the memories that intrude into my present life and justify the ragged and dangerous aspects of my base character. Lord, I want everything to be connected by Your work of redemption. May I remember the work You did on the cross as I consider my present prevailing mood and look forward to receiving a glorious inheritance that will maintain an upright status with You forever. Amen.

January 29

Scripture clearly instructs us to remember. But, what must we remember? It is clear that we choose what we remember and how we remember it. It is for this reason that we must be realistic about past events.

We need to consider how and why we remember that which has become the bridge that connects us to the present. Do we remember something because there is a sentimental value to it, but in reality, it has no real significance to the present and will produce disillusionment and discontentment towards life in the near future? Do we recall something bad in order to justify the deviant ways of our character? The one thing we can be assured of is that memories vary and are personal.

As believers, we must remember that in the past that we were indeed slaves to sin (*Romans 3:23*). We formerly served its deadly ways with foolish abandonment. We allowed the expectations of it to define our character and pursuits. We succumbed to its seductive delusion and called it reality. It is for this reason we must remember that we were once slaves, but because of the Lord's intervention, we now have a new status: that of being children of God (*John 1:12*).

Prayer: Lord, we all have our particular memories. We also have our own take on them as well. Lord, I want to remember that my life started with You at Calvary. I want to do away with the silly memories and be healed of the haunting memories, while making You the center focus of all that impacts my world. Amen.

January 30

Lately, Scriptures have reminded me of the importance of remembrance. It may sound like a moot point, but to God it isn't. He mentioned the discipline of remembering Him, His ways, and works in different Scriptures. For example, consider what Psalm 20:7 states, *"Some trust in chariots, and some in horses: but we will remember the name of the LORD our God."*

What was the purpose of this Scripture if it is not to challenge us about considering our source of reliance as we choose to remember what is true and sure? It is ironic what people put their trust in.

Through the years, I have learned the one thing I cannot put my trust in is memories. I do not trust *HOW* I remember something because I had a limited understanding of the situation at that time. I do not trust *WHAT* I remember because those who share such memories often differ in what they recall; therefore, it is clear that I cannot trust even the details that dot the landscape of each memory.

As I consider, the Scripture in *Psalm 20:7*, I realize I may not be able to trust the influences of the world, the strength of the arm, and the credibility of memories, but I can trust the One who never changes. I do not have to worry about my limited understanding about Him, for He is immutable and is able to remind me of what I need to remember, or He will enlarge my understanding of Him at the right time to bring wisdom to a matter.

When confusion abounds about Him or a matter, I am assured that in due time His truth will part any darkness or confusion, and the memories of Him will be stirred up by the Spirit. These memories have been established by the Word of God, "tasted" through experience, and upheld in the fiery ovens of trials and tribulations, and as a result they will bring all matters into proper perspective, settling the spirit and calming the soul.

Prayer: Lord, I just have to remember who You are for all matters to be put into proper perspective. Thank You for being the immovable and unchanging Rock of Ages. Amen.

January 31

The theme that has been brought to my attention is the importance of remembering eternal matters. *Deuteronomy 5:15b* states, *"And remember…that the LORD thy God brought thee out thence through a mighty hand and by a stretched out arm."*

Do you remember your salvation experience? I do because I became aware that the Lord set me free from the terrible burden of sin that weighed upon my soul. The Apostle Peter talks about how one becomes barren in their knowledge of Christ in *2 Peter 1:9*: They have forgotten that they were purged from their old sins.

There can be some type of sentiment and emotion attached to memories. Such attachments, whether bad or good, are what often set particular past moments or present events aside to become something we would reminiscence about. Such impressions may be shrouded by the fast movement of time upon the recesses of our minds, but nevertheless, they have made an imprint that can be uncovered by present situations. At this time such trajectories can come to the forefront as we recall the moment or event that had managed to plow up the fallow ground of our very conscience to consider its significance or importance to our lives.

The Bible tells us to remember those things that pertain to the ways of God. Such memories may leave an imprint on our lives but life with its demands often cover them up, causing them to become somewhat lost in happenings that have no real significance to our spiritual journey. It is for this reason, we must pause and choose to remember who, why, and what God has done on our behalf through redemption. This is why we have Communion Services to remember our humble beginnings in light of God's great provision of His Son's sacrifice.

Many times the command to remember is to remind us of who God is. *John 14:6* confirms this in an indirect manner. It tells us that Jesus is the Way, for He alone represents the glorious way of God. It is for this reason that out of loving devotion we must choose and strive to focus and concentrate on the Person, teaching, and example of Jesus to keep walking in the direction and way that will lead us to Him and the fulfillments of His many promises in our life.

Prayer: Lord, there is much I have forgotten, but what I do remember I want it to have an eternal significance. I want it to start with Your perspective and end with a greater revelation of Your abiding hand upon my life. Amen.

February

February 1

Ecclesiastes 12:1 states, *"Remember now thy Creator in the days of thy youth, while the evil days come not, nor the years draw nigh, when thou shalt say, I have no pleasure in them"* If you are reading my posts, you know I have been thinking a lot about our memories. It is not an obsession but a command that we remember certain things. We do choose to remember what we want to remember, and how; but what if we can't remember?

I pondered this much when my father was alive. He had Alzheimer's and the memories of the past simply encased him into a world we didn't recognize nor could we connect with him in the present.

We do not think much about the importance of our memories; however, if we do not have a memory in which to remember, we have no sense of who we are. Our identity or concept of self becomes lost in what appears to be fragments of broken glass. Ultimately, nothing really makes sense or connects in relationship to present reality.

I remember seeing a show about a man who had a certain amnesia where he could remember everything before a certain day and after that he would forget what happened from then on. He could live the same reality every day and forget it.

We are told to remember our Creator in the days of our youth because what has not been firmly established can do an unusual trapeze act where you fail to connect to the present happenings in light of past lessons. In these dark times, we need to exercise this particular choice of remembering our Creator in great measure if we are going to stand, withstand, and continue to stand. We need to be clear as to who will give us a sense of identity and purpose in a world that eventually will seem like it has lost its mind. When we lose our way in the mire of hopelessness and despair, we will know where we can once again find meaning and pleasure in life; thereby, salvaging the aspects of our memories that will bring substance and purpose back into our lives.

Clearly, the source of our residing memories must always find their origins in God if we ultimately are to realize and remember what is truly important.

Prayer: Lord, You are my all in all. You are my God who oversees every aspect of my life. You are the King who rules my life. You are the Lord who owns me. You are my place of safety that I hide in. You are my Defense that I run behind, my Rock I stand upon, my Hope that I cling to, and My Judge who will ensure justice when all is said and done. Thank You for being everything I need and ever will need in this present life and the next to come. Amen.

February 2

Yesterday it was about remembering our Creator in our youth, but consider what Psalm 143:5 states, *"I remember the days of old; I meditate on all thy works; I muse on the work of thy hands"* Obviously, we must have a working memory of the God of heaven to keep all matters in perspective. We must know Him to know who we are. We must recall that He is our Creator, and that He existed before all things, and because of Him all things function and work according to an unseen order. We must meditate on His incredible works to keep our confidence in Him center stage,

39

regardless of the changes around us. We must ponder how He has created all things, as well as His commitment and power to preserve us in every challenge.

Jehovah is God, and we must strive to keep that reality ever present, living, and important to us. The reason for this is because the present activities of life can cause us to quickly forget what is important. In essence, the initial value we put on the Lord and our relationship with Him can be replaced with that which has no real value. It is necessary for us to keep our precious memories and understanding of God alive in order to be prepared to recognize His present intrusion and intervention upon our needy lives.

Prayer: Lord the only one who can bring order to my chaotic world and purpose to my memories is You. I praise You that You are the only reality we need to seek, embrace, and hold on to, to keep our feet firmly planted on Your immovable truths. Amen.

February 3

When I read Matthew 13:22, *"He also that received seed among the thorns is he that heareth the word; and the care of this world, and the deceitfulness of riches, choke the word, and he becometh unfruitful",* I am reminded that I am apt to forget how important some of my scriptural discoveries and insights can prove to be. It's as if you try to enclose such times of revelation up in a nice place so that you can visit them at any time to recall their significance and then you realize that many times they end up in some trunk in the attic of the mind.

The truth of the matter is that we are forgetful people. This is because we are limited in keeping every important matter before us and past discoveries vivid. Our understanding becomes clouded by the world's intrusions and our activities rob us of the ability to keep all matters in their proper place.

I know for myself that when I strive to mark a certain truth or event as being a special moment, a priceless nugget, important insight, or life-changing event so I won't forget, I inevitably do. Granted, I have filed the memory away in a nice compartment and marked it with the word "Important." But worldly demands eventually cover such notations with the dust of vanity.

It is for this reason that we are reminded that the cares of the world can choke out the Word of God. Therefore, we must remember to keep the world's demands in a proper perspective to ensure that the weeds of vanity do not choke out the precious, eternal truths and fruits of heaven.

Prayer: Lord, so much of my life is covered by the dust of vanity. It covers up those things that are precious and vital to my spiritual well-being. Enable me to weed out the vanity of this present world and bring into focus the preciousness of Your truths and ways. Amen.

February 4

"Wherefore I take you to record this day…" (Acts 20:26a). God records everything. In the end, the earth will serve as a witness as to man's activities, as well as the witnesses of heaven, while the Godhead will serve as eyewitnesses as to man's doings, and the Word of God, the Holy Spirit and the blood of His covenant will also serve as witnesses as to the reason for man's spiritual state (*1 John 5:6-7*).

In the past I had to be honest with myself about my failing memory that plagues my humanness. Perhaps my compartments are full of non-essential information and like a computer, they need to be defragged at different times to revitalize areas of my life. Since I am so apt to forget things, I have kept journals. Journals serve as that flint or match that causes particular memories to rise out of the ashes of forgetfulness to be once again pondered.

As I read the meditations recorded in my journal entries, I realize how they are directed at the reality of God's goodness and faithfulness. But I also recognize that such exaltation was taking place because life teaches that we are indeed needy people, always poor towards God, and inept to change the face of the tides that are ebbing away the clarity of the shoreline of our lives.

I am so thankful that God and His Word never change. His Spirit can spark His truths within my soul and revitalize my spirit to once again rise in expectation of experiencing and seeing the majesty and greatness of the Lord.

Prayer: Lord, I am so needy. I am limited in what I can perceive about the world around me. My memories are clouded and untrustworthy, but I can still cling to the reality that You will never change in Your goodness towards me and the faithfulness You have continually bestowed upon my life. Thank You for being a loving and faithful God. Amen.

February 5

Numbers 15:40 remind us "That ye may remember and do all my commandments, and be holy unto your God" We must choose to remember what the Lord instructs us to do. This is a vital discipline that requires us to choose to remember what our Scriptural response needs to be to a matter.

I realize that memories lie dormant until there is something that awakens them out of their state of obscurity. For such a memory to exist it means that we had to experience it at some time. The Word of God is living and we are to experience the liberating truth of it, the joy of walking in it because it keeps us free of guilt and condemnation, the power of it because we can stand before the

Lord and our enemies in confidence of its heavenly authority, and to rest in its many promises because God is true and faithful to His Word.

Clearly, God used the reading of His Law to spark the people of Israel's memory as to His true identity, their high calling, and the inheritance they were given. Likewise, as believers, we must take the opportunity to always expose ourselves to that which will keep our spirit awakened with expectation towards God, and our soul ready to be lifted up by the everlasting wings of hope to gain an eternal perspective, while experiencing and possessing His promises.

Prayer: Lord, thank You for giving me a spirit and soul that can always receive more of Your Spirit, Word, and wisdom. Lord, touch each area to overflow with Your Living Water, always enlarging me to receive more from Your throne. Amen.

February 6

"The poor committed himself unto thee; thou art the helper of the fatherless" (Psalm 10:14c). Have you gone to the Lord? Spiritually, we start out as cringing beggars, but salvation places us in reach of the incredible blessings of God, but it takes faith to obtain them. An extent of a saint's richness is not based on the number of blessings they possess, but on the quality of their faith. *James 2:5* speaks of this very fact that we should be rich in faith.

As we live in these uncertain times, we must never forget the Lord is the One who is in control. In such darkness, we must remember this for we will discover how poor and vulnerable we are. He desires to be our helper, but He waits on us to cry out for His help and intervention.

We are powerless to change circumstances. We have no means to push back the oncoming tidal wave that is about to hit

43

the shoreline of our worlds. We are incapable of changing hearts and minds that are already inclined towards the ruin and destruction of the wickedness that is now enfolding the world into its evil designs. Let us always resign ourselves to remember that our hope is not here, our home is in a far distant land, and our life hidden in the eternal refuge of heaven.

Prayer: Lord, I choose to trust You, but the battle rages for my mind and heart. Keep my heart still before You and my mind sound in You. I need to trust You as I discern the environment around me. Amen.

February 7

I was thinking about devotion the other day. I have observed, not only in myself at different times in my religious growth, but in others as well, that there are four types of devotion displayed by religious people.

The slider: This group is comprised of the people who have an outward show of devotion. However, they eventually become lukewarm when the newness or excitement wears off. Behind the lukewarm show of devotion is someone who is simply trying to slide into heaven. He or she does not really want to run the race.

Religious: There is also a religious devotion. This is where people have a passion for being right. This passion is all wrapped up in their theology. The most devotion these people show is in the criticism of others who do not agree or live up to their religious notions.

Self-serving: There is a self-serving devotion. This is where a person is devoted to their personal causes. It is all about how such devotion makes him or her feel about self. These individuals must be recognized, exalted, and honored for them to continue in their devotion. It is mainly a pride trip. Ultimately, this type of individual's devotion must make them feel good about themselves before they can continue on with the same intensity.

Godly devotion: This type of devotion is where the person is truly devoted to God. His or her main desire is to know, love, serve, and please God. These individuals' love for God is enduring, their commitment is to His heart, and they have one cause—Christ crucified. Their whole life and heart are caught up with the reality of the one true God of heaven.

As for me, I desire the true devotion, but it is easy to give in to the other inferior types of devotion. As a result, many lose all sense of devotion as they become half-hearted or indifferent in their commitment and loyalty to God. Obviously, it all comes down to the heart, and whether one truly loves the God of the Bible.

Prayer: Lord, I do not want to have a zeal that has no real devotion or substance behind it. I want the necessary commitment that will establish in me a real inclination towards You in all matters of my life. Amen.

February 8

While I was never a "poster girl," I once was the girl behind the post. It was back in the early 1980's and after being encouraged— as in coerced—into attending a women's weekend retreat at a Christian camp by a friend who said, "You need this," I found myself on the church bus full of happy women. I remember looking forlornly out the window as we pulled out of the parking lot and thinking to myself, "No, I do NOT need this!"

I have never enjoyed camping or church camps and just the thought of eating unhealthy food and being bored to death for the weekend didn't appeal to me at all. Besides, just why did I "need this"? After all, I was saved as a young child, read the Bible, memorized verses, and believed every word of it. Admittedly, I had taken detours in my young life—many of them downright shameful—but I had always loved the Lord in my heart even though many major decisions I made were totally self-serving. However, it was all justified in my mind because God wanted me to be happy. Right? And as for those detours, the prevailing belief was "Once saved, always saved."

So, what could possibly be the problem? As it turned out, the speaker was anything but boring! She was a powerful, anointed, servant of God who was also a captivating speaker, author, and singer, with a wonderful sense of humor. But there was something else too, something a bit frightening, that caused me to want to be invisible. Since that wasn't possible, I chose to sit behind a load-bearing post in the middle of the chapel.

Maybe if I "hid" behind that post it would "protect" me from the awesome Presence emanating from her. But it didn't work. The speaker knew I was trying to hide behind the post, (as she later told me) and the Holy Spirit did too.

Visions of Jesus carrying His cross just for my sins began to fill my mind every time I closed my eyes. I could hear the cross dragging through the hardened streets. I don't know just when I finally came out from "hiding" behind that post, but the tears were flowing, and I cried through the rest of the retreat.

When the tissues ran out, I resorted to toilet paper. I cried so much the women started complaining that there wasn't any paper in the ladies' restroom. Holding up a soggy and tattered square in front of them I confessed that it was my fault. By then the skin on my face was red and peeling from wiping my face so much.

You see, YES! I really, really did "need this." I needed to get real with JESUS. I needed to totally surrender. Thank God for such a great speaker and servant of the LORD who knew the power of the cross. She went Home to be with her Lord and Savior in 2016. Her name was Zoanne Wilke. – J. Haley

Prayer: Lord, we may hide behind posts, religious garbs, deeds, and others, but You know where we are and Your Spirit will reveal our position and Your light will expose our great need. Thank You for not letting me hide from Your light of truth, healing, and restoration. Amen.

February 9

When I think of devotion, I must examine what I think on to focus on what is important to ensure right influence. I must also consider what I choose to remember in order to test my affections, and what I determine to maintain to ensure the integrity of my commitment.

We are told what to think on in *Philippians 4:8* and to direct our affections heavenward, but to ensure the integrity of commitment I must choose to remember what is vital, true, and righteous. For this reason, Paul reminds us of Jesus' instruction in *1 Corinthians 11* on the night He was betrayed when He took the bread and broke it and the cup to drink of it, He instructed His disciples, *"...this do in remembrance of me" (1 Corinthians 11:24c & 25c)*.

Memories are like the sand that runs through an hour glass. They simply mark the passing of time. However, certain memories can establish memorials in our lives. It is clear we cannot dictate the passing of those moments or events that serve as memorials. Like the memorials of the past, present memories will become tarnished as time erodes away their clarity and dulls down their impact. The truth is, memories eventually will pass away to be remembered no more.

It is for this reason that I want to establish a true lasting memorial that will have a touch of the heavenly to keep such memorials relevant. I want such memories that surround these memorials to affect the present, while constructively influencing the future. There is only one such memorial that can make the memories surrounding it last the test of time, and that is the work of the cross of Jesus.

The cross became the chisel, the hand of God the hammer, the love of God the die being cast, and the crucified Christ the eternal Rock, in which the everlasting memorial would be established. Daily I must make sure this living memorial remains vibrant and living in my heart to maintain the right intensity of my devotion. Even though I may stray from it, I will know that all I must do is turn around and come back to it to be once again established by that which is alive and eternal.

Prayer: Lord, thank You for the everlasting memorial that has been established by Your work of redemption. Amen.

February 10

I was reading *Psalm 9* today and its second verse reminded me of what joy we have even in this world, *"I will be glad and rejoice in thee."*. It is true I must choose to be glad and rejoice, but what a glorious song of hope and victory.

There is so much to chew on when it comes to meditating on God's words. Pondering the Word of God has been compared to "chewing it" like a cow chews its cud. It is vital that every part of it is broken down in order to receive the necessary nutrients from its ageless truths and wisdom.

God's words are full of life, serving as nourishment for the soul and a light that will spark our very resolve to act upon its truths in faith and obedience. In essence, His words will quicken our spirits to rise upon the wings of blessed hope and soar above the despairing darkness of this present world. We can truly rejoice from such heights of expectation in light of God's infinite power and eternal promises.

Prayer: Lord, thank You for Your Word. It is truly spirit and life to our very souls. We thank You that it is eternal and unchanging in its intent and capabilities. I choose to believe it by faith and obey it in loving submission to You. Amen.

February 11

I was thinking about the grave wickedness that has been exposed in this age. It seems that man is forever trying to establish a lasting memorial of himself, especially if he is wicked. Such an attempt speaks of independent man's desire to reign, his arrogance to come out on top, and his wickedness that reveals the utter darkness and delusion to such attempts. Whether it is a city as in the case of Cain or a tower as in the case of the people of Babel, they perceived themselves as leaving some type of memorial or legacy that will reach heaven and bring God down to an inferior position.

The Bible is clear that memories of such people will be wiped out. *Psalm 9:6c* puts it this way, *""...their memorial is perished with them."* It is clear that the tormenting memories that follow the wicked will perish. They will have no far reaching tenacles to bully, intimidate, control, rob, kill, and destroy.

As you study those who, like Satan, perceive that they can attain the heights of heaven, you realize how unrealistic they are. It is clear, as you study man's attempt to humble God and exalt himself in some way that the Lord always puts boundaries on people's evilness. Even though such individuals appear to be victorious at different times, eventually they will hit the wall of judgment that will stop them dead in their tracks. Such a wall is God Himself. As *Hebrews 10:31* reminds us, *"it is fearful thing to fall into the hands of an angry God."*

Prayer: Lord, we thank You that You determine the extent evil will reach in this present age. We desire to hide in You as our ark, while we seek Your wisdom and protection from the wicked designs of those who are sons of Belial in this present age. Amen.

February 12

The other day I mentioned that there will be a time the wicked will not even be remembered. In fact, *Psalm 9:17* tells us, *"The wicked shall be turned into hell, and all the nations that forget God."* This scripture brings sadness in one sense, but a comfort in terms of justice having the last say. There is nothing that causes such despair as injustice. In great darkness, it seems as if there is no stopping of the wicked to carry out their despotic agenda causing hope to be deferred in every direction but up.

We know it is God's heart that none perish, but if a man insists on his wicked, unjust ways then he will pay the ultimate consequence. It is for this reason that God's justice is what will cause me to rejoice in light of the great darkness that is coming upon the face of the world. It is true, I would love to see all come to salvation, but in light of the great covering of wickedness over the world, I would also love the wind of the Spirit to enfold me and translate me to heaven like Enoch. But I know that I have already been translated from the kingdom of darkness into the kingdom of God's dear Son (*Colossians 1:13*).

It is true that I would like to see vengeance come upon the wicked people of the world who love the ways of death because of the grave destruction they level at others. However, vengeance belongs to the One who is just in all matters. I must guard my heart and be assured that the memorial of the wicked will perish in the judgments of God.

As believers, we will never appreciate, agree, or become comfortable with the works or fruits of darkness, but we can rejoice in the glorious life, light, and hope of heaven.

Prayer: Lord, I am so thankful the battle belongs to You. I realized long ago that the soldier is only as good as the commander. Lord, I will "bomb out" in battle, unless You are directing my steps, preparing the way, and wearing down the enemies so they will fall into their own traps when the trumpet blows, calling Your soldiers to take up arms, and to stand and see Your salvation. Amen.

February 13

Have you thought about the promise found in *Hebrews 13:6*, *"…the Lord is my helper, and I will not fear what man shall do unto me"?* It is natural to see each of us as believers as being God's servants that are to carry out His bidding, co-laborers in the harvest field of the world, and soldiers that are prepared to march forward with orders, but in this verse, we see that the Lord is our helper and will enable us to get through this present world.

As we face this frightening time, it is important to remember that God is our helper through such times. We must keep in mind that as our helper, He is not above us, below us, indifferent to us, or fickle in what He does; rather, He is beside us. He will encourage us during frightening and uncertain times, He will comfort us during grave challenges and loss, he will guide us through darkness, and He will take our hand and lead us up the narrow path of righteousness.

To think that God, our Creator and Redeemer, offers Himself as our helper is incredible. It is His goal to lead us to a place of complete rest in Him. However, to reach this place, we must put our faith in Him as our Helper. We must trust His words, instructions, and promises. We must realize that we can and must cease from all attempts to change the circumstances around us and come to rest in Him, our real Ark, knowing He will lift us above that present darkness to experience the gentle light of His presence.

Prayer: Lord, I am reminded that after the sixth day, Your work was perfect and complete. Lord, I also realize it was after the creation of man that You ceased from work and rested. In fact, You went to the cross as man where the most trying and complete work was done: the work of redemption.

Lord, please help me to obey in small and great ways in order to ensure a completion of a matter. If a matter is completed it not only signifies order is present but one can now come into rest. At the place of rest, there can be sweet fellowship where You not only can enjoy me, but I can enjoy You. Help me to be obedient, help me to always be prepared to enter the Garden of sweet communion with You. Amen.

February 14

As many of you know, pictures, paintings and prints tell a story, and they can leave lasting impressions on small children.

I remember when I was around five years old, one such picture hung on Grandma's living room wall. It wasn't very big, but it captured my attention because of its "story." The domed buildings, stone walls, and tall "pointy" trees fascinated me so one day I asked Grandma if that was a picture of heaven. I have no idea why that picture brought to my childish mind "heaven." Grandma answered, "No, it's Jerusalem" and when I asked her what heaven looked like, she proceeded to try and explain what heaven looked like. Of course, that conversation was short, because describing heaven is impossible to do outside of what the Bible discloses.

1 Corinthians 2:9 sums it up best, *"But as it is written, Eye hath not seen, nor ear heard, neither have entered into the heart of man, the things which God hath prepared for them that love him."*

What I do know, at this stage of my life, is all that truly matters in this world or the next is the Lord Jesus Christ! *"That I may know him, and the power of his resurrection, and the fellowship of his sufferings, being made conformable unto his death; If by any means I might attain unto the resurrection of the dead." Philippians 3:10, 11.* – J. Haley

Prayer: Lord much of the beauty of what we see with the physical eye keeps us from imagining what we will see when this body falls to the way side and we will finally see You as You are in all of Your glory. Meanwhile, You are all I need to know, see, and fellowship with to know that what awaits me is so much more glorious than what I see and know here on earth. Amen.

February 15

Psalm 1:2 informs us, *"…his delight is in the law of the LORD; and in his law doth he meditate day and night."* We are to delight in the law of the Lord. How can we delight in that which is restrictive by its holy ways, its unbending instructions, and its perfect presentation of acceptable righteousness? *Romans 10:4* tells us that Christ is the end of the law for righteousness to everyone who believes. *Galatians 3:24* brought out that the Law was a schoolmaster to point us to Jesus.

The Law contained shadows of Jesus and His work of redemption. It veiled untold mysteries about God's plan to saved mankind. In fact, we know according to *Colossians 2:14* that the ordinances of the Law were actually blotted out by the work of the cross.

Henry Thorne best described the shadow that was cast by the Old Testament in this way, "There are clouds, but they are the dust of the Saviour's feet. No type of the Redeemer could be perfect that was destitute of the element of mystery. Think of the mystery of His Birth, of His Cross, of His vacated Tomb!"

Truly, we can delight in the Law of the Lord by delighting in Christ and His work of redemption.

Prayer: Lord, You are the beginning and end of all things when it comes to truth, life, and eternity. It is for this reason that I can truly delight in who You are and what You have done for me. I am so thankful that the shadows of the old turned into a living Person who not only walked among us, but secured salvation for our souls. Amen.

February 16

Have you meditated on what it means to "behold the Son"? After all John the Baptist and the Father in Heaven exhorted people to "behold the Son." We must behold Jesus in His humanity, deity, work of redemption on the cross, and as our present High Priest in the courts of heaven to ensure salvation and spiritual growth.

Before Jesus became a reality to me, God seemed far away and foreboding. It was not until I encountered Jesus in His humanity that I began to consider God in a personal light. He had seemed unreachable until the voice of the Son of God penetrated my heart. He seemed unfeeling until I realized the Son of Man cried over pending judgment and destruction. God, in fact, seemed indifferent to my struggles until Jesus became the Great Physician who came to bring healing to my pathetic, lost soul. He had appeared to be insensitive until I witnessed Jesus as the Lamb of God walking up Calvary with the cross. He also seemed deaf to the plight of all mankind until I realized that as the Man of sorrows His heart was actually broken on the cross for each of us.

While on earth, Jesus revealed the power of God in miracles and deliverance, the will of God on His way to Calvary, and the heart of God on the cross. Now as High Priest He manifests the goal of God by being the mediator that reconciles man back into a relationship with his Creator.

The question is simple, "Have you beheld the Son of God in His love, grace, and high calling?"

Prayer: Lord, in my ungodly state I knew things were wrong in my life and that I needed intervention. As a sinner I realized I needed a Savior, and as a struggling soul I knew I needed a Mediator. Thank You Lord for being my All in All, now I must let You become all things to me to realize the fullness of Your work, the greatness of Your mission, and the majesty of Your glory. Amen.

February 17

How do you keep your insanity in insane times? As I wrestle with the darkness of this age, I realize that we must wade through so much worldly terrain and influence to come to terms with what is real and acceptable to the Lord. This brings me to that point of connection that will keep matters in perspective and that is prayer.

Prayer is a privilege, allotted to each of us by redemption. It is the will of God that we pray about everything in line with His will. In fact, nothing can be done or accomplished without prayer. Prayer actually stands before the veil that separates us from the presence and glory of God. We must connect with heaven if we are going to have a perspective that lifts us above the darkness to see it for what it is. We must have a heavenly perspective in order for the light to reveal the way we must walk.

Prayer is what connects us to the throne of God. It will part the veil and open the way for us to gain the necessary insight into where we are and the direction we must travel. As a result, we must learn what it means to pray without ceasing (*1 Thessalonians 5:17*). It means that our heart is always in a state of open communion with God. In essence, we are always in a state of abiding in the place of sweet fellowship with the Lord.

Prayer: Lord, prayer is about learning to abide in that place with You. Granted, we may not always be communing with You, but we are in a position of being ready to commune with You in spite of what is going on around us. Help us to secure such a place with You. Amen.

February 18

The Word of God is clear how the Lord regards the righteous and the wicked. Consider *Psalm 11:7, "For the righteous LORD loveth righteousness; his countenance doth behold the upright."* We often consider God in an unrealistic light. We fail to regard His attitude towards a matter. For example, since we know God is love, we assume that He cannot hate. However, we know God hates iniquity. He will not even look upon any sin, which means He will not hear our prayers (*Isaiah 59:2*).

We fail to realize that if one emotion exists, the opposite must also be present. Hate is opposite of love. God loves those who are upright before Him. He regards, honors, and exalts them. As Christians we have been given the means to be upright through simple faith in the Lord Jesus. Faith establishes us before God in right standing, confirms itself with a right attitude, and expresses itself in godly conduct.

As believers, we must always consider how God regards our lives before Him. Does He consider it in light of Jesus' redemption or does He turn away from us because the darkness of iniquity is upon our soul?

Prayer: Lord, the Bible is clear about who You can bestow Your love upon. I choose the ways of righteousness to ensure that I will not just know about Your love, I will experience it. Amen.

February 19

There are those who want to see the promises of God now, but when you consider what *Hebrews 11:13* states about the saints who have gone before us, *"These all died in faith, not having received the promises, but having seen them afar off, and were persuaded of them, and embraced them, and confessed that they were strangers and pilgrims on the earth"* Even though they did not see the fulfillment of promises in their lifetime, they still believed by faith they were heirs to them because the Lord promised them.

Our spiritual journey begins with faith, and must also end with it. It was noted by Herbert Lockyer in his book, *All the Messianic Prophecies of the Bible,* that the same faith that inspired and formed Abraham's life and walk before the Lord was the same faith that sustained him in death. The Apostle Peter reminds us that at the end of faith is salvation (*1 Peter 5:9*).

Faith serves as those eyes that can see afar off in light of eternal hope. It is the muscle that allows us to walk in expectation of seeing the fulfillment of glorious promises. It is the eternal virtue of optimism that causes us to be a stranger and a pilgrim in this world, while being an ardent citizen of the next one to come.

Oh, to have faith like Abraham, confidence like Moses, assurance like David, and boldness like Paul would be to know the liberty that faith brings to each step, allowing us to advance in this present, dark world towards our final destination.

Prayer: Lord, thank You for the measure and gift of faith. There is no way we could walk through or survive this present world without faith towards You. Your mercy made faith available to us, Your grace provided it, and Your love inspires and sustains it in our lives. Amen.

February 20

The dreaded time came when we had to say "Goodbye, we love you" to our beloved little Tucker. He fought so hard to live and keep up his "job" as watch dog, protector, companion, music-loving dancer, and "gospel singer." Most of all, he was a thousand per-cent committed to me, making sure 24-7 that I was okay.

As my heart aches and tears flow from another painful loss, I keep asking myself how God could put so much boundless love into such a cute, little less than four-pound body. Only God Almighty, Creator of all things, visible and invisible can put feelings, including love and undying faithfulness, into His creatures.

The witness of God's power, personality, and presence is everywhere if we just take time to stop, look, listen and learn. We will always miss Tucker, just like we will always miss our other fur-babies who have left us.

How good it is to know, and sense the presence of the One who promised to those who love Him, *"I will never leave you, nor forsake you." (See Hebrews 13:5).* – J. Haley

Prayer: Lord, the good-byes of this life can be unbearable at times, but we live in light of the expectation of seeing You one day restore all of Your creation to perfection. Meanwhile, we take comfort in knowing that we never have to walk through those trying times by ourselves. Amen.

February 21

When I consider the two diverse ways of man, I remind myself of such scriptures as *Psalm 12:8, "The wicked walk on every side, when the vilest men are exalted,"* I make a determination to set my focus in the right direction in order to discipline my walk.

Righteousness has the ability to establish boundaries of discipline, especially when it is clearly seen in leadership. However, when the wicked are in leadership, those who have no inner restraint or moral discipline will succumb to vile ways as well. Darkness becomes more defined as light begins to bring contrast to the ways of others. For this reason, the wicked hate that which is righteous.

The wicked will rage against righteousness and try to destroy its testimony. They will falsely accuse it of deviation and set up traps for the righteous to fall into. The wicked are always looking for ways to prey on the righteous, to rob, kill, and destroy their life and witness. At times it may appear they are winning, but in the end, they will fall into their own traps and taste the bitterness of their destructive ways.

Prayer: Lord, it is hard not to see the ways of the wicked. It is also hard not to believe that evil will not win in the end especially when the systems of the world allow them to get away with so much. However, there will be a day of reckoning, and what is important is that I am not counted with those who are wicked. Help me to keep my eyes heavenward, to ensure that any envy of the wicked cannot take center stage in my life. Amen.

February 22

The hardest thing to watch is when the wicked are exalted, excused or even rewarded for their wickedness. Such an imbalance of justice causes great despair and hopelessness. In such an environment righteousness is constantly mocked. As believers, we must remind ourselves of what will be exalted in the end.

We have many such promises about the righteous being preserved and ultimately exalted, and when it comes to God's Word in all matters, we have *Psalm 12:7* that states, *"Thou shalt keep them, O LORD, thou shalt preserve them from this generation for ever"*

It is Satan's insane world where the wicked appear to get all the breaks, while the righteous appear to travel a hard road that is relentless in its ongoing challenges. However, we must remember the end of wickedness. The rewards of wickedness are temporary, while the judgments leveled against it will stand.

It is vital to realize that the wicked want to oppress the righteous to wipe out their testimony. Wickedness always expresses itself in indifference, cruelty, contempt, prejudice, arrogance, anger, and murder towards that which is pure and raises a mirror to reveal its dark ways. It will ultimately persecute righteousness.

As Christians, we are to hate sin in our own lives, be indifferent to its temptations, reject its cruel ways, show utter contempt towards its destructive ways, shun its prejudices, flee its arrogant attitude, resist its anger, and despise its murderous fruit. In essence, we must never have any part or agreement with the ways of wickedness. As the Bible instructs, we must come out and be separate.

Prayer: Lord, instill in me the same attitude towards sin as You have. Do not let me become enslaved by its wicked ways, evil attitudes, and tempting delusions. Amen.

February 23

I have meditated on what it means when it comes to the witness of righteousness being used to condemn the world. *Hebrews 11:7c* makes this reference about Noah, *""...he condemned the world, and became heir of the righteousness which is by faith."* We know that when we stand by faith it is counted FOR righteousness and when we act out of faith it is counted AS being righteous.

This brings me back to the example of Noah. What does it mean to be an heir of righteousness? It means in great darkness that you will be standing upright before the Lord. Perhaps the world will refuse to see your status with God, but when it is forced to acknowledge that righteousness exists, it will rage against it. In essence, it will attempt to snuff it out, but such righteousness will continue to stand as a witness against wickedness. It will speak of judgment and death.

The reason righteousness will stand is because it is not represented by one person; rather, it is a legacy that has been passed down by heaven itself. Noah was an heir of righteousness because he became identified to the legacy of heaven. He walked with God and found favor.

It is vital for every Christian to ensure that they are identified to this eternal legacy. As true believers, our main pursuit must be to become an heir of righteousness.

Prayer: Lord, I want to be an heir of righteousness, but I must learn how to walk with You by faith in order to find the type of favor that will reckon my life as being righteous in and before You. Amen.

February 24

Tears formed in my eyes, and my heart broke as I stared at the shattered pieces of what was once a figurine of Thumper lying at my feet. All I had wanted to do was hold orphaned Bambi's beloved rabbit friend for a couple of minutes, but even standing on tiptoe to reach him on the mantel with my small fingers obviously wasn't a good idea.

My mother heard the crash and immediately knew what had happened. In the midst of my sadness, I wondered if I was going to get a spanking, but she was understanding and calm as she swept the broken pieces into a dustpan. "Can't we glue him back together?" I asked forlornly. The answer was "No" and so poor Thumper went the way of many fine knickknacks back in the days before ugly plastic replaced collectable works of art.

Now, here's the thing: even though Thumper was no longer a visible item, his famous words never left my parents' lips whenever unkind words flew out of my mouth. I can't tell you how many times I heard, "If you can't say something nice, don't say anything at all."

We all know that it's impossible for anyone to ever totally gain control of their tongue, try as they might. It helps, however, to remember that God hears every word we utter, and we will be held accountable for it. King David prayed, in *Psalm 141:3 "Set a watch, O LORD, before my mouth; keep the door of my lips."*

He also sang, *"I WILL bless the LORD at all times: his praise shall continually be in my mouth" (Psalm 34:1). Proverbs 17:28* is one of my favorites, for it tells us, *"Even a fool, when he holdeth his peace, is counted wise: and he that shutteth his lips is esteemed a man of understanding."* May the LORD mercifully help His own to avoid the terrible aftertaste of having "our foot in our mouth." – J. Haley

Prayer: Lord, we do have a problem with our tongues. However, we praise You that You do not consider our words that are born out of frustration, but our hearts that are so very tender towards You that such words hurt our own soul, before they hurt Your heart. Amen.

February 25

Every time I read such scriptures as *Psalm 16:5, "The LORD is the portion of mine inheritance and my cup; thou maintainest my lot,"* I feel a bit sheepish. It always amazes me that I am so prone to pursue after vanity (that which is worthless and useless in the light of eternity), while being complacent towards what would prove satisfying and eternal. Such pursuits start out in an innocent way, but the emphasis ends up being all wrong.

Even though intellectually I know that worldly pursuits are silly, I have this ridiculous notion that I must at least experience its emptiness before I can let it go to the wayside because my imagination of what it will bring me has taken my affections captive. Now I can't simply let it go. I must partake of it to silent the torment that is operating in foolish expectation.

The Bible is clear that as believers we only have need of what was ordained to be our portion and that is the Lord Himself. He is the essence of our heavenly inheritance. It is only as I possess Him that I can be assured of maintaining my spiritual lot.

Prayer: Lord, help me to remember that Eve fell for the same foolish notion in the Garden of Eden. Take away the foolish idea that I must experience the vanity of something before I wisely let go of it. Amen.

February 26

How many people desire, seek after, and pursue an earthly inheritance? In fact, our liberal government thinks it has the right to tax, redistribute, and squander such inheritance because the recipient never really earned it in the first place. These evil individuals never stop to think that they will be taxing what already has been taxed in various ways, give it to people who never earned any of it, and eventually will squander it in wicked ways.

As believers we are told in Psalm 16:6, *"Yea, I have a goodly heritage"* The truth is the people of the world work hard to leave an inheritance to those who often do not know the value of it. It's clear that they were trying to leave a legacy behind that would establish a place of identity, security, and hope for those of their choosing, such as family members. Clearly, heritage should be regarded as sacred and not an opportunity to rob and destroy the blessing designated for others.

The one thing I am glad for is that my real heritage is not of this world. It cannot be taxed by wicked governments, taken away by despotic leaders, or squandered by the foolish. And the closer I get to obtaining it in the midst of temporary vanity and glory, the more I prized it.

Prayer: Lord, thank You for a heritage that cannot be taken away from me. It is living and eternal—it is You. Amen.

February 27

Christians must be disciplined to possess their life in Christ. King David stated in *Psalm 16:8, "I have set the LORD always before me: because he is at my right hand, I shall not be moved"*

As Christians, our Lord is our inheritance. However, to possess our inheritance, we must set the Lord before us. We must make

Him our right hand, the One who has our ear and who holds all authority as to our responses as well as what touches our lives and in what way it will impact us.

To have heavenly assurance in this manner will once again guarantee me that I will not be moved from that which is eternal. As believers, we must remember the Lord is our rock. He not only serves as our foundation, but he stands before us as our fortress, to the side of us as our companion, behind us as our protector, and in front of us as our guide. In essence, we are covered from every direction by Him.

Prayer: Lord, we have nothing to worry about as long as we direct our focus on You and trust you to work out all of the details. You have every aspect of our person and lives covered. As a result, we will never be moved from You as our eternal Rock of heaven. Amen.

February 28

The cascading rain was as unstoppable as my flowing tears. Somehow, I just wasn't prepared for the sudden chain of events that led to our final "Goodbye" to little Tucker, and now the silent emptiness and loss of so much love, like a powerful undertow, threatened to suck me under.

Later, while spilling out my anguish to the Lord, a small, black spot on the wall grabbed my attention. Now, I'm not the kind of a person who can ignore out-of-place "spots" on anything without taking action. Therefore, I grabbed a square of toilet paper, and carefully removed a little black beetle type of bug from the wall. Since I was already in a sentimental mood about God's living creatures, I decided to toss it outside.

So, there I was, standing in the middle of the house, trying to decide whether to free it into the back or put it out front. At this point, you may be thinking, "What difference does it make?" Well, in this case it made a huge difference, which, to us, was divine guidance indeed for when I opened the front door, there sat, much to my surprise, a rain-soaked box up against the door, waiting to be discovered.

As it turned out, and unbeknown to two of us, the third household member had ordered a box of textbooks for the children in her class. Since we rarely go in and out by way of the front door, who knows how long that box would've been soaking up rainwater, ruining the books?

We all had to smile and laugh a little at the greatness of our God, using a teeny-weenie bug to rescue textbooks just in the nick of time. We marvel at how intimately personal, detailed and aware of every little thing that concerns us the Lord is, and what a great sense of humor He has too! – J. Haley

Prayer: Lord in our sorrows, we sometimes forget that Your light will penetrate such darkness in unexpected ways that will always lift up the soul, encourage the heart, and allow a smile to outshine the stains left behind by tears. Amen.

March

March 1

In my recent meditations, I was reminded of my favorite song, "Amazing Grace." As I was thinking about it, I realized it puts things in perspective. For example:

1) If a person does not consider their sinful, wretched condition in light of God's grace, they will feel condemned in the end rather than forgiven.
2) If a person does not grasp salvation in light of God's grace, they can easily become religious and arrogant rather than humble.
3) If a person does not embrace God's sacrifice of His Son on their behalf in the light of His grace, they will end up bringing dishonor to the Lord, rather than honoring Him.
4) If a person does not understand God's promises in light of His grace, they can easily feel unworthy to receive God's best. It is for this reason we must trust the favor God wants to show us because of redemption in order to allow grace to freely reign through righteousness by faith.

God's amazing grace brings perspective because it walks hand in hand with His love, mercy, compassion, and commitment to us. After all, God's grace is not about us, but about God, and it inspires genuine faith in the hearts of those who believe.

Prayer: Lord, Your amazing grace overwhelms me at times. To know Your grace is humbling, to experience Your grace is sweet to the soul, and to walk in it is to discover the real virtue and disciplined life of a saint. Thank You for Your wondrous grace. Amen.

March 2

What do you want the Lord to see when He considers your life? Consider what *Psalm 14:2* tells us, *"The Lord looked down from heaven upon the children of men, to see if there were any that did understand, and seek God"*

The Word of God tells us that God seeks those who are seeking Him with their whole heart. In man's fallen state we know that he has no inclination to seek God. The reality is few of us seek FOR Him. Granted, we may seek knowledge ABOUT Him, we may seek some FORM OF RELIGION to connect with Him, and we may seek OUT THOSE who are considered experts in their religious field to answer our questions about God, but FEW seek Him.

Psalm 14:1 reminds us why few seek the Lord, because, there are many who say in their hearts that there is no God. Why would a person seek for someone whom he or she did not believe even existed? Sadly, most people are foolish because they walk in unbelief before God. I choose to believe what the Word has declared about Him. I maintain that all that is said in the Word of God is "amen, so be it on earth, for it is so in heaven."

Prayer: Lord, nothing is going to change the reality that You not only exist, but in the end, there will be no debate as to who You are, and that You are holy, as well as righteous in all of Your ways. God, I praise Your holy name and worship You in awe and adoration. Amen.

March 3

Life is a mystery as well as a gift. We must choose to receive this life as a gift. *Deuteronomy 30:19-20* says we must choose life and blessings instead of death and curses. Note, there are no lukewarm valleys that stand between these two choices. We are choosing either life or death by how we live out our life according to the master we choose to believe and serve.

As a believer, each day, I open up this gift called life to see what God has in mind. Most of the time I open it to discover the ordinary responsibilities of life, but more often than not, God has a surprise here and there for me to discover. Sometimes there are even miracles and extraordinary blessings that cross the bow of my ship.

The conception of life is a miracle and for the Christian, the end of it serves as a door that opens to the incorruptible. Mortality reminds us that physical death is part of the cycle of life, and that which is attached to the present world is temporary. Clearly, the present life is in constant flux. In a sense, mortality is meant to give us a reality check.

The purpose for our present life is to prepare for the next life. Some people are content to get by while failing to prepare for eternity, but as believers, we walk by faith as we prepare for heaven by choosing the ways of life.

I am so thankful that my Lord has and will conquer all enemies including the enemy of death. Praise His holy Name.

Prayer: Lord, keep me in Your ways. I choose to love Your truth and give way to the sharpness of it when it challenges my way of thinking. I prefer to leave this world possessing Your truth than possessing a delusion that will find me in the bowels of judgment and separated from You, for You are the essence of all truth and life. Amen.

March 4

It was during Seattle's evening "rush hour" traffic when I slipped out of the house and walked two blocks to a busy neighborhood intersection. My inexperienced and somewhat fearless pre-school mind decided this was the perfect spot for some excitement. Sitting on the curb's edge, I stuck my feet out as far as I could at each car that came around the corner.

Unbeknown to me, a neighbor who knew my family spotted me there, and not being able to park and snatch me out of harm's way because of all the traffic, drove straight to our house and alerted my busy mother who had no idea that I wasn't in the house. Since she was baking at the time, she snatched up the first thing in sight which was a sturdy metal pancake turner and dashed out the door.

Imagine my shock and surprise when I looked up and saw one mad mama heading my direction with that pancake turner in hand! I can still remember to this day that pancake turner smacking my behind with every step I took. It didn't actually physically hurt, but the "bawling out" I suffered for those two blocks was hard to forget. I learned about consequences that day.

Every one of us suffers in this world from the consequences of our wrong decisions, but the sad fact is, most people just keep on making the same bad decisions over and over again. *Proverbs 22:15* says *"Foolishness is bound in the heart of a child; but the rod of correction shall drive it far from him."* And our Lord said, *"As many as I love, I rebuke and chasten: be zealous therefore, and repent" (Revelation 3:19).* – J. Haley

Prayer: Lord, You are so longsuffering towards us, giving us a chance to repent and turn from our wrong ways, but You are also a loving Father. You will let us taste consequences for wrong decisions so we will learn doing what is right is the best way to walk regardless of the false promises and glitter of the world. Amen.

March 5

Ephesians 4:24 states *"And that ye put on the new man, which after God is created in righteousness and true holiness"* The daily challenge for the Christian is not to become comfortable with the old way. It is true that you first have to come to terms with the person you are in order to determine the person you desire to become to ensure real change. You must recognize the old and put it off so you can put on the new man.

Change is hard for most of us to consider. We like that old comfortable shoe or that tattered shirt that fits as it has melded into the very fabric of who we are. But change is necessary and can only occur when great travail of the soul has taken place. Like the butterfly, such change points to the inner man's struggle to come forth in a new life. Change entails being nurtured in the womb of adversity. A womb of this nature points to the dark night of the soul.

I cannot count the times that I have struggled in my innermost being with who I am and who I desire to be. I want to put off the old, but it is such a part of my landscape. I understand that for the new to come forth there must be travailing and a new birth. However, I need the courage to face the tidal wave of change that is close at hand after the travailing has passed and the new birth has taken place.

Prayer: Lord, in order to obtain life, we must face death—death to the self-life—death to the old ways—death to life as we know it. We avoid such death because we do not want to finalize it with the lonely sound of taps, a burial and a tombstone. Lord, the old must die for the new to come forth. Amen, so be it!

March 6

Psalm 42:7 states, *"Deep calleth unto deep at the noise of thy waterspouts: all thy waves and thy billows are gone over me."* Oh, how I have desired the deep things of God, but how deep am I willing to let Him go in my life?

I cannot understand the deep things of God until I have been prepared by the deep plows of God. Oh, how deep must He go in the soil of my soul before my heart is enlarged enough to receive the depths of His wisdom and truth?

Clearly, the soul must be overcome by the darkness of uncertainty. However, the darkness makes the nights of despair seem long and cruel. It seems as if there will be no end to such darkness, while the struggle seems to be endless. Despair nips at our heels and hopelessness becomes a heavy curtain upon our souls. Such times represent the winters that cause all to lay dormant under a blanket of uncertainty.

We must trust the fact that darkness is sometimes made by the extreme light of God upon the barren places of our souls. The Lord is faithful to reveal the darkness upon the different aspects of our soul in order to break forth with His light.

Prayer: Lord, it is in darkness that we learn the importance of Your light. Lord break through the darkness upon my soul and reveal the way in which I must walk in relationship to Your kingdom and will. Amen.

March 7

Jesus' great cry from the cross that should break every heart when they read it is, *"My God, my God why hast thou forsaken me!"* I believe in that one moment all the cries of the seeking, desperate souls throughout the centuries are heard. In that cry is what many would consider the ultimate betrayal. In His humanity, Jesus became sin for us, and God in His holiness hid His face from it revealing the great plight of man. (*Isaiah 59:2*)

Jesus's cry shows us man is separated from God. Man may not be aware of it or in his heart care about it, or in his mind give it any real consideration. However, man's great, deep loneliness is caused by the great spiritual separation between God and him caused by sin. It was not God that forsook man; rather, it was man forsaking God in his heart, mind, and will.

We know that Jesus' plight on that cross was temporary and would end in victory as made evident in His resurrection, but no doubt in His humanity it seemed like eternity. There are many struggles going on in the unseen realm of man's innermost being. The darkness is heavy upon his soul, the lies of the age thick, the wickedness of it stifling, and the despair of it overwhelming. At such times God may seem far away, as if forsaking us. Jesus gives us a slight glimpse into the tragedy of man being separated from God, and yet how many are seeking Him with all their heart because His promise is He will be found by them.

We can always blame what we perceive to be a gap, or separation from God, as the result of the age we live in. However, much of the separation can be due to the fact that Jesus is not being properly lifted up or is not sitting in His rightful place as Lord of our lives, our homes, and our churches.

Prayer: Lord, I do not want to miss You by tasting the bitterness of the soul caused by a leanness in the spirit, the dark garment of hopelessness, and the isolation of despair. Give me that great hunger and thirst for Your righteousness that will enable me to rise up out of the miry pits of this world and seek You with everything in me. Amen.

March 8

"The people which sat in darkness saw great light; and to them which sat in the region and shadow of death light is sprung up" (Matthew 4:16). We all start out with darkness upon our souls. Our journeys often lead us where darkness will enfold our souls, resulting in a state of utter, spiritual darkness. At such times it is as if the light will never again shine upon our weary souls. However, we must remember the heavenly light will mean nothing unless the darkness becomes intense upon our innermost being. Such intensity leaves us a clear contrast as to the state of our condition.

Today the shades of compromise caused by the abundance around us is gone. Self-sufficiency has taken flight due to the great need that now lays heavy upon souls. Arrogance has been rendered to a mere whimper because of the great losses that seem to be humbling man as he stumbles, falls, and feels great blows against his resolve to stand in such darkness. The darkness is overwhelming, but for believers we never have to settle for the darkness of the age. We must remember that, in a like age as ours, Noah walked with God and found grace.

How great of a light do we need in order to see through the grave darkness and the confusing shadows of the world we live in? It is not a matter of how great the light is, but how intense it is. Too much light can blind, but intense light can penetrate the darkness.

In Matthew we learn about the light that can break through such darkness. Jesus is the great light of heaven that came to penetrate the darkness of this world. My hope is that His light is penetrating every area of the darkness upon my wretched soul to bring hope, guidance, and direction as I rediscover a very simple truth: God's grace is always sufficient to get us through such darkness.

Prayer: Lord, darkness will come to my soul, but I have the promise of the heavenly light that flows through and out of Your grace. If I choose to trust You during such darkness, in due time the light will break through the consuming obscurity that plagues me. Amen.

March 9

There are times when the darkness that weighs upon our souls is so heavy that we perceive there is no way for the light to break through. We sense that if any light manages to part the heavy darkness, it will have to come from a giant source. When I encounter such darkness, I choose to remember Scriptures such as Revelation 22:16b, *"I am the root and the offspring of David, and the bright and morning star."*

We lived in an area that proved to me that any type of light can break through the grave darkness of night. Our home was located by a river in a quaint little community. One night Jeannette excitedly came into the house from the deck. She informed me that we not only lived by a beautiful river, but that the sky also emanated untold beauty.

When I went out on the deck and looked up in the midst of darkness, I saw one of the most beautifully lit skies I had ever seen. It was alive with the glorious lights of innumerable stars. I could even distinguish the light of the Milky Way. However, we later discovered that we could only see the beauty of the sky as the darkness of the night became more intense. It was the darkness that brought out the beauty of the night lights.

We may fear darkness, but if we want to discover the beauty and intensity of the light of heaven, we must embrace the dark night of the soul. It is only in darkness that the bright and morning star can arise to bring us the contrast of light in darkness and the beauty of a sun-lit day.

Prayer: Lord, we thank You that You are the real light of heaven. Your glory needs to shine upon my life and through it to cause the darkness of my soul to flee. Praise Your holy name for the light that penetrates the gravest of darkness. Amen.

March 10

I often meditate on what it means for Jesus to be the light of the world. We know He is the bright and morning star that must dawn in our souls to ensure salvation. I remember the instruction of Jesus that we are not to hide our light under a bushel because of fear or under a bed due to spiritual laziness and uncertainty. Clearly, this points to ensuring the light is not only allowed to shine in, through, and from our lives, but it must be lifted up so it can shine through the great darkness. Upon meditating on this fact *John 12:32* became more precious to me, *"And I, if I be lifted up from the earth, will draw all men unto me"*

Before Jesus can arise in our souls, we must first experience the foreboding ways of the grave darkness that rests upon the landscape of our souls. Once we experience His light, we must allow it to shine through us. This means that He must be lifted up in our lives so others can see Him as the light.

In *John 9:4*, Jesus made a statement about another type of night that was coming. This darkness would prevent man from working. When I consider the darkness Jesus was talking about, it was the darkness of death, His death on the cross. It dawned on me that in the travailing that occurred during His ordeal on the cross, that is when the light of the world was lifted above the darkness to shine in a greater way. For out of His death came a new dawning for those who experience the light's penetrating affect.

Prayer: Lord, the dark night of the soul represents some type of death. Enable me to embrace the death to ensure the light of Your life coming forth in greater ways. Amen.

March 11

The weather is so fickle and unpredictable these days, especially where we live, that the only "safe" way to dress is in layers. Some days I think that the "layering" procedure has been taking place for such a long time that I've forgotten what it feels like to dress lighter. I find myself thinking that it's a good thing I'm way past those days of trying to "keep up with the fashions." Besides, just who, when, where and why does everybody in the country have to conform to the so-called "fashions" anyway?

Most of the stuff we think we have to have, have to do, have to eat, and have to conform to as far as our outside appearance, our taste (or lack of it) of the arts and so forth isn't God's plan for us, but is instead totally the world's idea. And, who is the "god of this world"? None other than Satan. *("In whom the god of this world hath blinded the minds of them which believe not, lest the light of the glorious gospel of Christ, who is the image of God, should shine unto them" 2 Corinthians 4:4).*

As for fashions, Peter wrote, "As obedient children, not *fashioning yourselves according to the former lusts in your ignorance (1 Peter 1:14).*

When it comes to conforming, Paul wrote, *"And be not conformed to this world: but be ye transformed by the renewing of your mind, that ye may prove what is that good, and acceptable, and perfect, will of God" (Romans 12:2).*

Concerning those things that we cling to because we really do love them, John warned, *"Love not the world, neither the things that are in the world. If any man love the world, the love of the Father is not in him" (1 John 2:15).*

Finally, when you daily dress, don't forget the most important garment of all, and that is Christ. *"But put ye on the Lord Jesus Christ, and make not provision for the flesh, to fulfil the lusts thereof" (Romans 13:14).* – J. Haley

Prayer: Lord we get caught up with things whose glory is temporary, its importance leaves us hollow, its purpose proves vain, and any expectation we have about it flows through our fingers like water. Lord, cause me to set my affections above on You and not on this earth. Amen.

March 12

We are told in *John 1:5, "And the light shineth in darkness; and the darkness comprehended it not."* Spiritual darkness can't understand the light of heaven, and for the Christian such darkness is a type of night that enfolds the soul. This spiritual night comes upon us as a blanket. It appears as if it covers everything that can be seen in our lives. As a result, many people perceive they can do wicked deeds under the cover of such darkness.

They do not realize that the night reveals much. Granted, the light may give way to it, but only for a season. Once the light penetrates the darkness, it will reveal the types of deeds that were done in darkness.

The light will also reveal that there is a difference between the darkness of wickedness and the long night of travailing. The dark night of the soul represents a time or period in which one can find him or herself travailing to come to a place of rest. On the other hand, spiritual darkness represents blindness that will delude people about their spiritual state. They are not only blind, but they are spiritually lost. They must grope through their spiritual blindness.

I have learned that as a believer, night will surely come upon me, but not the darkness of wickedness. Like my Lord, I must travail in prayer and cling in faith and patience, while resting on Him, the Rock of Ages to survive the darkness that is forever trying to invade the hearts and minds of those who are loyal subjects of this present age.

Prayer: Lord, the night must come to my soul, but the grave darkness of wickedness must remain far from me. Keep me in the place of Your mercy, grace, peace, and rest. Amen.

March 13

When we think of the contrast between light and darkness, there is no greater contrast than this: God so loved the world, He gave His Son as light, hope, and salvation, but there is also a big "BUT," that follows that we must take note of in *John 3:19*, which brings a sobering contrast, *"And this is the condemnation, that light is come into the world, and men loved darkness rather than light, because their deeds were evil."*

We can get sentimentally caught up with how much God loves, but love is two-sided and must be present on both sides for it to be beneficial to the parties involved. No matter how we swoon over God's great love, the other side of the equation is that man does have a natural love or preference, but it is not directed towards God; rather, he so loves darkness that he prefers to remain lost in it to hide his evil deeds from the righteous, holy God.

Spiritual darkness clearly reveals a person's character and preferences. In spite of the darkness, the Lord sees our deeds. We cannot hide them from Him. In fact, the Lord provides the darkness so that the deadly fruits of the wicked can take root, be nurtured in an environment of evilness, and brought to full bloom in order to be consumed by His wrath.

As a believer, I must always look for the precious light of Christ in the darkness. However, I must realize that darkness is necessary for righteousness to be established and bring the contrast that the greatest darkness exists in man and not the present world. I must choose what I am going to love or prefer and remember as a believer I am to reflect the real light of the world. I must do so remembering, it was only in darkness that the lights of Noah, Job, and Daniel shined brightly in their generation, revealing the true ways of righteousness. (See *Ezekiel 14:14, 16, 20.*)

Prayer: Lord, when we hide in darkness, it is because we refuse to see Your light. We know it will reveal all of our wicked ways and deeds. Lord, shine Your light upon me for I desire all wickedness to be exposed in my life, rooted out by Your fire, and swept away by the winds of Your Spirit. Amen.

March 14

I mentioned three men yesterday. Whenever I think of overcomers and about the type of environment that produces wickedness in high places, I remember what *Ezekiel 14* stated more than once about these men, *"Though these three men, Noah, Daniel, and Job, were in it, they should deliver but their own souls by their righteousness, saith the Lord GOD."*

I realize that evil will occasionally prevail to test the patience of the saints, but only for a season until the Lord steps on the scene. The fruits of wickedness must come to fruition for it to be revealed and judged. However, God will deliver His people, but maybe not in the way we think He should.

In Ezekiel's day, being led away into captivity was a form of deliverance from the judgment that was about to be poured out on the people of Judah. God made it clear that only a few men would be delivered in it due to their righteous status. Meanwhile, wickedness would reign and evil would prevail in the form of judgment.

Noah, Daniel, and Job left a legacy of righteousness. Noah overcame the wicked world with faith, Daniel overcame paganism with an excellent spirit, and Job overcame the temptations of Satan with abiding resolve.

Truly, I want to be as these men in the midst of this present age of wickedness. I want to be delivered in spite of evil prevailing.

Prayer: Lord, give me the faith of Noah, the right spirit as Daniel, and the abiding resolve as Job to endure to the end of each test, knowing deliverance awaits. Amen.

March 15

The request is simple, but speaks of integrity when it comes to walking through this world, *"And lead us not into temptation, but deliver us from evil" (Matthew 6:13).* There is a saying "Evil reigns when good men do nothing."

To most Americans, "goodness" is a mediocre, tolerant state that avoids causing any real waves of conflict or discomfort. It operates in the comfort zones of shades of gray that have no real clarity or decisiveness. It is in such an environment that evil can overtake and prevail against goodness. In fact, it will enslave goodness into a tyrannical nightmare.

The only way to confront evil is with the light of truth. Those who spin the web of evilness do not work under the cover of night, but under the cover of spiritual darkness. They want people to be blinded by ignorance so that they can create their veil of seduction and delusion *(Isaiah 25:7; Hosea 4:6).*

It is clear that there is a difference between goodness and righteousness. Goodness is a matter of moral living, but righteousness not only entails upright living, it is also a matter of standing for what is true and right.

For righteous men, good living is a natural extension of who they are in Christ, while Jesus' truth is a passion that will not allow them to be silent by the evilness of the bullies, thugs, and infidels that hate and oppose it with their deception. I must ask myself if I am content to be "good" or have I come to a place of real righteousness to spiritually survive the darkness of the times I am living in?

Prayer: Lord, You have instructed us to be vigilant and sober for we are in a battle for our very well-being. Please do not let me settle for mere decency, but cause me to always strive for what is excellent in Your sight. Amen.

March 16

When I get overwhelmed by the present-day insanity, I choose to remember such scriptures as Matthew 6:33, *"But seek ye first the kingdom of God, and his righteousness: and all these things shall be added unto you."* The simplicity of this Scripture alone can take out any confusion created by the darkness of our times.

As I occasionally consider the wicked leaders of today, I often meditate on how their wickedness can grow to such an extent. This brought me to how evil operates. Have you ever witnessed what light does to the creatures of darkness? It makes them scurry and scramble to find a hiding place. This is also true for men who are evil. For this reason, they hate the light and rage against its penetrating power.

Because of Adam, we all are born into spiritual darkness. Due to what initially influenced us, our natural preference is to go along with such darkness. Sometimes we even manage to develop a moral code of sorts to live a "decent" or "good" life in a quasi-state of religion. In this state, we have no ill-will towards others so why should we suspect others of possessing evil designs? All is well in this type of "goodness," but this is part of the delusion of the darkness of this world.

Jesus said we are to first seek righteousness, not goodness. Righteousness possesses the cutting edge of truth and justice that are necessary to stand when spiritual darkness becomes all-consuming.

Prayer: Lord, it is my tendency to settle for mediocrity, but such an environment will put me to sleep spiritually. Cause me to awaken and stir myself up to demand what is right and excellent in all matters concerning You and life. Amen.

March 17

It was such a shock, but it shouldn't have been. After all, my mother had warned me that the chocolate squares she was melting in a saucepan on the stove were not sweet. But to my child's mind, she was wrong, so I did what I usually always did that oftentimes got me into trouble—I argued, protested and persisted.

That rich, dark brown liquid just had to be yummy and I so badly wanted a taste of it. Finally, she relented and with one last warning dipped a spoon into it and handed it to me. Of course, my instant dramatic reaction to the bitterness of that unsweetened chocolate prompted my mother to utter probably one of the most ancient statements known to man since the fall in the Garden of Eden— "I told you so!"

It seems to me, as I look back over my life, that most of what I've learned I had to learn the hard way. But the LORD knows this is true for most of us, and His Word is full of both heavenly wisdom and clear warnings. If only we would be wise enough to pray and ask God for wisdom! Even so, may we be eternally grateful for His faithfulness, longsuffering, goodness, mercy, grace and love, for without it, there would be no hope for any one of us.

"It is of the LORD's mercies that we are not consumed, because his compassions fail not. They are new every morning: great is thy faithfulness. The LORD is my portion, saith my soul; therefore will I hope in him" (Lamentations 3:22-24). – J. Haley

Prayer: Lord when we insist on our way, we end up tasting the bitterness of foolishness. Even though I may be faithless towards You, You are always waiting to show Yourself faithful to me. Thank You! Amen.

March 18

When I think of the different mixtures that can exist in my life, I remember *Matthew 9:10, "No man putteth a piece of new cloth unto an old garment, for that which is put in to fill it up taketh from the garment, and the rent is made worse."*

When I first became a Christian, the things that hindered me was trying to mix the old life with the new life. I desperately needed a new life, but I felt there were things that I could salvage from the old. I discovered that the old defiled the new and the new never could be mixed with the old.

It is not unusual to see people stand between two opinions about spiritual matters. They want the best of both worlds when it comes to their religious life. They pick and choose between worldly ways and questionable moral values that have been readily accepted by the religious world. They want to be politically correct to display a worldly savvy, while being decent and morally okay to silence their conscience. Clearly, this is a dangerous mixture.

Worldly savvy simply means a person is being influenced by the spirit of the world in the way he or she is thinking *(Ephesians*

2:2). The Apostle Paul stated that our minds must cease from being conformed to the world's way of thinking, and they must be transformed to grasp what it means to do what is the good, acceptable, and perfect will of God *(Romans 12:1-2)*.

The harsh reality is that a dangerous mixture of the world and religion will dull us down to what is righteous, making us ineffective to properly discern the times we are living in, thereby, preventing us from being prepared to stand against wicked tides. It is important to understand that righteousness will always prove to be far more excellent (or superior) beyond any worldly compromise. Righteousness only deals in the absolutes of a matter, causing a person to always shun the dullness that comes with the compromising ways of the world.

Prayer: Lord, the world may tempt us with the idea of compromise in order to ensure a veneer of peace with those of this particular age; however, it is a dangerous game where the soul is compromised as the truth is crucified. In the end, such people will be at odds with You. Forgive us for thinking that we can be at peace with both You and the world, when the world is at great odds with You. Amen.

March 19

The Apostle Paul gives us this warning in *1 Timothy 1:19, "Holding faith, and a good conscience; which some having put away concerning faith have made shipwreck."* How does one end up shipwrecked in their faith? It is easy. Faith is about letting go of any hindering attachments in order to pursue God with every bit of strength.

However, it is quite convenient for people to stand between two opinions and try to hold onto both the world and religion. Such people can maintain their own personal comfort zone. They never have to stir the water with truth and bring any uncomfortable attention on themselves. In essence, they simply can get along with everyone, hoping to keep anything from challenging their particular world. After all, they like it where they are. It allows them to give an appearance of being reasonable to the world, and a "good person" to the religious community.

From such a premise these individuals can believe that all is well in their worlds, when in reality such a conclusion is nothing more than wishful thinking. Wishful thinking becomes a tidal wave of wickedness that will fast approach the shoreline of their lives. In the end they will be left devastated. The truth of the matter is, this wave will leave all of those who are not properly prepared to stand and face it, shipwrecked in their faith.

As believers, we are all called to stand for truth. Truth will place us on the Rock of ages. On the Rock we will endure the tidal waves of destruction. These waves will take out the sand castles of wishful thinking, but they will have no power to move the Rock from its eternal foundation.

Prayer: Lord, You are the Rock. I must keep this in mind when I watch the waves of destruction aim at my foundation. Plant me on Your ageless foundation. Amen.

March 20

I have often struggled with how I am to respond to that which opposes righteousness. In my meditation about this matter, 2 Timothy 2:3 would often come to mind, *"Thou therefore endure hardness as a good soldier of Jesus Christ"*

As a Christian, I am to live as peacefully with others as I can, but never at the expense of what is right and true. It is not that any of us are really looking for conflict; rather, it is because the enemies of the cross do not know the ways of peace. Such combatants have only learned the ways of war because they are not at peace with God or within themselves.

These individuals are driven by that which is wicked and destructive as they rage against what is true and right. It is for these reasons that as a Christian I must learn what it means to be a soldier, always ready to take up my armor and sword, when necessary, as a means to stand against the enemy's tyrannical affronts, withstand the fallout of wickedness, and when all is falling in utter defeat and despair around me, remain standing upon what is true and right *(Ephesians 6:10-17)*.

Clearly, the battle does not come along the lines of people agreeing with my evaluation of a matter, but along the lines as to what they are going to do with the truth when presented with it. It is a sword that will clearly cut, expose, and will ultimately silence the enemy. It always brings people reluctantly to the valley of decision.

Prayer: Lord, our marching orders are clear. We are to try to keep the peace, but if war comes our way, we must not run and hide. We must stand sure in our armor, with our sword lifted up to push back the dark advancements of the enemy. Amen.

March 21

As I watch the ways of the world, I am constantly reminded of *John 10:10a*, *"The thief cometh not, but for to steal, and to kill, and to destroy"* Clearly the enemy of our souls wants to rob us our peace in Christ, kill our testimony, and destroy our life in Him, and it is for this reason we must guard our souls and possess them in patience.

It is easy to compromise with the ways and philosophies of the world. However, the world's systems are under another influence (spirit) that is totally contrary to the true God of the Bible. The Bible refers to this influence in different ways. It calls him the god of this present world or age, the spirit that is prevailing in the world working in the sons of disobedience, and the prince of the power of the air *(Ephesians 2:2; 2 Corinthians 4:3-4)*. However, this influence of darkness is best known as Satan or the devil. Since there is no truth in him, he is the father of all lies *(John 8:44)*.

The fruits that are being produced by the propaganda of Hollywood and the left media clearly confirm who is behind the twisted realities that are being presented. Jesus also said of Satan that he was a murderer from the beginning. The father of all lies will always start out with a lie to deceive, seduce, or beguile people into the deception that his lies are truth, wise, and superior. Once people buy his lies, he can rob them of sanity, kill any discernment, and destroy any moral conscience. This brings us to one of the main lies our particular age has bought, and that is everything is relative. In other words, there are no absolutes.

If no real absolutes exist, then man can establish his own moral code, creating an amoral environment that will eventually collapse in on itself. Such a collapse will reveal that Satan managed to once again steal discernment, kill good conscience, and destroy any distinction or contrast that could bring sanity back into a world that is going mad because of wicked practices and evil agendas.

Prayer: Lord, You are absolute and all that comes from You has no variance in it. Thank You for being immutable in Your character, Word, and ways. Amen.

March 22

In my last meditation, I mentioned the humanistic approach that all matters are relative. The Apostle Paul warned us in Colossians 2:8, *"Beware lest any man spoil you through philosophy and vain deceit, after the tradition of men, after the rudiments of the world, and not after Christ."*

According to the constant bombardment of godless philosophies that have passed through the ages there are no absolutes of truth, morals, and holiness in this world. In other words, there is no real God who is holy; therefore, all issues can be cast to the wind to see what will remain standing. Since there are no absolutes, man can establish his own particular conclusions, values, codes, and approaches to a situation.

There will be nothing to fear because there is no set truth, moral standard, or point of accountability. It is for this reason that the idea of one God, one way to eternal life, one truth about all things, and one immovable moral standard (the Law of God), causes these individuals to mock and rage against those who dare to adhere to such beliefs.

Jesus was clear that He is the truth about all matters. If a matter does not come back to the Lord's nature, person, work, teachings, and examples, it will ultimately prove to be quite the opposite of "relative" as each unrepentant person faces the absolute judgment and wrath of a righteous God.

Prayer: Lord, all is doomed that is of this world. I am thankful that I am a citizen of Your world to come. Thank You for allowing me to be part of Your unseen, eternal kingdom. Amen.

March 23

In my last post (March 17) I wrote about how, as a child, I begged and pleaded with my mother for just a taste of the chocolate she was melting in a saucepan, and how shocked I was at the bitterness that filled my mouth when she gave in to my persistence. This also serves as a simple illustration of the bitter consequences we reap when we insist on having our own way as opposed to obedience to God's ways.

Whenever we stubbornly refuse to believe and receive God's wisdom, instructions, commandments and warnings for our lives because we refuse to surrender our right to the self-life, we are setting ourselves up to reap the bitter consequences. Every time! Nevertheless, the temptation to give in to the world, the flesh and the devil is always there and will be until the coming of the Son of Man when He returns to set up His kingdom on earth.

In the meantime, we are called to be overcomers, to keep our light burning, to resist the devil, and to walk in the Spirit so that, instead of bitterness, we shall reap the sweetness of that good fruit that is well-pleasing to the Lord. *"WHEREFORE seeing we also are compassed about with so great a cloud of witnesses, let us lay aside every weight, and the sin which doth so easily beset us, and let us run with patience the race that is set before us"* (Hebrews 12:1). – J. Haley

Prayer: Lord, I wish foolishness did not always prove to be the vice of the young. It seems that the wisdom to avoid snares and pitfalls comes after pursuing vain desires of the flesh and empty promises of the world while falling into a cesspool of foolishness. Thank You for always giving me a way out as soon as I called out to You in humility and repentance. Amen.

March 24

There seems to be much confusion about what is real righteousness. I have struggled with this matter in the past. It took some studying and meditation of the Word on such Scriptures as 1 Corinthians 1:30, *"But of him are ye in Christ Jesus, who of God is made unto us wisdom, righteousness, and sanctification, and redemption,"* along with practical and challenging experiences to come to terms with this subject.

Some people think righteousness is a matter of what you do, but this is not completely correct. Righteousness has a lot more to do with where you are standing in relationship to God. This brings us to the absolutes of God's righteousness.

There is no deviation or swaying when it comes to what must be considered true and right. Righteousness means right standing with God. To have right standing with God is to know there is no righteousness in any of us outside of Him who is righteous. In fact, the Lord must personally count a matter for the sake of righteousness in the place of personal obedience, or as being righteous. Therefore, upon salvation God must place us in Christ who serves as the essence of righteousness for us before the Father.

In Christ we positionally have right standing before the Father up front, but it is as the life of Christ is worked in us through the sanctifying work of the Holy Spirit that we are established in such standing before God in our character; and, it is when, by faith through obedience to the Word, that we are able to do right in regards to others that God is able to count or reckon our actions as being acceptable to Him.

Prayer: Lord, You are the essence, place, and revelation of righteousness. Hide me in You so that there will be no resemblance of the old me left to stand completely stripped and undone before You in Your holiness. Amen.

March 25

Have you ever meditated on *Philippians 2:5, "Let this mind be in you which was also in Christ Jesus."*? I have meditated on this verse because I see it both as an instruction and a discipline. To "let" points to a decision that will prove contrary to what I am used to. How can I let the mind of Christ be my mind when it is carnal and contrary to the disposition, attitude, and ways of God? The whole purpose of "let" is to ensure my mind is transformed by walking in a new way.

Righteousness is a disposition of Christ that I must give way too and an attitude I must develop that displays the integrity of His mind towards the matters of good and evil. This disposition will express itself in acceptable, godly conduct that is able to discern the will of God. People cannot do right by others unless they are right before the Lord. They cannot be considered right unless they have right standing in God.

For example, Job knew that he was righteous before the Lord, but he did not realize that he was righteous because of his standing in the Lord *(Job 1:1)*. It was not until he understood that righteousness is not just a matter of doing what is right, but it also involves God counting a matter for righteousness, while walking in obedience in regard to others is what carries the mark of God's approval *(Job 42:1-6)*.

Clearly, right standing implies that one is standing by faith on the Rock of who God is, while hiding in the cleft of His promises, and knowing that His hand is upon us in all that we do out of love for Him according to His Word *(Exodus 33:18-22)*. Such righteousness will be necessary to survive the attacks that will always come with the advancement of grave spiritual darkness.

Prayer: Lord, I truly strived to have a right relationship with You. I know that there is no real righteousness outside of You and Your perfect word and ways. Amen.

March 26

There's an old saying, "What goes in is what comes out." And, this is what happened around 60 years ago when I was "put out" for dental surgery.

My jaw bone had to be cut in order to extract a wisdom tooth because the roots had wrapped around it. Now, I think most folks know that when a patient is coming out of Sodium Pentothal, they are probably going to be vocalizing some things without being conscious of it.

So, to this day, I'm very thankful to the Lord for what came out of my mouth according to my somewhat shaken mother who was with me. When I had recovered and was fully conscious, she told me that I had loudly stated, "Jesus is coming soon, and I want you to be there!" When asked about the attending nurse, she stated that she ran for the door, and never came back.

This short story is an example of how important it is to guard what we put into our minds and hearts for that is what will come out in our words, deeds, dispositions, and attitudes. *"For the word of God is quick, and powerful, and sharper than any twoedged sword, piercing even to the dividing asunder of soul and spirit, and of the joints and marrow, and is a discerner of the thoughts and intents of the heart"* (Hebrews 4:12). – J. Haley

Prayer: Lord, Your Word is eternal and once it is planted in the heart, the heart remains true to Your truth. It not only springs forth in life and fruit, but it can come out in a simple testimony. Thank You for giving me a love for Your Word and firmly planting it in my life when I was young. Amen.

March 27

We all can relate to David's cry in *Psalm 13:1, "How long wilt thou forget me."* Spiritual darkness causes one to feel forsaken or forgotten by God. I cannot begin to count the times I have felt God has forgotten me. Granted, when I feel as if I am on top of the world, I feel infallible, as though nothing could possibly go wrong. However, such a state is delusion caused by my arrogance. I am never on top of matters. If anything, I am just flying high in my imagination as I allow my fickle feelings of self-sufficiency to define my reality.

The truth is I am very needy, and if I do not keep my spiritual plight in perspective, I will set myself up to fall into the abyss of utter despair. After all, life knows how to knock me off of my all-knowing pinnacle of arrogance and sever the all-knowing weak branches of folly.

It is in the dark abyss of uncertainties and despair that we are most prone to question if God is aware of our plight. In our need we desperately desire to see Him. It is only when we humble ourselves before Him by faith that we can be assured that He is with us. He will never leave nor forsake us no matter how great the darkness.

Prayer: Lord, You are my hope and stay. I pray You show me mercy, for in my logic I see myself as being wise. In my religion, I see myself as okay, and in my good deeds, I see myself being acceptable. Lord, all of these things prove I can easily be deluded about myself. Help me to have integrity and discernment in all matters. Amen.

March 28

Some of the greatest personal battles and revelations for the saint occurs in the night. King David even admitted it when he declared in Psalm 17:3a, *"Thou hast proved mine heart: thou hast visited me in the night."*

I have discovered that night is clearly part of our spiritual growth. It is in the night our souls can sorely be tested. This is when the reins of the heart are being tugged at by despair, plagued by seeds of doubt, and shrouded by the darkness of unbelief. Our resolve is being bombarded by adversity and our emotions feel as if they have been tied into a pretzel, preventing them from flowing or functioning in a proper manner. In the end, we find ourselves free-falling into an endless crevasse of fear.

The one hope we must keep in mind is that the Lord visits us when the light is shrouded by times of testing. We cannot see Him, but we can believe and trust that He is there. After all, the real test of faith is to trust God in the midst of such darkness and to continue to seek Him. However, before He can be found He must become our only source of hope in such uncertain times. It is the assurance of hope that allows us to see Him when we least expect it.

Prayer: Lord, we know that You allow the night to come upon our souls. It is a time for You to go deeper so that eventually we can come higher in You. I know these things, but knowledge does not take away the impact of such darkness upon my soul, even though I choose to trust You. However, in the end I will not be ashamed or disappointed that I put my faith in You. Amen.

March 29

I have often meditated on such Scriptures as *Psalm 18:21, "For I have kept the ways of the LORD, and have not wickedly departed from my God."* Holding tightly to God is a must when all matters of life challenge our resolve to continue our spiritual journey.

The Bible tells us that God will never leave nor forsake us. Oh, how we cling to such promises when the spiritual darkness upon the soul is thick and suffocating. Yet, there are times we hardly can believe that the great Rock of heaven is in the same place He has always been.

The problem is not that God has moved from His foundation of truth, but our vision or position in Him has changed. Sometimes the darkness of despair blinds us as to where we are located. We cannot see the Lord and we begin to grope for that which is firm. However, God has not moved, but like Peter who got out of the boat to walk to Jesus, in our gawking at the circumstances that loom around us, we can unknowingly move away from the Rock and lose sight of Him.

Sometimes we move or depart from the Rock because something has caught our attention and we begin to seek it out. By the time we realize that we have left the protection of the Rock, the storm clouds of adversity and challenge have already move in to enfold us in darkness.

Clearly, I must choose to believe and know that the Lord will never depart from who He is, but I can, in my desperation or even fear, depart from the place He is to hold in my life. How I must learn to cling to Him, regardless of the challenges.

Prayer: Lord, You are the One who holds and preserves my very soul. Instead of panicking when I become lost, help me to remember that I can humbly cry out in such times and You will hear me and bring me back into Your protection. Amen.

March 30

Most of us live in at least one "world within the world" depending on where our interests, talents and curiosities lie. One such world is the culinary world which presents an endless array of possibilities that include flavors, textures, herbs, and spices ranging from the exotic to the sublime—sweet, salty, sour, spicy, savory, tangy or bitter.

Sometimes the Word of God can be described, or compared, to these universal culinary experiences. For example, just as sugar is often classified as an addictive substance, God's people crave the sweetness of God's wonderful promises. However, just as too much sugar causes grave imbalances in the human body, so too leaning on God's promises while ignoring the conditions that come with them results in a dangerously unbalanced, spiritually weak and shallow Christian.

Jesus said that man is to live by *"every word that proceeds out of the mouth of God (Matthew 4:4)."* We cannot partake of the "sweet" without also tasting the bitter.

Revelation 10:20 says, *"And I took the little book out of the angel's hand, and ate it up; and it was in my mouth sweet as honey: and as soon as I had eaten it, my belly was bitter."*

Let us, therefore, if we are to truly follow Christ and "endure to the end," enjoy the sweet, but also embrace the bitter, for *"He that saith he abideth in him ought himself also so to walk, even as he walked" (1 John 2:6).* Remember, He walked up a hill called Golgotha. – J. Haley

Prayer: Lord, we usually want only that which tastes good, but we must experience all of the different spices found in Your Word to have balance in our lives. I desire the promises, but I must be prepared to walk in light of the conditions that will prove to be bitter to my fleshly attitudes and ways, trusting that You will use both to bring forth fruit acceptable to You. Amen.

March 31

The world we walk though is dark and foreboding. This reality becomes more obvious as we consider the wicked activities of the world. Granted, the present age has the glitter of delusion, the temporary light of destruction, and the fading light of vanity, but such light masks the empty vacuum of darkness and hopelessness that blankets the soul.

In my meditation at such times, Scriptures such as *Psalm 18:28* allows the light of hope to dawn in my sagging spirit. *"For thou wilt light my candle: the LORD my God will enlighten my darkness."*

As I learned long ago, I stand as a small candle in this dark world. I am meant to cast some type of light. This light will be determined by the type of wick and life that I possess. Do I have a crude, base wick that will not respond to the fire of the Holy Spirit? Is the type of life I hold capable of casting a light, and if it does, what will it say about the life that resonates through me? The Lord is the only One who can penetrate the darkness of my soul with His Spirit and life. His life is the light of my soul that will penetrate the darkness before me with His Word and promises.

Meanwhile, if my candle fails to cast the light, I must question where I am in my life before the Lord. Is my wick charred by indifference? Is the wax of my strength reduced to ashes by lifeless activities? Obviously, there have been many times my relationship with the world has caused the flame to lose its luster. I need to once again position myself close to the fire of the Spirit and the igniting power of my Lord's life in order to become the candle that shines through the darkness.

Prayer: Lord, You are my source of light, Your Spirit is my oil, and Your Word is my flint. Lord, I submit my life as Your wick. Set it ablaze with Your power and glory so others may see You. Amen.

April

April 1

"My times are in thy hand (Psalm 31:15a). Even though I know the words of *Psalm 31:15* are true, I still struggle with trying to maintain and uphold the life I possess. In spiritual darkness there is a great struggle to come to the light. I have pondered the numerous times I have wrestled with the matters of life. I have lamented over lost opportunities, chided myself over missing cues, and shook my head at the foolishness I have succumbed to along the way. I have also wondered how much I have wasted in getting the issues of the heart and life right.

It is only as I grab hold of such promises as *Psalm 31:15* that I am able to take comfort in the fact that my times are in God's hands regardless of the events taking place around me and my inept responses. He is not shocked or caught off guard by any aspect of my life. He foreknows and foresees every minute, day, and hour. However, He is also the One who situates my test, helps me gain hindsight about the past, as well as necessary insight for the present, and foresight in light of my future inheritance.

It is for this reason that time can prove to be a decent companion. I do not need to let time bring an indictment against me; rather, I can take the present time to first glean from the fruits of its many lessons and opportunities before I allow it to dissipate into the ongoing annals of bygone time.

Prayer: Lord, I am so thankful that my times are in Your hands. You are trustworthy in Your ways, pure in Your intentions, righteous in Your works, and powerful in Your actions. I humble myself before Your blessed ways, as I choose to trust You with each moment of my life. Amen.

April 2

One of the great questions in the Bible I often consider was asked in *1 Kings 18:21*, *"And Elijah came unto all the people, and said, How long halt ye between two opinions? If the LORD be God, follow him; but if Baal, then follow him. And the people answered him not a word."* The great prophet Elijah asked the people of Israel how long they would stand between two opinions. While they neglected the altar of God, they had been erecting altars to idols. Although they had some semblance of representation of God in their midst, His presence and blessings were clearly missing.

If a person is swaying between two opinions, it becomes clear they are standing for nothing and neglecting and sacrificing their life in God. They will move according to what is popular in the world, acceptable to the crowd, and pleasing to the flesh. It is for this reason I examine myself to see if I am swaying with the times I am living in or standing on God's Word. Am I just getting by or am I faithfully occupying as I walk in the ways of obedience?

As you read about the physical environment during that time, you realize it revealed their spiritual environment as well. The people of Israel were clearly in both a physical and spiritual drought. Since God's desire is that His people come to repentance to be saved, spiritual crises will often manifest in natural disasters. Although unbelieving man who lives in denial that there is a holy, just God and is actively involved with the affairs of this world would mock and rage against such a thought, it would serve those well, who believe there is a God, to consider the ways in which He tries to get man's attention *(Haggai 1:4-11)*.

101

It is God's will that none perish, but if people choose spiritual drought of the soul and refuse to receive by faith the giver of Living Water, Jesus Christ, and stand on His truth, then they are indeed doomed to know the great thirst of the torment of hell. In the end, they will be deemed wretched fools who have no recourse but to face His wrath.

Prayer: Lord, all is doomed that is of this world. I choose You and am thankful that I am a citizen of Your kingdom that is yet to be revealed to this age. Thank You for allowing me to be part of Your kingdom and giving me the strength to stand in these trying times. Amen.

April 3

"And I called for a drought upon the land, and upon the mountains, and upon the corn, and upon the new wine, and upon the oil, and upon that which the ground bringeth forth, and upon men, and upon cattle, and upon all the labour of the hands" (Haggai 1:11). Today, there are means to control our weather, but I have also learned that if there is a drought, flood, earthquake, or outbreak of horrific storms, that God's people must check out the spiritual environment in their life, the present environment of their community, state or nation. If there is spiritual indifference towards God, a physical drought may well be mirroring such a condition.

If the world around you is being flooded by the foolish, ridiculous, and heretical ways of the age we live in, perhaps the river banks are also overflowing, resulting in contamination and destruction. If there is an earthquake, perhaps faulty religious and worldly foundations are being shaken to get our attention. If there is an outbreak of storms, all you have to do is consider the present storms that are raging in homes, churches, this nation, and in many cases on an international level. The storms of the world have left many cold, defenseless, and open to destruction.

The truth is, God is actively involved in the happenings of this world and permits the folly of man to create crises. He may be loving, but that love has been extended for the purpose of saving our wretched souls. He could very well allow the elements, circumstances, and personal challenges to shake, expose, and bring down all personal and worldly defenses to cause people to realize that they are in a spiritual crisis, vulnerable to destruction, and they must look heavenward for their solution if they are going to survive the elements and storms of this world.

Prayer: Lord, thank You for Your faithfulness to draw and save people. Anoint that which will be used to bring one's soul into the fullness of Your salvation. Amen.

April 4

No doubt most folks can fondly recall certain bygone days that stand out as being especially "fun." Of course, everyone's personal definition of "fun" could, if jotted down on a 3" x 5" card, probably cover an entire football field. And, maybe, just maybe someone's memories would coincide with one of my "fun" activities, but then again, maybe not—for you see, this particular fun event involves a couple of dumpsters.

The first dumpster adventure I had was back in the 80's when I lived for a very short, very hot, and very broke time in Phoenix, AZ. It began one morning when I went to take out the garbage, and what to my wondering eyes should appear but a dumpster full of very nice, and very much needed, items! There was a lot of kitchenware including good cutlery (which I still have), beautiful serving bowls, soup bowls, drinking glasses, a brass pole lamp, and other items. And, not only did I need all these treasures, but they were all mine for free!

Believe me, this was such a blessing because company was coming for dinner and I couldn't even offer them a glass of water because I didn't have any glasses! I felt so overjoyed as I rescued everything I could reach, and was reminded of the four lepers in *2 Kings 7:3-16* who found the camp of the Syrians abandoned so that all they and the Israeli army had need of was theirs for the taking.

The other super fun day took place in a cemetery two weeks after Memorial Day a couple of decades ago. One of my friends told me that the caretakers throw all of the flowers away! And sure enough, when we arrived at the cemetery the dumpster was piled high with chrysanthemums of every color and hue. We loaded up with all we could reach, overjoyed at the thought of how gorgeous our yards would be with all the free plants. (And, once they were revived and planted, they were indeed beautiful.)

In the first situation, the LORD knew what I had **need** of, and therefore He provided it, and in the second dumpster run, the LORD knew what I really **wanted** for our yard, and He provided that too. How great is our God! *"Behold, God is my salvation; I will trust, and not be afraid: for the LORD JEHOVAH is my strength and my song; he also is become my salvation. Therefore with joy shall ye draw water out of the wells of salvation" (Isaiah 12:2, 3).*

Fun has more substance to it, and meaning, and is much more "fun" when the LORD's presence is in it! – J. Haley

Prayer: Lord, You are so amazing. You show Your faithfulness by meeting our needs and bring awe to our spirits when you provide us with pleasures that satisfy a want. Praise Your holy name. Amen.

April 5

The results never change when it comes to the matters of right and wrong in this world. *Proverbs 10:30* establishes an important principle, *"The righteous shall never be removed: but the wicked shall not inhabit the earth."* As I consider the fruits and ways of wicked people, I cannot imagine what these people think they will gain in the end. However, the one thing I know is that they will never inherit the land.

The land will not hold or maintain them. It will become as lifeless and barren as they are, causing them to experience hunger and death. The land will resort to the same extremes that these individuals have practiced in becoming mean spirited, hateful, and unforgiving towards those who they see as being inferior. It will ultimately spit them out with the same disregard they have shown others.

To survive the darkness engulfing the world, we must make sure that we know, worship, regard, obey, and morally line up to our holy God. God knows how to deliver the righteous, but He also will destroy any remembrance of the wicked out of the land *(Psalms 34:16)*. As Christians, we must come out and be separate from such wickedness. If we fail to separate, we are in danger of not only experiencing God's wrath, but discovering what it means for the very land to spew us out like disgusting vomit, revealing that we have indeed been part of something that was foul, repulsive, decaying, and dead to God.

Prayer: Lord, You have called us to separate from the unholy in order to protect us, but we often rebel and go our own way to discover the vanity of the profane. Forgive us for our stiff-necks. Amen.

April 6

Psalm 28:3 states, *"Draw me not away with the wicked, and with the workers of iniquity, which speak peace to their neighbours, but mischief is in their hearts."* It is natural to go our own way that seems so right to us, and turn off our discernment towards those we like or agree with. However, if we are being honest about the state of mankind, we will have to admit that discretion is called for at all times and not blind trust. We must discern what is so to ensure that what attracts and draws us is not the works of the flesh and the present world.

I have been quite aware about my inclination towards the base ways of the old man in me. Due to my past condition of sin, darkness can attract me, at which point, I can easily be drawn away by the seducing, delusional worldly ways of the wicked. I can find myself becoming attracted to the works of iniquity. I can see such ways as bringing me happiness and peace. However, worldly happiness is a temporary façade at best, and the idea of the illusive peace offered by the world is the destructive bait that will cause me to fall prey to the mischief of the wicked.

The only way I can avoid falling into the traps of wickedness is by loving the truth. The truth of the matter is I am weak and vulnerable in certain areas. I must be honest about such weaknesses, humble myself before God and ask Him to put the necessary reins on me as a means to pull me back from the destructive traps of the world.

Prayer: Lord, there are certain aspects of the world that can at times tantalize my freshly appetites. I know, Lord, the only way I can avoid the traps is become crucified, dead to the "old man." Expose such areas and give me the strength to outright mortify them. Amen.

April 7

Do you play the blame game? Sadly, this game started with our first parents, *"And the man said, The woman whom thou gavest to be with me, she gave me of the tree, and I did eat" (Genesis 3:12).*

When things go terribly amiss in the world we live in, who do we blame? A person with integrity will never blame anyone; rather, they will take responsibility for their part, but those who lack such integrity will either nobly accept the blame while justifying their rebellious actions in light of circumstances or find others to transfer their faults onto.

It is interesting what happens when there is a terrible tragedy of tremendous proportions because both faith and character will be tested. At such times finite man grapples with issues that are not only out of his control, but beyond comprehension. After all, "Bad things only happen to bad people." However, when bad things happen to innocent, unsuspecting people, the tendency is to resort to the blame game.

Why do we, as individuals, resort to such levels? The Bible tells us why we experience such sorrows and anguish in this world. It goes back to the disobedience of man. Instead of choosing the way of righteousness, our first parents gave way to delusion and/or chose the way disobedience, bringing a curse upon all mankind *(Genesis 3:17-19)*. This curse involves toiling in our environment, experiencing the sorrow of loss and despair, tasting the vanity of our labors, and experiencing death.

Due to being deceived, Eve found herself in transgression, but when you consider how Adam responded to his sin, you can begin to realize why man often finds himself in a destructive cycle that will often leave him empty and sorrowful. Instead of owning up and repenting for his blatant rebellion, Adam blamed both God and Eve for his action.

It is mankind's tendency to blame others for their unhappiness and God for their miserable state. Although, God gave man free-will to choose to love and obey Him, people often use their freedom to disobey the Lord, and then when confronted, they will turn around and blame Him for the mess, along with the "Eves" who are in their world for their disobedient actions. Meanwhile, the fruit that reveals that they have committed such offense exposes their real character. Such individuals will shed tears while they wallow in self-pity because the consequences they are paying are too great to bear.

Prayer: Lord, we do not naturally want to obey, but then we turn around and blame You for the results because You did not stop us or bless us in our sin. We indeed have the folly of selfishness, arrogance, and hypocrisy bound in our hearts. Forgive me for such foolishness in my life. Amen.

April 8

Since there's "nothing new under the sun," there has to be other people who, besides myself, talk to their plants—at least once in a while. Somehow, I felt better assuring the beautiful, blooming Campanula (Blue Bells) which was safely tucked in its temporary container in a corner between the back porch and the house to protect it from the blustery wind and pouring rain, that it was not forgotten.

I think the one-sided conversation went like this, "You'll be okay, you've got a home now, but you're not planted yet." It was then that it dawned on me that those of us who belong to our LORD and Savior are in a comparable position as the Blue Bell plant.

We know we've been bought with a price, we're part of the household of faith, and we're citizens of God's Kingdom, but in our present physical body we're not "fully planted" until we receive our new, glorified body at His coming at which time His Kingdom will be established on this earth and He will then position (plant) us to rule and reign with Him. (See *Revelation 5:10; Daniel 7:27; 1 Corinthians 6:1-3; 2 Timothy 2:12*.)

In the meantime, let us steadfastly remain as *"trees of righteousness, the planting of the LORD, that he may be glorified." (See Isaiah 61:3.)* – J. Haley

Prayer: Lord we have promises of the glory that awaits us and glimpses of it by faith and highlights of it in Your Word, but there is no way we can begin to imagine it. Lord, I just want to thank You for the promises, glimpses, and highlights of the expectation of glory that awaits us. Amen.

April 9

It is a tendency to get caught up with the debate of which one was the main culprit when it came to our first parents' fall in the garden. It is natural to put the blame on Eve, while giving Adam a pass because he was some poor victim. The Bible is clear Eve was beguiled while Adam was not (*1 Timothy 2:14; 2 Corinthians 11:3*).

Eve fell into Satan's traps while Adam knowingly rebelled. Eve shows me in my fallen state I can be easily deceived when it comes to the temptation of sin and fall into it, but when it comes to Adam, *Job 31:33* reveals the reason for Adam's response, *"If I covered my transgressions as Adam by hiding mine iniquity in my bosom."*

Adam reminds me that once I blow it, I must struggle with the tendency to skip out of taking responsibility for the wrong attitude behind it and the dishonorable conduct that follows. I must avoid explaining my foolishness away, justifying away my transgression, or qualifying the stench of my iniquity. I can't abide with covering any treachery towards God's sovereign authority, while hiding my moral deviation as a means to feel good about myself in order to avoid feeling the biting shame of being wrong.

The truth is no one really wants to be wrong. Being found in a wrong state is like taking a big stick to our pride. Our great tendency is to cover the shame of our spiritual nakedness by keeping our fragile pride from being exposed and wounded. This is what happened to Adam in the garden. Apparently, he had been toying with being independent from God's authority. When he gave way to his rebellious thinking, instead of owing up for his actions, he tried to hide his moral deviation behind false accusations.

I realize that I must possess integrity to overcome such a foolish state. There is no logical explanation for sinning, for it is what it is. And, any sane reasoning concerning it will only bring us into agreement with God's evaluation about a matter. Ultimately, we need to become silent before Him in shame, and repent and confess our sin.

Prayer: Lord, it is so easy to delude myself about what is wrong in my life, but if I am to silence my guilty conscience, I need to shut up and come into agreement with Your take on it. Forgive me Lord for preferring the dark way of self-justification, rather than repenting so that I can know justification that comes by way of Your blood. Amen.

April 10

What do we need to understand about our spiritual state of affairs? At the core of it is iniquity, a state of moral deviation that wants what it wants when it wants it regardless of how wrong, poisonous, and destructive it will be in the end.

Due to the iniquity present in each of us, we must struggle with the tendency to skip out of taking responsibility for our attitude and conduct if we are going to ensure the integrity of our prayer life. *Psalm 66:18* states, *"If I regard iniquity in my heart, the Lord will not hear me."* Who wants to face the moral deviation that so plagues us in our attitudes and decisions?

When I am in denial about my sin or a wrong attitude, I so much want to explain my foolishness away, justify away my transgression, or qualify the stench of my iniquity. I want to cover my treachery towards God's sovereign authority and hide my moral deviation as a means to avoid facing my real depravity. I do all of this to avoid feeling the biting shame of being guilty before God.

The truth is no one really wants to be wrong, and Adam was no exception. He had been thinking about transgressing against what was already established by God. (See *Hosea 6:7*.) When he gave way to his rebellious thinking by eating of the fruit of the tree of knowledge of good and evil, he created a big gulf between his Creator and him. Sadly, the only one who could close it was God.

Prayer: Lord, I so much want to do right to avoid being found wrong, but my motive is even self-serving and wrong. Lord, we so much need to be saved from our way of thinking, and being. Save me Lord Jesus. Amen.

April 11

The only acceptable response towards any sin, whether iniquity or transgression against the law, or covenant of God, is found in *Psalm 32:5, "I acknowledged my sin unto thee and mine iniquity have I not hid. I said, I will confess my transgressions unto the LORD, and thou forgavest the iniquity of my sin."*

In the past I have played the blame game. Tossing the blame onto some other poor soul reveals immaturity. Sadly, playing the blame game is natural to avoid accountability that is repulsive to pride. For this reason, I take valuable lessons from life and try to assimilate them into my spiritual life as a means to exercise and practice them.

Every Wednesday I clean house. It may not seem like much to most people, but it is important to keep on top of housework as well as our life. A cluttered, unclean environment makes for a cluttered, oppressive life. In such an environment one can become complacent because clutter can become overwhelming and uncleanness depressing. To ensure my complacency does not take center stage, I regiment my life as a means to schedule certain activities on particular days.

Obviously, clutter and the presence of uncleanness is not just a problem in the physical realm, it can also be a spiritual problem. Our lives can become cluttered with besetting sins, irritating ways, unhealthy attitudes, and unclean due to unbecoming ways and wicked practices. As a result, I need to schedule in my spiritual life house cleaning as well. I need to make sure those unacceptable spiritual hindrances are dealt with through humility, repentance, and forgiveness.

Prayer: Lord, we need to clean up the temple of our lives. Help us to consecrate our all so that You can sanctify that which You have ordained for Your purpose. May we do nothing but bring glory to You. Amen.

April 12

We are given this incredible promise in *Psalm 27:5, "For in time of trouble he shall hide me in his pavilion: in the secret of his tabernacle shall he hide me; he shall set me upon a rock."* As I consider the times we now live in, there is no debate as to the fact that they are troubling.

Great storms seem to be forming on the horizon, strong winds are blowing, waves are roaring, the waters are raging, and anger and hatred are rising like rogue waves that will leave great devastation behind. This should not surprise anyone. Due to our first parent's rebellion, the curse of trouble came upon this world and there is a time in the near future that it will be dealt with. Meanwhile, man would know failure, taste sorrow, experience distress, and feel the heaviness of despair upon his soul.

However, I also know we are approaching the end of this age where all enemies of God will be brought under the feet of His Son. The trouble that is coming upon the world will be that of great travailing, but we must remember there can be no new life come forth without first travailing. The spiritual kingdom that is being established and the Promised King will emerge at the end of this age, but the old will not easily give way to it. Therefore, there must be the travailing of judgment, the purging of wrath, and the cleansing of separation.

The key for me as a believer is to know there is a hiding place. In Christ, we are already positioned in His heavenly pavilion, and firmly placed upon our Rock of eternal ages that can't be moved by fierce storms of this age.

Prayer: Lord, thank You for being my immovable place of safety. We take so many things for granted when life is clicking along. However, time can cause the sands to shift underneath our feet as the waves of uncertainty grab at our ankles to attempt to uproot us from Your stable foundation. Amen.

April 13

Have you ever felt like a "sitting duck", ready to be picked off by unseen forces that have no concern for who you are? One of the things that can cause men to feel vulnerable and out of control are plagues, and we certainly have been inundated by planned plagues in order to rob people of their finances, kill people's health, and destroy any real quality of freedom and life they can have. We know that all such destruction can be traced back to the father of lies, Satan, who was a murderer from the beginning.

In *Numbers 16:47-48*, we have an interesting event that took place that involved a plague, *"And Aaron took as Moses commanded, and ran into the midst of the congregation; and behold, the plague was begun among the people: and he put on incense, and made an atonement for the people. And he stood between the dead and the living; and the plague was stayed."* What makes man a "sitting duck" is idolatry and what brings healing is the intervention of God.

I have often noted that men appear to be nothing more than pawns that must be sacrificed as a means to protect some ruler, agenda, or force. The truth is man is at the center of one of the greatest battles that has been waged and fought from the beginning of his existence.

This battle is for men's souls and who he will ultimately worship and serve. Who will influence the mind, gain the attention of the will, and own the heart of man? The war is between light and darkness, truth and deception, flesh and spirit, and wickedness and righteousness. It is between the forces of heaven and the forces of hell. It is a matter of life and death. Man often tastes the bitter fallout of this war, while God is the one who is often accused or blamed for the outcome. However, man alone chooses the outcome for himself.

The one thing we can be assured of in this battle is that like Aaron, the Priest of old, the Lord Jesus stands between life and death. I do not know about others, but I am assured that because of believing God's Word about the redemption of Christ, I stand on the side of life and not in the frightening shadows of judgment and death.

Prayer: Lord, You not only bridge the gap between life and death, You are the One who has pushed death back. Thank You for drawing me to You, allowing me to choose Your life. Amen.

April 14

So many beautiful teacups, and so little space to display them! Teacups, artfully crafted with their alluring designs, colors and shapes can somehow bring a splash of happiness into a world full of daily drudgery, endless work, and weariness. Some of the cups in my small collection are petite, and require constant refilling. Others are made to hold a couple of ounces more, while some of the larger cups give more promise to the enthusiastic tea drinker. One way or the other, the pretty cups are all unique and special, and all are made for the same purpose.

In a way, teacups can be compared to Christians who all hold the treasure of Jesus in their hearts, with some being "weaker," (holding less), some being "middle age" (holding more), and others being "of full age" with a greater capacity. The difference is, however, a teacup cannot enlarge itself, or hold more than it was designed to hold; but as God's children, we are expected to grow in the grace and knowledge of God, seeking to be enlarged and filled to overflowing with the Holy Spirit, and seeking to know Him as the Apostle Paul did who said, in *Philippians 3:10, "That I may know him, and the power of his resurrection, and the fellowship of his sufferings, being made conformable unto his* death" and *Galatians 2:20*, "*I am crucified with Christ: nevertheless I live; yet not I, but Christ liveth in me: and the life which I now Live in the flesh I live by the faith of the Son of God, who loved me, and gave himself for me.*"

John the Baptist declared, "*I indeed baptize you with water unto repentance. but he that cometh after me is mightier than I, whose shoes I am not worthy to bear: he shall baptize you with the Holy Ghost, and with fire*" (Matthew 3:11).

Are you ready to "hold more"? - J. Haley

Prayer: Lord, we are clay vessels that can be broken down, reshaped and enlarged by You. Have Your way because You alone know the type of vessel I must become, knowing that which is overflowing of Your Spirit will flow through me to others for their edification. Amen.

April 15

It is easy when we see trouble coming to faint in our minds with fear. However, when I see trouble coming my way, I must choose to remember what *Psalm 27:13* tells me, "*I had fainted, unless I had believed to see the goodness of the LORD in the land of the living*"

King David spoke this, a man who had to run for his life and hide in caves. According to his other psalms, David had a hiding place that would not be shaken by events. As Christians we have such a hiding place, but we must believe what the Bible states, that in the end we will see the goodness of the Lord prevail among His people.

The Bible is clear that believers must not faint in their minds because of fear. (See also *Hebrews 12:3*.) They must avoid accepting the judgment of the circumstances and seek the abiding faithfulness of God. They must look beyond the present troubles and believe that they will taste God's goodness in the land of the living.

I must constantly remind myself that I am just passing through this world and that my citizenship is not here, my future is not based on the present age, my hope is not founded in the temporary, and my expectation is not dependent on the unpredictable seasons of this present age.

It is by remembering my true inheritance that I will keep myself from fainting in unbelief and hopelessness no matter how much I feel like a sitting duck in this world. The world is clearly not my home. And, the home that awaits me will be glorious. For this hope and expectation, I can do nothing more than rejoice.

Prayer: Lord, I must keep my eyes on You to avoid fainting because of the darkness and circumstances that loom before me. I must trust the light of Your life in me to guide me through the darkness and keep my feet from slipping into the abyss of destruction. Amen.

April 16

Although God is sovereign, He will not step over man's will to demand, or insist on having life on his terms. Although God is the God of the universe, He gives the god of this age the right to rule over his systems. Even though Satan is limited by the seasons and ages set before him by the Creator, Satan still rules much of the activities that take place within the systems of this world.

This enemy would have us to believe that we are sitting ducks, pawns that have no say over our plight. It is true that we cannot control circumstances, but we can decide how we are going to respond to them. Will our spirit be downtrodden because we do not have any hope outside of circumstances, or will we realize that God is the solution? The Apostle Paul best described the positive paradox of a believer in *2 Corinthians 4:8*, *"We are troubled on every side, yet not distressed; we are perplexed, but not in despair."*

As the Rock, the Lord will not, nor can He be moved. Whether we are standing in Him, hiding in Him, or abiding in Him, all the forces of earth and hell can come against us, but we will never be moved. Even though all can be thrown at us, we will never be destroyed. This is our promise, our hope, and our inheritance as believers.

Prayer: Lord, we are a blessed people. Whether in the ovens of adversity, the fires of persecution, or the abyss of hopelessness, You are our immovable foundation of hope, sanity, and promise. Thank You for being who You are. We can rejoice in You. Amen.

April 17

"God, who at sundry times and in divers manners spake in time past unto the fathers by the prophets, Hath in these last days spoken unto us by his Son, whom he hath appointed heir of all things, by whom also he made the worlds" (Hebrews 1:1-2). I so marvel that God so loved the world, because many people choose to not love Him.

God looks for the one lost sheep, while men pursue other gods who are lifeless. He called out to Adam in the garden when he was hiding his shame behind fig leaves. He warned Cain before he murdered his brother Abel to recognize the sin that was at the door. He gave the people of Israel the Law so that He could show them their need for atonement and intervene on their behalf and bring them forth as a blessed people. He sent prophets to warn of impending disasters and judgments, but they were shunned, persecuted, and murdered.

And, not least of all, He gave His only begotten Son so each of us could be saved, but in spite of His overtures many continue to show contempt towards Him, while some connive and devise wicked advancements in darkness against His light of truth to destroy it along with His people. God has good intentions and thoughts towards each of us, and has done all He can do to reach out to, and warn mankind that many are dangerously heading towards the brink of destruction, with their eyes closed and their fingers in their ears.

Clearly, people insist that they prefer their lost state to hearing God's call, turning from sin, fulfilling the Law with love, and receiving Jesus Christ as Lord and Savior (*Romans 13:8-10*). So, what is God trying to do to get our attention in this age? If we are going to spiritually survive, we must individually make sure He is not trying to stir us awake just in time to face the great darkness that is working to consume us.

Prayer: Lord, You have never ceased to call, invite, and talk with those who believe upon You. Lord, give me the ears to hear Your voice and to properly respond to Your invitation and instructions. Amen.

April 18

In the last meditation, I considered what length God will go to get our attention. As we face the enormous crises brought on by the elements of the world we live in, we wrestle with the why's or how's that allow such events to happen. The inspiration behind our wrestling matches is not attached to this world, but to the next one.

We have our own ideas of how God must respond to the matters of life. We often walk according to the false promises of this world instead of in light of the promises of the next. Consider what we have awaiting us according to *1 Corinthians 2:9, "But as it is written, Eye hath not seen, nor ear heard, neither have entered into the heart of man, the things which God hath prepared for them that love him"* However, note who the promise is directed to—those who love Him.

We must realize just how vulnerable we are in our fallen state. We struggle with our concept of God. Some even feel the need to defend Him if there is the slightest suggestion that He is behind any disastrous, unfolding event.

The truth is, nothing happens without His foreknowledge and involvement. Is He trying to reveal the real spiritual condition of man in an attempt to save his soul? Will He use the circumstances of the times to wake up the sleeping saint in an attempt to prepare him or her? Will He unleash the destructive elements and forces of the earth that many worship to try to expose the foolishness of their gods?

Trusting God in the bad times is what will put our faith to a real test. We can think we have great faith, but let adversity touch that part about our life that is pleasant and we will find out what attitude we have truly developed towards God, and whether we love Him for Himself or are we in love with what He can do for us.

Prayer: Lord, you walked through the ovens with Shadrach, Meshach, and Abednego, and I will trust that You will walk with me through my fiery trials of faith as well. Amen.

April 19

I think we can agree that we are living in the end of the last days. Consider what *2 Peter 3:3-4* tells us, *"Knowing this first, that there shall come in the last days scoffers, walking after their own lusts, And saying, Where is the promise of his coming? For since the fathers fell asleep, all things continue as they were from the beginning of the creation."*

It has been my natural inclination to try to defend God's reputation at different times because of the scoffers. For me, there have been many incidents where I felt the need to defend God when He was viciously attacked by angry souls. The truth is, God needs no defense.

Man's choices often create the terrible events in the world. If man would care to listen, he would be made aware of pending disasters. If man was obedient to the sovereign authority of God, sin would not demand His judgment upon it. If he was observant, he would discern the times he lives in and be prepared for what is coming. However, the unbelieving become scoffers. Case in point, the Bible has already warned us of the times we are living in, but how many people are ignoring and scoffing at such warnings? Obviously, as the darkness of sin grows in this particular age, many will prefer the darkness of unbelief to being prepared to spiritually survive the times they are living in as they wait for the blessed hope of His coming.

In time, such individuals will begin to taste the bitterness of such events. As darkness escalates, they will falsely accuse and rage against God for not sparing them from the consequences and destruction that are now upon them.

As believers, we have been called to be prepared. Such preparation entails watching for His coming, faithfully occupying, fervently praying, and making sure that we are walking in the ways of righteousness so we will be found worthy to escape what is about to come upon the world.

Prayer: Lord, You have told us what we need to do in the days we live in, but will we believe You and like the preacher of righteousness, Noah, respond to Your instructions? Lord, I want to be a Noah in relationship to the days I am living in and not like the scoffers of his time who continued to live without any consideration of You and Your impending judgment. Amen.

April 20

The words of Mark 10:45 have always been a source of hope and expectation to me. *"For even the Son of man came not to be ministered unto, but to minister, and to give his life a ransom for many."* I know when Jesus comes back to earth the second time, it will be as King to rule over all, Lord over all estates, and Judge over all. Meanwhile His ministry is revealed in Him being the Son of Man who came to die as the Lamb of God so I could be reconciled back into a relationship with God.

The more I see souls in turmoil, families in disarray, societies in chaos, and nations reeling under the grave sin of leaders and its people, I have become more aware that Jesus came to ransom people from the destructive, tyrannical masters of this world. However, people are the ones who insist on remaining under the curse of death, as well as risk the well-being of their souls for the darkness of this present world.

It is sad to think that we have a tendency in our fallen condition to hide behind, or run back to these wicked, unmerciful masters because our deeds are profane. We do not want to accept the ownership of Jesus as Lord in our lives. We want to belong to the blessings of heaven while laying claim to the darkness of the world that serves our purpose. In such a state, people will find themselves standing in the decaying clothes of foolishness and vanity.

I must surely examine my attitude towards God and the world. Is God trying to spare me in some way from the destructive, evil entanglements of the world, but am I choosing to ignore His warnings and hold onto wishful thinking that all will turn out right in the end? The one thing I am aware of is that all words, deeds, and plans will be brought to the light. Idle words will judge us as being foolish, hidden sins will be declared from the rooftops, and wicked plans will be thwarted.

In such a state, I can only cry, "Oh Lord, my flesh rages against being disciplined by Your timing. My pride cries foul at having to wait, and my logic would want me to think that waiting is a sick game, but I choose to believe in Your very character and know that Your ways are perfect." My last declaration is, "Amen, so be it on earth for it is so in heaven."

Therefore, I say to myself, "Away with the foolishness of the flesh, the arrogance of pride, and the conceit of my logic."

Prayer: Lord, save me from the foolish, worldly, wishful thinking of the "old man." Amen.

April 21

Have you ever found yourself cornered in an awkward, distressing or bad situation with no way out? What you are about to read is true, it really did happen, and I will never forget it. It took place in the early 1980's. It was early evening, and I was reading alone in my motor home which was parked alongside other RVs in the South Center Mall in Seattle, WA.

The reason a group of us were there is because we were all professional artists who were exhibiting our artwork in the mall for three days. I could hear the muffled and somewhat excited voices of the others that had crowded into the RV parked next to mine, but I had no desire to join them, I didn't know any of them personally, and I was tired from a long day.

That's when the woman who owned the RV came over and rapped on my door, insisting that I come join them. She wouldn't take "no" for an answer so I reluctantly followed her. Once inside the cramped space, I found a place to sit as far away from the center of attraction as possible for, much to my dismay, she was "reading cards" and then telling people all about their lives.

The excitement was escalating as one person after another exclaimed how "right" she was, and "how did she know?" Since there was no exit through which I could escape, I prayed for help. Finally, the dreaded moment came when she called me up to the front while the others enthusiastically joined in with her. That's when I flatly stated, "It won't work for me."

She replied, "Of course it will. You'll see! Cut the deck." I repeated, "It won't work for me." She insisted, "Just cut the deck." So, I did, and it turned up a Jack. She blinked, and said, "Give it to me," which I did. Then she said, "Go ahead and cut the deck again." So, I cut it again, and again the card was a Jack. Her body noticeably stiffened in obvious agitation as she took the card. "Turn over the card on the top" she flatly stated. Obediently, I plucked the top card off the pile. It was another Jack!

By now the others had quieted down as they watched their heroin card reader begin to unravel. Tersely she commanded, "Take the card off of the bottom." You guessed it! It was a Jack! Trying to conceal anger, she suddenly stood up and said, "Let's all go to dinner!"

The following Sunday after the art show, I told this story to a couple of Christian men in the church I attended, and one of them said, "Do you know why she couldn't read a Jack?" I answered that I didn't have a clue. He explained, "She couldn't read it because it stands for JESUS CHRIST!"

Now, I don't know if this incident fits the theological definition of a miracle or not, but I do know for sure that there definitely was Divine intervention and protection from a familiar spirit, and that God's powerful, living Word never fails. *"Ye are of God, little children, and have overcome them: because greater is he that is in you, than he that is in the world" (1 John 4:4).* – J. Haley

Prayer: Lord we often innocently fall into things, but when we do, we quickly discover that You are not asleep at the helm, or surprised. As a result, You are always there to protect us from our enemies, keep us safe when our enemies are on the prowl, and preserve us when others are being swallowed up by the darkness. Amen.

April 22

I have been thinking about balance. Balance keeps the fragile from breaking and the strong from falling off the edge of sanity into a pit of insanity. Sadly, the tendency for most of us is to go into the extremes.

Sin causes us to either overcompensate or scramble to justify. Hurt or offence causes us to become bitter or fractured. Guilt causes us to hide or be driven by torment. It is for this reason that we as believers must understand what it means to come back to what is balanced, centered, and sure.

In *Haggai 1:5*, we read these words, *"Now therefore thus saith the LORD of hosts; Consider your ways."* The prophet, Haggai, told the people of Israel to consider their ways. He not only said it once but twice *(Haggai 1:5, 7)*. "Consider" in this text means to come back to center of what is true, right and important.

Because the people of Israel had failed to come back to center, their environment was out of order. They found themselves in a physical drought, but it was simply mirroring their spiritual condition. They had come back to the land of Israel over almost six decades of absence. Their precious city, Jerusalem lay in ruins, the land was unproductive, and the task to establish some semblance of order in the midst of destruction was monumental.

In their attempt to establish some semblance of life, they forgot a very important part of the equation. They forgot to begin at the center with God by first establishing His presence in the land by building the temple. Granted, they laid the foundation in the first two years there, but it was not until sixteen years later they began to build the structure and it was exactly seventy years after the temple of Jerusalem was destroyed that the new temple was finally completed.

Prayer: Lord, You are the center of everything that is right, true, and pure. If we are going to get matters right, we must start from the center of who You are, discipline our lives according to the center of Your example, and never sway from the center of Your Word. Amen.

April 23

When I think about our nation, I cannot help but think of the people in Haggai's day. The Hebrew people had not just returned to their original inheritance to reestablish their presence in the land, but to reestablish God's presence. The fact that the temple was not established in their midst after years of being back, caused the people of the land to pay consequences. *Haggai 1:10* states, *"Therefore, the heaven over you is stayed from dew, and the earth is stayed from her fruit."*

If God is not in the midst of the people, the center of what is true will be missing, blessings will be thwarted, purposes unfulfilled, and activities will prove to be empty and useless. For the last six decades there have been moves to kick God out of every aspect of this country and the devastating consequences of it is now coming to full view for many to see.

Godless, immoral, humanistic people have not only attempted to wipe God out of the rich legacy and history of our nation, but to outlaw any reference to Him. It is evident that the further people get away from the true center of the Universe, the more chaotic, perverse, insane, and lawless their environment becomes.

Keep in mind, God is the only source of true light, and wherever He is missing in the equation, darkness is not only present, but it will invade and consume every area where the light of truth has become dim, compromised, or sacrificed. If we, as a people and nation, are going to survive this present darkness, we need to come back to center as to what is true and right.

Do you need to come back to center in your life to survive the present darkness?

Prayer: Lord, have mercy on this nation and stir up Your people to once again become the salt of the earth and the burning light in the world. Amen.

April 24

King David declared, *"As for me, I will behold thy face in righteousness. I shall be satisfied when I awake, with thy likeness"* *(Psalm 17:15).* Regardless of how dark and wicked the times we live in are, as believers we should have only one goal and desire, and that is to wake up in the very likeness of Christ. We should realize we will never know satisfaction until we reach our highest potential in the kingdom of God—to be conformed to the very image of Christ.

In my lifetime, I have sought for that which I thought would make me happy. I have pursued after that which I perceived would give me purpose. I have desired those things that I thought would bring me inward satisfaction. However, all of it proved to be vanity. Whether my search brought me to disillusionment, my pursuits ended in despair, and my desires proved to be unrealistic, it all proved useless.

The reality is, all that I need and desire are found in Christ. To look for anything outside of Christ is to know and taste the bitterness of vanity.

Prayer: Lord, You have designed me to reflect You. Unless I submit to Your ways of righteousness to reach my potential, I will never know complete satisfaction. Amen.

April 25

One of the things I must consider is what my desires, agendas, and goals are when it comes to the kingdom of God. It is up to me to direct my attentions and affections heavenward, while discerning my desires, agendas, and goals to see if they line up to the Word of God and His will for my life.

In *Psalm 27:4*, King David clearly stipulated the essence of his heart, desire, and goal, *"One thing have I desired that I may dwell in the house of the LORD all the days of my life, to behold the beauty of the LORD, and to enquire in his temple"*

Desires, agendas, and goals will be greatly affected by the direction of my affections. My affections will be confirmed or reinforced by my preferences or they will be greatly befuddled, causing an inward battle of torment and despair. It is for this reason we are told to set our affections on things above (*Colossians 3:2*).

As a believer, my desire should be as David's. I must seek it with all of my heart. I must realize that by desiring to dwell in the house of God in this present world, I will be assured of dwelling in His glory in the next. Ultimately, I will indeed, in the end, behold the beauty of my Savior, Lord, and God.

Prayer: Lord, Your will should be my desire, worshipping You my agenda, and bringing honor and glory to You my goal. However, to ensure Your place in my life, I must dwell in Your presence. Lord, hear my heart's cry, and bring me into those secret places of communion with You. Amen.

April 26

When it comes to our nation, we must consider what we value. What is really important to us as a collective people? Much of what we value today has been determined by the way we have been conditioned by wicked Hollywood and indoctrinated by the lawless, perverted media and a corrupt educational system.

It is important to come to terms with how we have been influenced as to our worldview. Paul stated in *2 Corinthians, "And what concord hath Christ with Belial? Or what part hath he that believeth with an infidel?"* It is hard to believe that everything attached to this world is subject to the spirit of the world which is Satan. Therefore, what we value is what we pursue, put our energy in to acquire, and what we ultimately will try to possess as a means to ensure our survival.

People have different ideas of what it means to survive. Some attach survival to the quality of life. Granted, none of us wants to be deprived of the lifestyle we are used to, but the first thing we must acknowledge is that as a nation, life as we know it has, and is, quickly changing before our eyes.

Some people attach what is important to security such as savings, etc. Yet, we know that such security is false. It is based on worthless paper and standards that can fluctuate and lose their value overnight.

There are those who perceive that their quality of life is based on things or material possessions, but Jesus is clear that we must beware of covetousness because a man's life does not consist of the abundance of the things which he possesses. In other words, the one with the most toys will not be considered a winner in the end. Others are trying to devise schemes in which they will cleverly outmaneuver the present destructive tides, but there will always be those who will ultimately prove to be better chess players in the end, proving that all that is of this world is doomed.

We must remember as believers, our life is not of this world which is not only temporary but will prove to be useless and vain in the end when it comes to eternal matters.

Prayer: Lord, we live in a world that does everything to rob You of Your throne and authority and take what people think, or believe captive in order to demote You. However, each attempt miserably fails because You will never cease to be Who You are. You will reign forever and ever. Amen.

April 27

The "green thumb" in my life was apparently lost and gone forever. It was just another little thing that added a depressing smudge onto my growing mental list of "gone forever" issues. After one failure this spring, I carefully replanted the nearly invisible seeds of great promise into three little ceramic flower pots, placed them in the matching tray, and put them in the kitchen window. Then came the watering part.

Keeping in mind that those seeds were so tiny, I took care to mist the dirt several times a day. After all, I thought to myself, it wouldn't take much to drown them. The memory of healthy, thriving basil, parsley, and rosemary plants last year served to prop up my flagging patience.

So, long after the normal germinating process should have taken place, I waited and watched for the first wee sign of life. Finally, the day came when I made a decision. Not even one little shoot was popping up out of the dirt, so I decided (with an "I'll show you!" attitude) to "flood" them under the faucet, and give them three more days to show up. What a shock it was for my unbelieving eyes to see green shoots everywhere, and it was so fast I think I could've actually watched them grow if I had nothing else to do!

This brought to mind how many people think that they can simply "mist" the good seed of the Word of God in their lives by grabbing a verse of Scripture that gives them a little spiritual "energy" boost for a few minutes a day instead of plunging into the Living Water, and drinking deeply of His Word. David sang, in *Psalm 63:1, 2, "O GOD, thou art my God; early will I seek thee: my soul thirsteth for thee, my flesh longeth for thee in a dry and thirsty land, where no water is; To see thy power and thy glory, so as I have seen thee in the sanctuary."*

If your heart cry is that of King David's, then don't settle for a mere "sprinkle" (a "touch of the Spirit" here and there) when you can be fully immersed. Jesus said, *"But whosoever drinketh of the water that I shall give him shall never thirst: but the water that I shall give him shall be in him a well of water springing up into everlasting life" (John 4:14).* – J. Haley

Prayer: Lord we pursue the best the world has to offer, go to great lengths to accomplish what we think is important, and so often land on what is vain and nominal because it has nothing to do with eternity. Mankind has it wrong because they have it backwards. Lord, we need to pursue You so that we can partake of what is eternal, lasting, and satisfying. Amen.

April 28

When I thought about the vanity we can often pursue, I had to consider the idea of legacy. Legacy points to some type of inheritance or memorial that one leaves behind. In a way, the power or impact of legacy is determined by the reputation one leaves behind. Sometimes legends are born out of such legacies.

Consider the type of lifestyle and reputation Jesus had when He was put on the cross as a common criminal. *Philippians 2:7* describes the Son of Man's ordeal, *"But made himself of no reputation, and took upon him the form of a servant, and was made in the likeness of men."* He had become of no reputation, He had no place to lay His head, His physical beauty stripped from Him by the indifference and hatred of those who mocked and beat Him, and He was stripped of even His robe as He hung naked on the cross.

Even though we have the best intentions, our level of commitment comes down to what am I willing to lose of my present life and this world? The truth is we may feel ourselves quite committed and dedicated but when we are required to offer something up of great value for the Lord's use and glory, we find out just what we value and the real price we put on possessing the life of Christ.

Jesus died to obtain a spiritual inheritance for us. He gave it all and obviously, what we need to value in order to spiritually survive the onslaught of this present age is our relationship with God above all else. It is in a relationship with God that He can pass down the legacy of the inheritance that was secured on the cross.

Prayer: Lord, it is easy to chase after legacies that will turn into ashes and dust at the end of the age. I prefer to pursue an eternal legacy that will be declared from the corridors of heaven. Lord, be glorified in my life. Amen.

April 29

The Lord is clear about who we as believers can come into agreement with. Paul clearly brought this out in *2 Corinthians 6:16a, "And what agreement hath the temple of God with idols? For ye are the temple of the living God."*

We must remember, agreement has to do with the spirit you allow to influence your way of thinking: that of the natural man, the spirit of the world, which is Satan, or the Holy Spirit. Do we expose ourselves to that of temporary vanity, become ensnared by the evilness of the age, or maintain our life in the Lord by ensuring we are walking after, being led by, and walking in the Spirit.

We must remember we are part of a legacy. The legacy of this world is often signified by the mounds of dust and dirt that covers the debris of past civilizations, while many memorials stand silent. The truth of the matter is that the legacy of the self-life and the world ends up in the grave of silence, death, and decay to never rise again.

The problem with the legacy that is being purported by the wicked in America is that it harbors the ways of death. It has already been judged and in due time it will be covered by the winds of time and completely forgotten.

It is clear that the godly legacy in America is under attack. At best, God has been tacked on to religious activities, sentimentally fitted into worldly, self-serving lifestyles and practices. At worst His glory, authority, and power have been adjusted to fit the wicked philosophies of the world, or it has been shrewdly stripped from Him in the minds of the vulnerable by various quasi-religious presentations.

When you consider these attempts to fit a holy God into America's fleshly lifestyles and worldly cultures, you can see how it is religious man's attempt to force a marriage between present man-made religion and the present politically correct philosophies of those who resent or hate God. However, His presence and blessing will be conspicuously missing from all such fruitless attempts.

Such a marriage is not only doomed, but it will prove to be the ultimate downfall of this nation and those who purport to know God. Sadly, those who fail to wake up to the ramifications of such a marriage made in hell, will fail to see that they have been sheep, purposely fattened up and put to sleep for the sole purpose of being led to the slaughter.

Prayer: Lord, the godless legacy of the world will never make it past this age. We need to value the eternal inheritance over the foolishness of the vanity of the world in order to ensure a right attitude towards Your kingdom. Amen.

April 30

I have wondered why America fell into her present state. It is obvious that one of the reasons is because of her prosperity. It is for this reason that *Psalm 30:6* caught my attention *"And in my prosperity I said, I shall never be moved"*.

David is declaring that in prosperity he would not be moved. What was he talking about? He would not be moved from the center of truth, righteousness, and life. There is a real temptation in prosperity to float away from the center of God on the ripples of self-sufficiency.

In such a state, there is an inclination to ride the high waves of "so-called" infallibility and live in the luxury of arrogance and indifference toward the harsh reality bombarding the world. Such a condition causes people to perceive that they have need of nothing including God. They become unrealistic and hard toward the truth.

David knew what it meant to be abased in his position as well as exalted. However, his past experience taught him that he must not let his present status of prosperity move him from the center and source of his eternal inheritance.

The truth is we will always have need of God to be the center of our lives. All great saints keep the prosperity of the world in check by remembering what their real inheritance consists of: Jesus Christ.

Prayer: Lord, we must keep our attitude towards the world in check. We must not allow the world to influence us in the wrong ways causing our attitude to sour or become indifferent towards You and eternal matters. Keep me on a tight rein. Amen.

May

May 1

Recently, we heard a preacher declare that we have nothing to offer the Lord. When it comes to salvation, this is true, but when it comes to service, we do have something to offer Him: our lives, our hearts, our all. The Apostle Paul makes this clear in *Romans 12:1*, *"I beseech you therefore, brethren, by the mercies of God, that ye present your bodies a living sacrifice, holy, acceptable unto God, which is your reasonable service."* However, we will be unwilling to consecrate our lives in such a way unless we first put the necessary value on our relationship with the Lord.

The truth is, we will never sacrifice what we truly value in this world unless we recognize that there is something far more worthy of our loyalty and pursuit. However, we are the ones who determine what will become valuable or worthy to us. Ultimately, we will not sacrifice or die for something unless we have first decided to live for the purpose of possessing that particular treasure.

There are examples in Scripture of this very fact. Solomon tells us to sell everything and buy truth. Jesus speaks of selling all to possess the pearl of great price. As believers, we know that the great treasure He speaks of was Himself and His kingdom. We must value, prize, and desire to possess Him in this present world above all else in order to be part of His unseen kingdom and ensure we gain Him in all of His glory in the next world. Obviously, to survive the age we are living in we must gain Christ. In order to gain Him, we must see Jesus as the worthy and greatest treasure of heaven. We do this by personally putting the highest regard and price on Him so we will begin to pursue Him with relentless diligence and fervor.

Prayer: Lord, what I have valued in the past has all proven to be vanity. However, You are the great prize of heaven. By being in You, and You being in us we will inherit all You have promised. You are worthy of being pursued until possessed. Give me the right heart attitude towards the importance of gaining You. Amen.

May 2

Finally, it had quit raining enough one fall day when I lived in Everett, WA many years ago to take my big golden shepherd (or whatever he was, I never knew for sure) for a walk. Bruce was just the best dog ever: I called him a "Christian dog" because he had all the attributes Christians are supposed to have, plus more.

So, leash in hand off we went down the short street to a main road. I felt good that morning, all cleaned up from head to toe, in a fresh pair of jeans, nice sweatshirt, and hair fixed "just so." Yep, I was definitely "on top of it."

The woods on the other side of the road were beckoning, and the hill wasn't too steep for my knees back then, so my faithful companion and I started to make our way down through the trees. Then it happened! Suddenly the leaves I was stepping on gave way to the gooey mud underneath them, and the next thing you know I found myself sliding down the hill on my back.

Covered with mud, I managed to get up while Bruce patiently waited to see what was going to happen next. Well, there was only one thing to do and that was try to get back up the hill, and go home! One thing about Bruce, he was so smart he always knew when he should turn into a service dog, so he helped pull me back up the hill.

I'm reminded by this little story of how we can sometimes think we've got it all together—you know, all "cleaned" up spiritually because "we" have worked so hard to be "clean" or righteous in God's sight. But more often than not, this is usually when we find ourselves flat on one side or the other, and greatly humbled by the Lord. How much better it is to simply come to God with all our "mud" and "uncleanness," and seek His face for help and forgiveness. A good verse to remember is *1 Corinthians 10:12, "Wherefore let him that thinketh he standeth take heed lest he fall."* – J. Haley

Prayer: Lord, when we think we are on top of it, we will quickly find ourselves face down in some mess. Lord, I know when pride exalts us, You use the smallest things to humble us. I also know this must be because when we are caught up with self, we are blind to those things that will trip us up and bring us down to size. Have Your way Lord. Amen.

May 3

"The meek shall eat and be satisfied: they shall praise the LORD that seek him. Your heart shall live forever" (Psalm 22:26). When I study the concept of "meekness," I cannot help but remember Jesus' words, "Blessed are the meek: for they shall inherit the earth."

Meekness is an interesting term. It simply points to strength being under control. Clearly, such strength is not unruly, unyielding, undisciplined, or unmanageable. It does not hide behind some veneer of discipline; rather, it gives way to that which is allowed to channel it in a productive way. For the Christian, it simply means that his or her strength is yielded to the authority of heaven, disciplined by the Spirit, managed by the hand of God, and ruled by the Lord of lords.

Meekness allows me to receive from God. Once the mild spirit of meekness distinguishes that something is from God, the now tempered soul becomes satisfied as it partakes of it. From this premise, the heart attitude takes on a thankful pose for the blessing as it recognizes the grace that has been afforded to it.

Strength under control is disciplined enough in its focus that it is able to seek God out in purity and confidence, knowing that in the end the person will see God and live.

Prayer: Lord, You instructed me to learn of You for You are meek and lowly. I so desire to develop Your very mind and disposition towards all matters. I submit all to You as a means to give way to Your wondrous example. Amen.

May 4

"I will love thee, O LORD, my strength" (Psalm 18:1). When I was thinking of meekness, I had to ponder what affords us the desire to become meek under the gentle leading of God's Spirit. The answer is simple, it is love. When you love someone, there is an agreement present.

Love is a choice that brings a powerful agreement between the parties involved. As I meditated on this Scripture in *Psalm 18*, I was once again reminded of this fact. King David wrote this psalm. He clearly declared, *"I will...love thee, O LORD."* (Emphasis added.) David did not make this declaration on the clouds of emotional sentiment; rather, he made it in light of the revelation that the Lord was his only real strength.

We usually love someone else because he or she can add something to our lives. However, those whom we love first become the very essence of our lives. In other words, we cannot do without him or her. It would be like losing our breath, our right arm, the essence of our very life.

Clearly, this is the love that David had for the Lord which brought such strength to him, and this is what I must also possess for the Lord to ensure He becomes the essence of my strength.

Prayer: Lord, there is no life, strength, or hope outside of You. I so much need Your love to abound in my heart towards You to keep You ever before me in my affections and pursuits. Amen.

May 5

There are many people seeking some form of happiness. *Psalm 16:11c* tells us what and where we must seek to experience true happiness, *"At thy right hand are pleasures for ever more."* However, many people seek it from a state of arrogance and not meekness. They want to feel happy, yet joy remains far from them.

The question is in light of this worldly pursuit, how can I come to a state of joy in my own life? I must own my prevailing mood regardless of the circumstances. I must come to this state on my own volition. I must seek it out in the right places.

The Bible is clear that real joy is found at the right hand of God. The New Testament states that Jesus sits on the right Hand of majesty. He possesses all power and authority to ensure a matter comes to fruition.

I know that Jesus is my place of wisdom, righteousness, sanctification, and redemption. I know in Him I have the full revelation of God. In essence, He is all I have need of, for He is all in all.

Sometimes the clouds of life come between me and my place in the heavenlies, taking my focus elsewhere. All I can see are the foreboding clouds of adversity and uncertainty. But I must choose to remember that my solution resides above the clouds, sits in a place of authority, and awaits for me to call upon His precious Name so that He can show Himself mighty on my behalf, leaving the world around me with a record of His majesty, and me with a greater testimony of Him.

Prayer: Lord, I do call upon Your precious Name. I know that there is power, hope, and salvation attached to it. You indeed have been given a name above all names. Praise Your Holy Name. Amen.

May 6

The life of Christ can truly end in incredible joy. King David declared, *"In thy presence is fullness of joy" (Psalm 16:11b)*. In fact, *Nehemiah 8:10* tells us the joy of the Lord is our strength. Once again, I come back to the subject of strength. Meekness is associated with strength, but so is joy.

Joy is likewise an interesting subject because many do substitute joy with worldly notions that are associated with partying, having fun, or being happy with the vanity this world affords them. However, joy is an eternal virtue that never ceases regardless of the circumstances. Granted, I must choose to enjoy a matter, but the state of joy is an anchor that I must let down into the depths of my character according to my unchangeable God. After all, God never changes but my state can be easily enough changed unless I first anchor my faith to the Rock of Ages. I must choose to visit such a state when fear knocks at my door, uncertainty haunts me, insecurity torments me, and unbelief tempts me.

In order to visit such a state, I must follow the line of this anchor and come to the state of joy. As stated, this joy is found in the presence of God. It leads to peace and rest in the Lord.

Prayer: Lord, You have made available everything we have need of to experience the abundance of Your life in the midst of this lean world. I thank You for giving us Your life. Amen.

May 7

'Oh, what a tangled web we weave/When first we practice to deceive,' is a very 'Shakespearean' phrase, however, it is not from Shakespeare. It comes from an early nineteenth century Scottish author, Sir Walter Scott, best-selling writer of novels, plays, and poems.

That famous saying reminds me of a certain dainty, yet strong, creeping weed that hides itself wherever it can take root. I find it in my big oregano patch, in amongst the ground cover, and even in the grass. What gives it away are the miniature yellow flowers that innocently bloom along its slender green vines. The only way to get down to the roots is to gently but firmly grasp the top of the "stem" and then try to "follow" it as much as possible through whatever it's entangled with until you get down to the center. It was while pulling out this particular weed the other day that it came to me that some folks are a lot like that weed.

They can act innocent for a while, or give the impression that they're a genuine, "sold out," born again Christian, but as you become increasingly involved with them over time, you begin to discover that there are some major deeply-rooted problems underneath it all.

Just as the roots of the creeping weed are grounded in the soil of this world, so too are the roots of an unrepentant heart towards the things of God. *"Looking diligently lest any man fail of the grace of God; lest any root of bitterness springing up trouble you, and thereby many be defiled" (Hebrews 12:15).* – J. Haley

Prayer: Lord, due to our old man, we all have "weeds" in us, but we can humble ourselves and give You permission to pull them out, regardless of how far the roots go and are entangled with the world. It may hurt at first, but it is liberating in the end. Thank You. Amen.

May 8

In the midst of a troubling world and its activities, I choose to ponder what it means to be meek and joyful. Both virtues are associated with strength, but they also point to the quality of life. *Psalm 16:11a* states, *"Thy wilt shew me the path of life."* Sadly, most people start with the virtue rather than starting with the source that produces meekness and joy. As a believer, I know there is only one source that ensures such virtues: The Lord.

The Bible tells me that if my strength is disciplined under the Spirit, I will possess meekness, and if my strength becomes one with the strength of the Lord, I will know joy. The truth of the matter is I must be in His presence to secure both virtues in order to experience the fullness of His life.

In our fallen state we are lost to God and He to us. We find ourselves groping in the darkness from one experience to another trying to secure some semblance of life, meaning, and happiness. Each attempt to secure some meaning or semblance of life often finds us being cast into a pit of despair.

We desire order only to be entangled in utter chaos. We seek after joy only to taste bitterness and we pursue pleasures, only to end up being swallowed by vanity.

Prayer: Lord, I spent more years lost than I want to talk about. However, my testimony is that You found me. I no longer have to grope in darkness in search of that which has no eternal value in it. Because of You I can possess the Christian's virtues of heaven that will add much to my life as they ensure a right relationship with You and will bring satisfaction to my soul and contentment to my spirit. Amen.

May 9

"And he said unto him, Why callest thou me good? There is none good but one, that is, God" (Matthew 19:17a) We had a primary yesterday and the results revealed that the "old guard," no matter how wicked, hypocritical, mean-spirited and ruthless it has been, is entrenched in the politics of our day and uses all the dirty tricks to maintain its position. Sadly, there are those who are not interested in character or how dirty one gets, just so they get what they want; therefore, they are willing to partake of these individuals' sins without any concern of the destruction it leaves behind.

In one of my previous meditations, I talked about the difference between man's "goodness" and true righteousness. Goodness points to "good" character that will prove to be morally beneficial for all involved, while righteousness is about right standing and doing right. The idea of goodness varies with different individuals. However, the one thread that connects all such concepts of "goodness" in this world is the desire to get along with others.

The idea that most people have about what constitutes "goodness" is that its main intention is to show some type of "goodness" towards others. For example, it you are "good" you will not murder, steal, or do harm in regard to others. In many incidents, such goodness will also become compliant to maintain some semblance of peace, which allows such individuals to fit into what I call the "good ole boy's" group.

However, Jesus made it quite clear in the Scripture reading that only God is "good." Goodness is part of the fruit of the Spirit, clearly revealing that if it does not come from God in order to serve as an extension of Him in regard to that which is beneficial to His kingdom and pleasing to Him, such "goodness" will amount to but a mere mask or man's humanistic presentation of common decency. Such decency may impress others, but God will not be in it *(Galatians 5:22-23)*. It is for this reason that we are called to righteousness.

The Apostle Paul made this statement in *2 Corinthians 5:21*, *"For he hath made him, (Jesus), who knew no sin, to be sin for us, that we might be made the righteousness of God in him."* (Parenthesis added.) I had to ask myself if I was settling for the common courtesy that should be allotted to everyone, or am I reaching to embrace the excellent ways of true righteousness?

Prayer: Lord, we are always being called to walk in Your ways of righteousness. Give us clarity of heart, vision, and purpose to walk in them. Amen.

May 10

How many times have you heard *Proverbs 14:34, "Righteousness exalteth a nation: but sin is a reproach to any people."* Sadly, we are tasting the bitterness of wicked leadership and the tyranny of evil men. Righteousness exalts a nation, but sin is a reproach to any people. Sadly, because of a casual attitude towards sin, even among church-goers, we have been tasting the oppressive bitterness of it.

As previously noted, righteousness, not man's "goodness" exalts a nation. Due to this nation's destructive leadership and ways, we are now tasting the reproach of sin. Sin's evilness vexes the spirit, its wickedness causes despair to the soul, and its darkness produces anger and disgust that will prove hard to bear.

As a people, we are clearly reaping the misfortune of experiencing firsthand the consequences of what happens when a nation becomes complacent towards righteousness, ignores the responsibilities of righteousness, or compromises righteousness to live in peace with any form of wickedness. We now can see that in such a state of sin, foolishness replaces wisdom, folly mocks sobriety, insanity trumps reason, ignorance rejects truth, and lawlessness and rebellion rage against justice.

To spiritually overcome the wickedness that has taken center stage in this nation, we must choose the ways of righteousness. But we must remember that there is nothing nominal, complacent, or indifferent about righteousness when it comes to sin. It is wise enough to see that to be silent when evil reigns is suicidal, to be complacent when wickedness tears at the moral fiber of what is right is to sign a death warrant, and to lay down when righteousness demands you to stand against the tidal wave of injustice is to prove that one is not courageous or worthy to know or experience the goodness that will naturally flow from what is right, just, and honorable.

However, the key to righteousness begins with true repentance that turns from sin, humility that is a product of brokenness over sin, and true conversion that comes out of seeing a matter according to God's holiness.

Prayer: Lord, there are only two ways in which man can live: according to righteousness or sin. I choose the blessed, wise ways of righteousness. Amen.

May 11

In the last meditation, a clear challenge was put forth to my spirit in regard to righteousness. As a nation, we stand at a very precarious crossroad in our history. What clearly stands before American citizens is a blatant contrast between light and darkness, righteousness and wickedness.

This was clearly brought out by Joshua in *Joshua 24:15*, when he established that the people had to choose between the idols of their fathers and the God who delivered them to the Promised Land. We often quote this scripture in part but consider all of it in context, *"And if it seem evil unto you to serve the LORD, choose you this day whom ye will serve; whether the gods which your fathers served that were on the other side of the flood, or the gods of the Amorites, in whose land ye dwell: but as for me and my house, we will serve the LORD."* As in Joshua' days, the fence that once stood between these two realms of righteousness and wickedness is all but gone. In its place a line has been drawn in the sand as to who one is ultimately going to serve.

Clearly, there is no room for non-committal fence walking when it comes to what is right or wrong in today's world. To choose to be neutral is to choose the ways of darkness and not light. People now must choose who they will serve, what they will stand for, and what current of agreement they will step into. The truth is, this nation will not survive unless the people make a clear distinction and stand for what is right and true.

The grave spiritual darkness that is now encroaching into our lives has the potential of consuming us unless righteousness personally reigns in us. I am constantly being reminded of Noah who was a preacher of righteousness. Due to his right standing with God, his witness of the ark ultimately brought the flood upon the world of the ungodly *(2 Peter 2:5)*. Clearly, man's so-called "goodness" is not enough to stand in such darkness. It will be judged as bringing a reproach to what is right and true.

I don't know about others, but personally I would rather be in the position of bringing judgment upon a matter because of standing and declaring righteousness. I want to lift up the standard and mirror from which the light of heaven can reflect rather than experiencing judgment because I was clinging to some type of personal goodness that allowed me to stand mute concerning the havoc that the injustice and insanity that the present-day wickedness is having on this nation and its people.

Prayer: Lord, there is a line in the sand and it begins at Your cross. I choose to stand on the same side as You and Your righteousness. Amen

May 12

It's a real blessing to know others are enjoying pictures of some of my paintings, most of which were done in past years. God is the giver of gifts and talents, and I never wanted to ignore, "bury" or misuse any gift He has given to me even though I know the world is full of truly great art accomplished artists that I could never measure up to.

I believe what God requires is that we recognize what He has entrusted us with, or put on our heart, and then choose to be faithful with it. Whatever He gives us and whatever we have is from Him and not ourselves. Therefore, even if the "table" of others seems to be fully furnished as for a royal banquet, and all you've been given is one fork, knife and spoon (or maybe even just a set of chopsticks) all that is required of you is to be faithful with what you have.

Ask the Lord to help you, then do your best for the glory of God and for the enjoyment or benefit of others. *"Freely ye have received, freely give" (Matthew 10:8b).* Trust in the LORD with all your heart, learn of Him, live for Him and then watch how He will not only meet all of your needs, but fill your heart with joy, love and peace. - J. Haley

Prayer: Lord, You have freely given out of grace and by faith we freely receive in order to impart it to others out of love to You and obedience to our commission. Thank You for giving us the best, providing us with that which is better, and offering that which is excellent in every way. Amen.

May 13

I was pondering the matter of judging others. *Proverbs 16:2* states, *"All the ways of a man are clean in his own eyes; but the LORD weigheth the spirits."* We often try to weigh people as to their substance and worth in order to determine if they are worthy of our recognition and consideration. For example, in the world we judge them by their status based on various standards from educational degrees to wealth. In the religious realm we judge people according to their outward piousness and deeds. But, how does God weigh a person? In order to be fair and just how should we personally weigh people?

According to *Proverbs 16:2*, God weighs individuals according to their spirit or motives. We are told to discern or test the spirits as well, but we often judge according to how someone or something makes us feel about ourselves. If something makes us uncomfortable, then we often conclude something is wrong with the person or situation. This is where people often regard something according to jealousies, biases, and prejudices that have been conditioned and established in them. Hence enters in what we personally value or regard as being worthy and important of our consideration and attention, and unfairly judge them.

Jesus condemned such judgment and warned us that the way we judge others is how we will ultimately be judged. Clearly, it does not matter what veneer we put on our judgmental ways, the Lord will always deem the prideful spirit behind it as being wrong and profane.

Prayer: Lord, You are the righteous Judge. You have told us to take the beam out of our own eye and judge righteously. Lord, I need Your wisdom to not only judge righteously, but to properly discern. Amen.

May 14

How many times did the Lord tell Joshua and others, *"Be strong and of a good courage" (Joshua 1:6a)*? It takes courage to do what is right. It often means going against the present currents of the world and being made out to be a fool for being different. It is for this reason we must rightly judge a matter to ensure the integrity of it.

We all judge a matter based on what we consider to be substance or character. For Christians, character has to do with integrity. Such character is often forged in people through trying circumstances that will require them to go against the natural grain of what is considered acceptable and religious. In such times integrity will actually demand excellence, courage, and honor, when taking the easy way out would be understandable and acceptable.

If Christians are going to survive the spiritual darkness of this present age, it is vital for them to insist on the way of personal integrity. It will take such integrity to go against the tidal wave of wickedness and darkness that is engulfing the world, swallowing all that is nominal, and sweeping away that which is being consumed by compromise, fear, and despair.

It is integrity that allows us to take courage in making the right judgment calls in our lives. Granted, the world may very well curse us for such judgments, but in the end, we will be able to face our Lord and Savior.

Prayer: Lord, I must be strong in light of Your goodness and take courage in Your righteous ways. If I do, I will never be moved from Your abiding protection on my life. Amen.

May 15

Fear is a major battle that must be often fought in different arenas, especially as we look into the spiritual darkness of this world. The one arena that anxiety can gain a stronghold in our lives is when we have to wait as the uncertainty of our times enfold us. However, we are instructed in *Psalm 27:14, "Wait on the LORD: be of good courage, and he shall strengthen thine heart: wait, I say, on the LORD."*

There will be much fainting going on as we witness darkness consuming this age. However, I realize I must keep close to the center of what cannot be moved by events of the world. In fact, I must stay close to that which is moving and shaking the very foundations of the world.

It is by clinging to the center that I can take courage in my situation by knowing it is the Lord who will strengthen my heart to endure the testing that comes with the darkness. It is the Lord who will deliver me though darkness and from any tyrannical claim it may have upon my life.

In order to experience such deliverance, I must learn to wait on Him. It does not matter how close the tidal wave of destruction is to me, I must wait for His instruction. It does not matter how much the water of anxiety is rising, I must wait. It does not matter how the current of urgency is prompting me to move, I must wait. God's timing is perfect. He knows how to deliver me in and through the storms of life.

Prayer: Lord, I hate waiting, but I also dread becoming foolish because I failed to wait for the right timing to move. I choose to wait upon Your leadership, knowing that You will lead me to higher ground. Amen.

May 16

David declared as a reminder in all challenges in *Psalm 18:8b*, *"…but the LORD was my stay."* There will always be much debate in the mind, but to give in to its arguments will cause us to be double-minded. It is not what we know that keeps us steady, but who we know.

What does it mean for the Lord to be my stay? Is He that immovable stake that never moves from the eternal foundation of truth? Is He that secure place that will never be humbled in times of adversity? Is He that Rock that will serve as a place of refuge from my enemies? Is He the tree who can become a shady place of protection from the searing heat of judgment? Is He that place of oasis who offers refreshing waters as we journey through the barrenness and darkness of this present world?

David understood what it meant for the Lord to be his stay in all matters pertaining to his life. He knew that he would never be moved from that which proved to be eternal, powerful, immutable, and immovable. He knew what it meant to trust this place in the storm, hide in it when his enemies were ready to prey on him, and cling to it when the dark was trying to consume him.

Like David, I also must learn what it means for the Lord to be my stay. Note, it is a learning process because this place is discovered in greater measure when we learn of the character, attitude, and ways of our Lord and begin to walk in them, knowing we will reach the destination of eternal glory.

Prayer: Lord, I so want to make You my stay. Help me to learn of You so that I can come to a place of complete rest in You. Amen

May 17

Once upon a time it was fashionable to have a pretty candy dish filled with sweet treats displayed on living room coffee tables. My Grandma always had a candy dish as did friends we used to visit.

As a little kid back then, nothing was more fascinating that looking at all the assorted colors and shapes of the popular, artfully crafted hard candy that was almost eye level, and my mother knew it. Her goal was to raise a "lady" and that meant not ever touching anything, no matter how tempting, that did not belong to me. Therefore, she would wait until I was quietly seated before she would tell me to ask if I could "please" have a piece of candy. Just one piece, mind you, not two or a handful. But before I could even muster up the confidence to ask, I was strictly reminded that whichever one I touched was the one I had to eat.

That old fashioned candy wasn't something that could be devoured in two gulps! As the hard coating slowly softened in your mouth, a delightful combination of sweet and tart was released. Finally, the once hidden soft fruity center began to emerge, releasing its own special flavor, and for a brief moment it took center stage before melting away as the whole "candy drama" came to an end.

You know, God has given all mankind something far more satisfying to our mind, soul, and spirit than a dish of fancy hard candies, and that is His eternal Word. I remember when, long ago, His Word was also a center piece on many coffee tables across the land. Like the tasty treats in a candy dish, God's Word has elements of both sweet and tart, with textures of hard and soft. But, unlike candy, His Word is life-giving. *"Thy words were found, and I did eat them; and thy word was unto me the joy and rejoicing of mine heart: for I am called by thy name, O LORD God of hosts"* (Jeremiah 15:16).

The wonderful invitation to "eat His Words" has no limit, and offers eternal satisfaction. *Psalm 34:8* says, *"O taste and see that the LORD is good: blessed is the man that trusteth in him."*

The Master is calling to "come and dine" (*John 21:12*). Will you accept Jesus' invitation today? – J. Haley

Prayer: Lord, Your invitation has gone forth, but sadly many are not hungry or thirsty. Lord, cause Your Word to make me thirstier to know Your ways, and hungrier to never settle for the world's decaying bread and self's foul-tasting meat. Amen.

May 18

Those who refuse to humbly bow to seek mercy, will always meet with judgment. Consider David's request in *Psalm 25:4, "Shew me thy ways O' LORD, teach me thy paths."*

God's ways are righteous and His paths narrow and challenging, and the question is, am I willing to learn both about His ways and paths with the intent of walking His ways out in obedience and allowing His paths to disciplined me. When I think about what it means to learn the matters of heaven, I have to keep a couple of things in mind.

1) What I need to understand cannot be comprehended on an intellectual level. It must be believed and embraced on a spiritual level. It must be received in the heart as being true.
2) The Holy Spirit is the One who must lead me to the truth of a matter so that heaven unveils the wisdom and revelation of it to my heart, but then I must exercise my faith in walking it out.
3) Learning is not just a matter of hearing something as being true, it is a matter of seeing how it works in our life. In other words, it must be assimilated into our lives for it to become truth.

This is why, as a believer, I have been given the precious indisputable example of Jesus. I am to walk as He walked. His example shows me what the Christian life looks like. His example reveals the ways of holiness, His disposition that of meekness and excellence, His attitude defines righteousness, and His conduct stipulates godliness. Man may do his best to share the way with others, but it is the Spirit, who not only leads the way to such a life, but He is the One who establishes the life in us, while establishing us in the life of Christ.

Prayer: Lord, thank You for the hope we have in You. Without it there is no real future regardless of worldly blessings. You are our future. May we learn to abide in that precious hope and expectation of Your promises. Amen.

May 19

You will not find true wisdom among the opinionated dogmatic, bigoted, and experts of the age. With this knowledge do I really believe such scriptures as *Psalm 26:10 "All the paths of the LORD are mercy and truth unto such as keep his covenant and his testimonies,"* or am I adjusting my own way of walking out my Christian life to some religious code?

Scripture is clear as to what comprises the paths of God. They are not composed of unbending religious standards, but of mercy. They are not constructed by doctrines or theology, but by His everlasting truths.

The Lord's path does not lead to men's traditions, but to places of righteousness. They do not constrict; rather, they guide and restrain as a means to protect. They do not demand that one adheres to their boundaries; rather, they encourage and inspire a person to see the "goodness" or "benefit" in walking according to the covenant and testimonies of heaven.

The problem is, we see the boundaries of God as being oppressive, unfair, and unrealistic, but the truth is they are liberating to one's soul. Such liberty allows people to know God, reach their potential, and know the sweetness of what is good and right.

Prayer: Lord, our fleshly independence would have us believe that Your ways are unfair. The truth is they are not only just and right, but they lead to life. Have Your way in my life oh Lord. Amen.

May 20

"The secret of the LORD is with them that fear him; and he will shew them his covenant" (Psalm 25:14). I have met people who are in search of unveiling the mysteries of the world around them. They are seeking some type of enlightenment as to what makes things work. It is not that they desire to enjoy a matter for what it is, but their motive to gain insight is for the purpose of controlling their reality for their personal benefit.

At the base of the old man is to be as god when it comes to controlling his or her world. The pride of the flesh is bent on understanding a matter in order to get on top of it.

This Scripture tells us that the secret that will unlock much for the believer is the fear of the Lord. The "fear of the Lord" is the beginning of heavenly wisdom. Since such fear has humble beginnings, it possesses a sincerity that will accept a matter for what it is. Its desire is to not displease the Lord, but to also do that which will not bring any reproach or distress to Him. It is from the premise of the fear of the Lord that God can reveal much to a receptive heart, knowing that the wisdom that is unveiled will be appropriated in a beneficial way.

Prayer: Lord, genuine wisdom always comes from Your throne. I desire wisdom more than gold, and truth more than all the riches of the world. Thank You for making both of these eternal virtues available to me through Your grace, and may I be in a state of humility to properly receive them. Amen.

May 21

It is clear that, *"A wicked man taketh a gift out of the bosom to pervert the ways of judgment" (Proverbs 17:23).* How many are saddened by the harsh reality that the highest seats in the offices held in our federal government are up for sale to the highest bidder? This is not only true nationally, but state-wide and locally. There is nothing so frustrating and discouraging than to know that people in influential positions of life can be bribed, because they have no concern for what is right.

In fact, the operations of this present world comprise nothing more than one big scam because many people are on the take and can be easily enough bought, and whether the scam is directed at taxpayers, the innocent, the vulnerable, and the miserable, it does not matter because there is no mercy and compassion in any of it. In fact, in most cases it is nothing but raw, cruel lust for filthy lucre, power, and influence.

The Word of God tells us if a man can be bribed, his judgment will be perverted and untrustworthy. This brings us back to character. What is a man's worth if he can be bribed with money, influenced to compromise what he knows is true and right by the pressure of others, and proves to be unpredictable in what he says or promises? Clearly, what we value or treasure will determine our worth, to not only those who depend on us to be trustworthy and true to our word, but to ourselves as far as the type of person we allow ourselves to become.

Whether it is bribes, scams, con-games, or what we call dirty politics, it is all a lie, propped up by skeletons of past victims and promoted by the wicked games and lies of the present, and it has put this nation on the fast track to spiritual ruin in every arena. The lies are nothing more than a house of cards that will not withstand the strong winds of truth and judgment. Keep in mind, that Satan who is the father of lies, is the overseer of these individuals and the inspiration behind their wicked darkness, and like their master, they will also have their part in the lake of fire.

In the right conditions it would be easy for any of us to accept a bribe and fall into the different traps of this world. Perhaps the bribe will silence the conscience for a time, but eventually it will expose the treachery that lies at the heart of every person who lacks the conviction of integrity and righteousness.

Prayer: Lord, You call us to excellence; therefore, we must avoid the base ways of treachery. Help me to become the person You are calling me to be. Amen.

May 22

It was just a reel to reel black and white presentation, but way back when I was a kid it was fascinating. To think that the Green Lake Evangelical United Brethren Church in Seattle would show it to the congregation was so exciting, wonderful and faith-building that I never forgot it.

The film was about the wonders of God's creation from time-lapse pictures of seeds through the germinating process to budding, full-grown plants and flowers to photos of beautiful and intricate snowflakes, along with frost and how salt changes under a microscope when a drop of water is added. Of course, compared to the incredible advances in the realm of true science of today, what dazzled my young mind was quite elementary and simple.

Nevertheless, first impressions are lasting impressions, and the impact it had on my soul and spirit awakened within me a deep and abiding curiosity and appreciation for God's creation that has remained with me to this day. At times when things get overwhelming, I just take a good look at the purity and beauty of a flower, or watch the colorful little birds, and consider all the majesty around me and simply tell myself that God is bigger and more powerful than anything!

"Thine, O LORD, is the greatness, and the power, and the glory, and the victory, and the majesty: for all that is in the heaven and in the earth is thine; thine is the kingdom, O LORD, and thou art exalted as head above all" (1 Chronicles 29:11). – J. Haley

Prayer: Lord, I do not have to look far to see Your power in action, know Your abiding care is at work, and experience Your presence and peace. All I have to do is look up, look around, and choose to see the beauty and power embellished in Your creation. Amen.

May 23

"Even so every good tree bringeth forth good fruit; but a corrupt tree bring forth evil fruit" (Matthew 7:17). The world has various resources to offer a person. It makes many false claims as it attempts to deceive or seduce each of us away from truth and reality. It is when we value the things of this world more than the things of God that we will find ourselves tempted to compromise our character, sell our integrity, and take on a pose of arrogance and indifference towards others.

For example, if we value the material things of the world, we will become quite indifferent to the needs of others. If we value our reputation over our moral responsibilities towards others, we will end up sacrificing those around us. If we value our religious dogmas over what is of Spirit and truth, we will become judgmental and unforgiving towards those who dare to disagree with us. If we value our self-life rather than prefer others over ourselves, we will become cruel and foolish in our dealings with those who do not bow down to us.

As we have seen time after time with our leaders, our attitudes will clearly reflect what we value. Even though individuals can angrily justify accepting bribes or succumbing to some type of peer pressure at the expense of others, such people prove that their so-called "convictions" or treasures were for sale. Jesus was very clear that we can know what is in a man because the fruits of his life will ultimately reveal what he truly values.

Prayer: Lord, the fruit of my life will tell what kind of tree I am. It will also reveal my source. Lord, I have striven to make You the source to all that flows through my life. Thank You for the perpetual eternal life that flows from You to Your people. Amen.

May 24

"But we have this treasure in earthen vessels, that the excellency of the power may be of God, and not of us" (2 Corinthians 4:7). Jesus revealed that the worth of a man comes down to what he truly treasures. Man in and of himself has nothing substantial to offer others; rather, it comes down to what he truly values that will determine his worth and impact where others are concerned.

If what man treasures has no real substance or worth, then he has nothing of worth to offer those who cross his path. This brings us to the harsh reality that we have only two assets of any worth that we can offer a person. We have the treasure of heaven (Jesus) and our character. If we are void of both, we will be counted as untrustworthy and having no real substance that will make any lasting impact on those whom we encounter along the way.

If we lack Jesus, but have a bit of character, we might be able to offer man our word, but we will not be able to add any real treasure to his life. If we are going to survive the present darkness, we must possess the treasures of Jesus and personal integrity. Without Jesus we will have no reason to stand in the midst of darkness, and without character we will have no means to withstand the affront of such darkness.

Do you possess both treasures or will you ultimately be bribed to compromise your very soul by the encroaching darkness that is engulfing this world?

Prayer: Lord, the only way we will offer any value to others is if we possess You as our treasure. Thank You for becoming that Prize that is worth pursuing in this dying world. Amen.

May 25

"And he said, I beseech thee, shew me thy glory" (Exodus 18:33). A. W. Tozer made this statement, "Remember this: The man that has the most of God is the man who is seeking the most ardently more of God." As I pondered this statement, I had to agree. It is easy to lose one's desire for God.

There are so many other attractions and tastes that can consume us. In fact, we often develop a taste or desire for something because it "tastes good" and brings much pleasure to us. It is clear that without the desire, we see no need to partake of it.

We must partake of God's goodness, experience His abiding faithfulness, know His honorable intentions, and walk in His ways to develop a desire for more of Him. Once we begin to taste His goodness, witness His glory, and experience His grace, we will not settle for trickles from heaven, we will beseech the throne of heaven to reveal more of Himself to us. Each revelation will cause the Lord to become more precious to us, while His life in us makes us more precious to His kingdom.

Prayer: Lord, the value of my life hinges on how valuable Your life is becoming to me and in me. Lord, I do beseech You to show me Your glory in greater ways. Amen.

May 26

God's glory! It is a wondrous thing to consider God's majesty in light of His attributes, ways, and works. We want to wait in His presence, rest in His goodness, marvel at His great works, and stand on His promises, but each new discovery causes us to realize how little we know or even can comprehend about the One who is eternal, the One who is all-knowing, ever-present, and unchangeable.

We can sense His presence and want to bathe in it. We can taste His goodness and know satisfaction, we can witness His works and can't imagine ever doubting Him again, and we can find great hope and expectations because of the promises that await us; however, since everything about us is temporary, such times end up fleeing from us, leaving us with a sense there is more to experience, there is more to discover, and that at best we have just encountered the tip of the iceberg.

The question is how will we respond? Will we try to hold on to that which is fleeting or will we discover a greater hunger and thirst that only God can fill? At that time, we might remember that God's thoughts and ways are always higher and, that at best, we are on some spiritual plateau, and the great heights yet to be discovered are before us, not behind us.

I have always discovered that heights in God are never reached because He is eternal, but I can look into the face of His glory. For Moses, he was only allowed to see the backside of His glory, but for every believer we never have to look far to see His glory. John summarized it best in *John 1:14, "And the Word was made flesh, and dwelt among us, (and we beheld his glory, the glory as of the only begotten of the Father,) full of grace and truth."*

Prayer: Lord, by Your grace You put the desire in me to look up from a point of humility and I need to look into Your lovely face to see the glory and riches of heaven in Your eyes of love. Lord, never let me settle for the fading revelations of yesterday when it comes to You, the decaying crumbs of past experiences, and unrealistic molehills of silly, fleshly notions about my life in You. Cause me to hear Your invitation, cause me to come. Amen.

May 27

It seems like I'm always looking for something, but at least I know what I'm looking for when I'm looking for it. So back around 1981 it came as a shock to me when the thought flashed through my mind, "This is what I've been looking for!"

You see, I didn't know I was looking for anything, but in reality, I was. Whenever an evangelist spoke in the church I attended, or even in other locations, I went. And, one such evangelist was a powerful woman who was also an author from Flagstaff, Arizona.

This woman (Betty Swinford) "had the goods" as we used to say, she emphasized knowing God, and I couldn't get enough. She had something I wanted, something that drew me to her, so I got a copy of her speaking schedule, and followed her for the short time she was in the area. People had been genuinely physically healed, delivered, and filled with the Holy Spirit. All quietly, reverently and with power.

Towards the end of her annual tour, I found out after her meeting that she was going to a local lady's home for lunch so I joined in. I distinctly remember that she was weary, but I had just one burning question for her, so I made my way to the side of her chair, knelt down and asked in a low voice, "How did you get your power?" I didn't know what to expect, but she softly and simply said one word, "Suffering."

Well, I can tell you, THAT is one word none of us wants to hear! I went home with that depressing word surfacing every time the thought of asking God for power surged through my very being. It was a wrestling match at that point—either continue living a shallow, surface ho-hum, "safe Christian" existence, or yield to the Spirit, take the plunge and tell God I was willing to "pay the price", no matter what, and trust Him with everything.

If only there could be another way! But, suffering? Yes, suffering. *"That I may know him, and the power of his resurrection, and the fellowship of his sufferings, being made conformable unto his death" (Philippians 3:10).* It was true, I had found what I was looking for before I even knew I was looking for it, and it was to know God, not just about Him.

The intense wrestling match between my flesh and the Spirit ended when I finally yielded and tearfully exclaimed, "Yes. LORD! Your will be done, not mine, no matter what!" From that day forth everything "went up into the air" in my life, but Jesus has never left me nor forsaken me. Suffering? Yes, but "tailor-made" just for me, and with God's help, I know that *"I can do all things through Christ which strengtheneth me" (Philippians 4:13).* – J. Haley

Prayer: Lord we often don't know we are looking for something, because it's not of this world, but that which is attached to the treasures of heaven. That is why a thirst and a hunger must be first put in us before we realize we are settling for crumbs and not pursuing the full-meal-deal. Give me that hunger and thirst. Amen.

May 28

"A little that a righteous man hath is better than the riches of many wicked" (Psalm 37:16). Righteous people often leave a dichotomy behind them. Many times they are considered the scourge of the earth rather than blessed. It is true that the righteous are not always those who are blessed from a worldly standpoint, but the righteous are not after the material goods of the age they live in. They are not caught up with the temporary glory of the present world. Their desire is to be rich in faith towards God.

A person can possess all the goods and riches of the world, but still be considered poor in the sight of heaven. The Bible is clear that we treasure what our heart values. What we value will reveal what possesses our heart. What possesses the affections of our hearts is what we will ultimately pursue. What we ultimately pursue is what we end up serving and worshipping.

Once again, I must continually put value on my Lord. I must strive to possess Him regardless of the glitter and false promises of the world's riches.

Prayer: Lord, there is so much of the world that wants to take my affections captive, but I choose to direct them heavenward towards You. This is the only way I can keep my affections from becoming vile and useless. Amen.

May 29

"And Jesus answered and said unto him, What wilt thou that I should do unto thee? The blind man said unto him, Lord, that I might receive my sight" (Mark 10:51). One of the most interesting questions Jesus would ask someone was, "What would you like Me to do for you?" I often meditate on such questions because it seems so obvious as to the need and answer.

Can you imagine the Lord asking the blind or lame man what can I do for you? Obviously, the blind and lame wanted healing, but did they? Such intervention would revolutionize their life in a way that would also require changing how they would think about their responsibilities and whether they were willing to accept such a transformation.

For example, for some people it would mean getting rid of their excuses for not doing something constructive, while for others they would have to cease from justifying their possible personal failures that abounded in their lives and relationships, and begin to take accountability for the type of life that they were about to pursue or embark on.

We often consider certain changes through romantic notions. We see how such change could benefit us, but we often do not realize that it will put us in a strange arena that we have no knowledge of. It may be exciting, but the unknown can cause us to fear.

For Christians, the only way they can tread into the unknown is to trust God. Clearly, change will come, but to ensure advancement comes with change, it must be done in light of heavenly expectation and excellence.

Prayer: Lord, change can be a popular chant, but real change that will change the course of the world is an inward change of the heart and not of ideology or philosophy. Lord, You are the only One who can change the heart. Have Your way with my heart. Amen.

May 30

"My son, fear thou the LORD and the king; and meddle not with them that are given to change: For their calamity shall rise suddenly, and who knoweth the ruin of them both" (Proverbs

14:21-22)? Yesterday I was meditating on change. At the last presidential election, a liar, fraud, and despot was deceptively put into the highest office with false promises of making our nation better by promoting the worse filth possible. Clearly, if we do not understand the direction of change, it can prove to be destructive instead of beneficial.

This present change is clearly a downward spiral that involves unseen evil powers. When things are unpleasant, we want change but we are quick to settle for surface change. However, real change will not occur until hearts are humbled, knees bow in repentance, and cries of mercy are sent forth.

We must discern not only the direction of change, but our personal motive for wanting it. Some people simply want relief from what is unpleasant, but not the responsibilities that might come with any real transformation or deliverance. In such times it is our inner character that is being tested because we understand that any real change will result in a complete transformation that will take us out of what is considered normal.

When Jesus came the first time, the Jewish people were looking for change. They resented being under the tyranny of the Roman Empire. As a result, they were looking for the Messiah to come and deliver them. However, when Jesus stood in their midst, many did not recognize Him. Change came, but not in the way that many desired.

Believers are looking for Jesus to come, but how many are prepared to have their understanding about Him shaken and ripped asunder by events that will not fit into their narrative? I fear at times that I have my own idea of how change should occur. As a result, I can miss the beneficial change that is being inspired by heaven itself.

Prayer: Lord, we must beware of the call for changes. We must discern the motive behind such changes. Lord, expose my real motive and intent behind my present attitudes and prepare me to accept the extraordinary, the unexpected, and yes, that which will shake my very foundations. Amen.

May 31

God works according to principles that operate according to His unchangeable character and Law. Whatever law we give way to brings us under the same principle for it says in *Galatians 6:7, "Be not deceived; God is not mocked: for whatsoever a man soweth, that shall he also reap."*

Regardless of how foolish man becomes, he must not deceive himself as to the reality that God will not be mocked by the ways of rebellion and unbelief. There is a day coming that will unveil the works of the righteous, and the foolish ways of the scorner. This day of reckoning is coming when the truth will highlight that which honors the Lord, or it will cut through the dark curtains of rebellion, wickedness, hypocrisy, and unbelief. People will face Him according to His grace or they will fall into His hands of wrath.

Such a day will prove to be a terrible thing for those individuals who fall into the hands of an angry God. Granted, there are those who are banking their very soul that a Holy God does not exist. Others are flattering themselves with a god that they have created to their own liking, while some believe religious affiliation will get them into the kingdom of heaven. However, there is only one way to meet God and that is at the point of redemption. This redemption was secured by what Jesus did on the cross.

The question still remains: am I ready to meet the Lord, and likewise, are you ready to have everything about your life uncovered by the light of God's truth?

Prayer: Lord, we can prove to be wretched and foolish in our notions about eternal matters. Such notions often set us up to fall into the abyss of desperation to reveal our true need for You. Help me to steer away from the pinnacles of self-sufficiency as I remain steadfast in humility, while I walk along the slippery slope of doubt and uncertainty. Amen.

June

June 1

I was thinking about the change that has taken place in this country. As I consider the insane times we are living in, I often meditate on *Daniel 7:25, "And he shall speak great words against the most High, and shall wear out the saints of the most High, and think to change times and laws: and they shall be given into his hand until a time and times and the dividing of time."* Let's face it most politicians are liars who speak great words as a ruse to cover up their wickedness.

Most would agree we are living in the end of the last days. The godless are trying to change times in light of history, traditions, sound principles, and moral laws. Ungodly change in any arena will prove to be an affront against the Law of God and the resolve of saints. Such change will prove to be a disgrace.

Consider the wicked change that has taken place in this country and the abominable acts that are presently happening even in so-called "Christian" churches. In a way, it has wiped out over 200 years of the sacrifices of those who maintained the vision for something that was godly, unique, and excellent. The attitude behind this change has deemed godly principles and sacrifices as obsolete and insignificant. Sadly, this was all done in lieu of that which has proven over and over to be evil, hateful, and destructive.

Change sounds great in the midst of drudgery, but we must realize that change will occur; therefore, we must decide in light of the future as to the type of change that will serve as a legacy, for not only the present generation but the next generation. In doing so, we must take responsibility for the character that is being presently established in our lives, the church, and this nation. To take such responsibility we must first become accountable for who we have become, and who we will eventually become, because of our inner character and preferences.

Prayer: Lord, I feel we Christians can become too smug in our Christianity instead of realizing that we will always miss the mark in our own strength, but I will praise You for You are the mark. All I have to do is press in and strive towards You, and I will not be disappointed. Amen.

June 2

Character will determine what we treasure about our present life. The Apostle Paul stated, *"For now we live, if ye stand fast in the Lord" (1 Thessalonians 3:8).* If what we treasure is not considered worthy of sacrifice and possession, we will ultimately sell it down the line when we are being tested. For example, Judas Iscariot did not value Jesus; therefore, he sold his loyalty to Him for thirty pieces of silver.

Peter's resolve was also broken down by what he did not understand, and he fell into the trap of betraying his conviction concerning Jesus to avoid identification with Him during His greatest trial.

What about the masses following Jesus? He said of them that many followed Him because He fed them with earthly bread. You wonder how many of those people who fed on the earthly bread provided by Jesus yelled for the crucifixion of the heavenly bread (Jesus) when stirred up by the religious leaders to do so.

It takes inward character of integrity to stand. We can only stand fast in our faith in the Lord. If we remain planted on the character of God, we will find the strength in our personal character to remain standing regardless of what slams against us.

Prayer: Lord, there is so much against us when it comes to this world. But Your promises remain true. If You are for us, who can be against us? Thank You Jesus! Amen.

June 3

When I think about feeling after the Lord, I realize that the type of impact He makes on my senses has a lot to do with my own mood. When I am in a foul mood, I will not give the Lord any real consideration; therefore, any enlightenment on His part would not be regarded in a receptive light. If my mood is that of selfishness, He will have no place in my desires. If my mood is that of conceit, I will see no need for His wisdom. If it is self-sufficient, I will see no need for His intervention.

The Apostle Paul stated in *1 Corinthians 2:10*, *"But God hath revealed them unto us by his spirit: for the Spirit searcheth all things, yea, the deep things of God."* It is clear that I must be following after the Spirit. My moods and emotions must be under His gentle direction. I must step over wrong moods, and bring all emotions in line with the Word of God. It is from this state that the Holy Spirit can revive my inner man and lead me to the truth about the Lord in relationship to His mind and His ways.

Prayer: Lord, Your Spirit brings springtime to weary souls. Right now, spring is still officially upon us. Thank You for the spring that reminds me of new life. The sounds of Your creation are all around. It reminds me of the newness of life coming forth. Thank You for the gift of both Your Spirit and Life that abounds in the season of revival. Amen.

June 4

Her name was "Mrs. Spoon" because that is just what she was—a spoon. Not a small, weak, spindly spoon by any means, but a thick, sturdy, substantial wooden spoon such as aren't made anymore.

"Mrs. Spoon" had a hand-painted face on her rounded side which Grandpa "Pop" carefully crafted. Her big eyes, long eyelashes and petite lips seemed to be looking straight at you as she stood, in her fancy long skirt, on a top shelf in the kitchen. "Mrs. Spoon" had a special job to do and that was to keep both eyes on me whenever I was left for a few minutes alone in the kitchen, or if Mommie was busy with kitchen chores.

I knew at a very young age that if I did anything I wasn't supposed to do, "Mrs. Spoon" was watching and would tell on me, and the knowledge that her "face" might smack my tail end kept me in line. Fast forward 75 years, and guess who "lives" in my kitchen? "Mrs. Spoon!"

Her face long ago wore off through many years of making jams and jellies, soups, stews and chowder, but even though she's been "retired" from her first job, she's still a valuable and hard-working utensil in my kitchen. Maybe the sobering thought of "Mrs. Spoon's" big eyes watching me left long, long ago, but I still "know in my knower" that God's eyes are always upon me for He is Everywhere Present, All-Knowing, All-Powerful and Unchanging. *"Neither is there any creature that is not manifest in his sight: but all things are naked and opened unto the eyes of him with whom we have to do" (Hebrews 4:13).* – J. Haley

Prayer: Lord, it is easy to convince yourself that You do not care and if You do, You are tolerant enough to understand any "sound reason" behind wrong actions. However, Lord, You do not change. Your attitude towards wrong is the same and the reality is You see it all. Forgive me for making You small and thinking my questionable ways are hidden from You. Amen.

June 5

I take such comfort in Scriptures such as *Jeremiah 29:11, "For I know the thoughts that I think toward you, saith the LORD, thoughts of peace and not of evil, to give you an expected end" (Jeremiah 29:11).* I have often become concerned by the environment that has been created in America. For years we have been told by others how to classify our lives.

For example, when I was in the fifth grade my family and I were living in what many would consider the poverty level. However, I felt I was one of the richest kids on the block because my family was intact and I had friends and an environment where imagination was encouraged and the possibilities incredible.

Today in our high-tech society, if a child does not have a computer, chrome books, smart phones and the assortment of latest technology gadgets, he or she is considered to be poverty stricken. Who determines such an unrealistic value system?

The truth is, many in the generation coming up cannot even communicate or interact with people unless they have some type of keyboard, cell phone, or means to text their latest message. They sit mesmerized by the blinking cursor that glides them across their screen as they express their thoughts or ideas to someone else or become conditioned and indoctrinated by wicked video games.

I, for one, am thankful for the means to interact with my Lord. As a believer, He has given me His Spirit to communicate with Him. I don't have to use some type of indifferent technological tool to try to make contact with an idea, image, or anonymous entity. I know who I am communicating with, and I can trust His intentions towards me.

Prayer: Lord, You never change towards those who belong to You. You have the best intentions towards each of us. Thank You for Your goodness and kindness. Amen.

June 6

Many people are fearful, joyless, and confused. As a believer I refuse to give in to any of the fleshly states that fear losing the fading life as I know it, as well as a joyless reality because the fruits of this present world is hateful, bitter, and foul, producing endless confusion due to colliding realities. I choose to trust the Lord when He hands the key to endure this world in *Philippians 2:2, "Fulfil ye my joy, that ye be likeminded, having the same love, being of one accord, of one mind."*

The high-tech environment we live in strips away the humanness of people. High tech has no regard for personality, identity, talents, and character of people. It is indifferent and soulless. In such an environment we can present any front without ever exposing ourselves. We can interact with others without having to have any real personal encounter.

The casualty in this environment is that people are found to be emotionally inept to have any real relationship with others. The ability or skills to personally communicate in a natural or constructive way are missing. Few are able to connect to reality making the innocent vulnerable to fall victim to predators, as relationships become susceptible to being shipwrecked by the challenges of every-day life, causing and allowing people to end up living in small selfish worlds that are void of any real substance.

What many fail to realize is that the quality of our relationships with others will bring the greatest satisfaction to our lives. The truth is people will not survive the darkness of the times we live in without some type of support. Each of us must know how to discern the times, communicate with those who are likeminded, and learn to submit and be part of that which is worthy and greater in substance and purpose for our sake and the glory of God.

Prayer: Lord, the value of earthly relationships will depend on what kind of value we put on our relationship with You. All greatness will always find its origins in You. Amen.

June 7

"And when he putteth forth his own sheep, he goeth before them, and the sheep follow him; for they know his voice. And a stranger will they not follow, but they will flee from him; for they know not the voice of strangers" (John 10:4-5). The question is how many of us recognize the voice of the Lord? Yes, we have His Word, but how many equate it to His voice? We have impressions and revelations from the Holy Spirit, but how many know how to discern them?

I have been thinking about the technology that runs our lives. Admittedly, I have not been attracted to it because no doubt it is leading to a one-world society. The truth is that technology reminds me of the Wizard of Oz. Everyone seems to be sitting behind the curtain, or I should say, their various screens. Instead of pulling some kind of switch to give the effect they want to produce, they type words on their devices to make an impact or communicate in some way.

As I meditated on this concept, I had to ponder what would I write to try to influence my reality? There are so many voices and every one of them have legitimate opinions and concerns that they need to communicate. However, should we be more concerned in speaking our mind, or listening to what is being said?

As I considered the voices that are being expressed through the various communicative avenues, Jesus' words in *John 10:4-5* came to me. As believers if we are going to survive the times we live in, we must be able to recognize the voice of our true Shepherd in the midst of the many voices that are vying for our attention.

The question we each must ask ourselves is do we truly know the voice of our Shepherd? Only He will be able to lead us through the darkness presently engulfing the world.

Prayer: Lord, thank You for offering protection and life in the midst of uncertainty, doom, destruction, and death. Uncertainty points to confusion, doom to sin, destruction to the world, and death to the body and soul. However, Lord, You are the essence of sanity, hope, and life even in the midst of the many voices of the world. Amen.

June 8

Proverbs 23:23 tells us to, *"Buy the truth, and sell it not; also wisdom, and instruction, and understanding"* How many of us would be willing to sell our present realities to buy truth that would challenge our foundation and conclusions? How many of us are willing to face harsh reality when we prefer to believe fables to avoid confronting the grave darkness of our times?

When I thought of the many voices penetrating the various avenues of technology with opinions, education, and indoctrination, I could not help but think that in such a time as this real communication is actually missing. For most people they are hitting a stone wall of deafness. I was reminded of another period in time when darkness engulfed the world under the Roman Empire.

Politically it was oppressive and unbearable to the people who had to live under the tyranny of the times. People responded to the environment differently. Some became zealots in trying to change the times, some decided to play along to see what they could get out of it, and others tried to get their religious bearings to make sense out of what seemed like a world gone mad. No doubt frustration was hitting the height of anger and despair because those in leadership could be bribed, while some in the powerful religious arena had their own personal agendas and were willing to sell truth and justice for political favors.

However, the environment was ripe for something to penetrate the hearts of men. What needed to penetrate the hearts of men was the light of truth and hope. Truth would set them free to embrace the true hope that would come through one man, Jesus Christ, one message, the Gospel, and one act of sacrifice on an old wooden cross.

Prayer: Lord, You came to set your people free and deliver them from the oppressive tyrants of this world. Thank You for delivering me. I praise Your holy name. Amen.

June 9

"For this is he that was spoken of by the prophet Esaias saying, the voice of one crying in the wilderness, Prepare ye the way of the Lord, make his paths straight" (Matthew 3:3). It is obvious that in each generation there is one voice that must be heard.

When you think about the battle going on for hearts and minds, you realize how people are indeed like sheep. In today's world there are very few voices that seem to get any real attention. These voices belong to those who have special interests and personal agendas, but in between all these factions that seem to take center stage, stand the common people.

As for the masses, they are happy to live their lives. Their hope is to avoid the conflict brought about by the wave of corruption caused by a few. However, such corruption finds them as it erodes every ounce of hope with each oppressive, perverted decision, policy, or compromise that is made in darkness. It was in a time much like this that 20 centuries ago, a voice came forth from the barren wilderness.

We know who possessed that voice, John the Baptist. He did not bring another political speech, nor was he trying to con, flatter, or devise a plan to change the times. Rather, he brought a message that not only penetrated the darkness of the times and man's soul, but it prepared people to embrace the solution.

Like the days of John the Baptist, the solution will not be found in the present attempts of the human race to try methods or measures to change indifferent or corrupt governments, but in a message that is not only inspired by heaven, but can penetrate and change hearts. The harsh truth is environments can only change as one's life and heart are transformed by the hope and truth of the light of the world.

I must ask myself, has the true light of heaven, Jesus, penetrated my life and heart to influence or change the destruction that darkness is having on those around me?

Prayer: Lord, I must not assume anything about my spiritual state. I must know if I am right before You. Amen.

June 10

There it stands, surrounded by grass, out in the back yard, fully dressed in the green leaves of summer. Its innocent loveliness, rather than a stately appearance, is nevertheless pretty enough to have a way of deceiving casual observers as to its "inner branch work." The truth is, anyone who sees it "naked" in the springtime quickly determines that it's an awkward specimen of a tree.

It's amazing to me how such a healthy tree in summer, and a flaming beauty in early fall can appear to be so ugly in late fall and winter! If trees had a contest for "bad hair days," that tree would certainly be the winner. When we bought it a few years ago, we were told it's a boxelder tree, but from my Internet searches, I'm beginning to doubt that.

Whatever it is, this tree reminds me of overcoming Christians who start off "all elbows;" spiritually "gangly" and sometimes "out of joint." As the Lord faithfully allows them to go through their "pruning, and "process," they begin to develop deep roots in the life-giving soil of God's Word. And, as they experience the sifting of Satan, the boiling of the Refiner's fire, the breaking and crushing of their pride, along with the mundane life of daily irritations, they begin to make progress in their life in Christ—a life that brings forth good fruit for the glory of God.

We may not like it, but we need to embrace our "process" because without it there is no "progress." God's goal in redemption is to make us whole and blameless. *"And the very God of peace sanctify you wholly; and I pray God your whole spirit and soul and body be preserved blameless unto the coming of our Lord Jesus Christ" (1 Thessalonians 5:23)* – J. Haley

Prayer: Lord, we are called to "overcome." It is not optional but necessary to stand strong in our faith, regardless of how dark the night becomes. However, we must be pruned back at times to develop the means to be overcomers. Have Your way. Amen.

June 11

Jesus asked a simple question in *Luke 9:25*, *"For what is a man advantaged, if he gain the whole world, and lose himself, or be cast away?"* One of the things that has always amazed me is what man will sell to gain the world. As I watch the insanity around me taking center stage, it saddens me that the first thing man is willing to offer up on the altars of this world is his own soul.

Man is forever willing to lose his soul to gain a false sense of security through money and power, as well as a false sense of peace. He is willing to embrace darkness in order to hide his deeds behind various masks. He complicates matters so others will not see that he is also willing to offer their souls on the altar for his own self-serving purposes. People who will sell their own soul have no qualms about selling or destroying the souls of others. Perhaps this is the most frightening aspect of the darkness that engulfs the world.

The world requires our souls, while Jesus gave up His life on our behalf. The world demands our all, while Jesus gave up His all so that He could become all in all to us. The world will sacrifice us, while Jesus became a sacrifice for us. The contrast is obvious, but sadly most people choose the world instead of Jesus. In the end, all they gain is emptiness and a foreboding sense of doom.

Prayer: Lord, I remember what it was like when I was selling my soul to the world. It was so lonely, so empty, and so miserable. Thank You for giving me a choice. I choose You and Your glorious redemption. Amen.

June 12

Have you ever meditated on Paul's words found in *Romans 8:36*, *"As it is written, For thy sake we are killed all the day long; we are accounted as sheep for the slaughter."* I know that Jesus allowed Himself to be led away to the cross and that Paul understood that in ministry to lead, he must also allow himself to be led where he would be required to pour out his life at times, become a spectacle at other times, and to be led to the different altars of the world to be offered up as a sacrifice in order to share the Gospel.

I have long ago realized that to the world my soul is considered, at best, a cheap commodity that has no real purpose or significance to it other than to be offered up for the sake of the godless, the hateful, and the despots of society. If I do not serve such people's purpose, I must be destroyed. If I do not agree with them, I must be devalued, stripped of any virtue that might bring a contrast to their insanity. If I dare think outside of these infidels' insanity, I must be persecuted, tortured, and left for the remaining vultures of the world to do as they will with me.

Since many people are being isolated by their present environment, it will not be hard to use such individuals to fall into line in carrying out the wicked deeds of a few. Meanwhile these very same followers will be offered up on whatever altars that are being erected along the way.

The Bible warns us that the sheep are often led away to be slaughtered, but if we are truly believers of the most High God, we can learn what it means to leave a witness behind as we possess our souls in patience, knowing our body may be killed by those who serve as Satan's instruments, but our soul will be preserved by the God who knows how to deliver us through, from, and out of the wickedness of the age in which we live into His glorious kingdom.

Prayer: Lord, thank You for delivering us. You have delivered us from so many trials and tribulations as we struggle to advance forward to our destination. We do look forward to Your next deliverance, knowing that one day we will be completely delivered from this present world. Amen.

June 13

We often think of the victorious Christian life in relationship to the world's idea of success. However, the Bible purports a different presentation of what it means to be rich and an overcomer. Consider what *Psalm 9:18* states, *"For the needy shall not always be forgotten: the expectation of the poor shall not perish for ever."* Jesus stated that the poor will always be among us and *James 2:5* tells us being rich in God's kingdom has to do with faith, and from experience I can tell you faith that is exercised the most when a person must depend on God for their basic needs to be met.

When we embark upon the concept of embracing something new, we must first come to terms with what we have need of. So many times, we assume we understand what our needs are and they should be obvious to any onlooker, but our ideas of needs sometimes turn out to be desires that have nothing to do with maintaining our life.

It is not unusual for these desires to become obsessive, driving us to pursue them. We think to ourselves, "If only this was a certain way." Those "if only's" may represent some dream, but they are rarely realistic. We can assume if circumstances change, we will be quite another person, but is such an assumption realistic? After all, we are who we are.

We often assume that Jesus knows what we have need of, but are we prepared to receive that which will often challenge us to step outside of comfort zones to discover what is excellent. So many times, we are blinded by the ruts we often dig for ourselves. We assume we know what we have need of, when in reality we have never faced the harsh reality of our depravity and that it is God alone who provides what we have need of.

We all start out blind by the depravity of the old. It is only when the light of Jesus penetrates the darkness of our soul that we can begin to see what we really have need of. This is when we will realize that God does not overlook us in our need, and we will not perish in our poverty.

Prayer: Lord, I know that I am needy, poor in every way, but You are the One who adds eternal value to my life. Thank You for comprising the real wealth in my life. Amen.

June 14

There is one statement in the Old Testament that summarizes the hope of all saints, past, present, and future. It is found in *Job 19:25-26, "For I know that my redeemer liveth, and that he shall stand at the latter day upon the earth: And though after my skin worms destroy this body, yet in my flesh shall I see God".*

The Apostle Paul stated that without the resurrection of Christ our faith would be in vain and we would remain dead in sin. After all, it was Jesus' resurrection that proved He was victorious over death.

One of the most interesting people of the Bible is Job. Job knew what it meant to possess abundance and to be brought to the base point of losing it all. Even though he tasted the abundance the world had to offer, he also had to taste the bitterness of losing it. Through it all his only sustaining comfort was that he knew in the end that the future life that awaited him would wipe out all bitterness.

Job believed in resurrection. David said it best when he spoke of coming forth in his Lord's likeness in *Psalm 17:15.* Job declared that he would see his Redeemer. Both of these men were looking towards a future that had not yet been secured by the work of the cross. They looked forward through a shadow of promise with clarity and hope towards a future inheritance.

As a believer, I must believe and live in expectation of my future inheritance. This inheritance points to realizing the fullness of redemption secured by Jesus, the Son of God's death, burial and resurrection. It is heavenly and eternal.

Prayer: Lord, I possess in my life the guarantee of inheriting an eternal inheritance. You provided that guarantee for me through Your redemption. Thank You Lord for Your grace. Amen.

June 15

I need to consider what my response should, and must be, towards evil. *Psalm 27:27* states, *"Depart from evil, and do good; and dwell for ever more."* I know Satan can come as an angel of light and his cohorts as ministers of righteousness to deceive or dull people down to the state of evil that abounds and the workings of wickedness.

I also must not forget the tendency, or how easy it is, to call evil good and good evil in order to avoid confronting it as a means of getting along with the world. The natural response towards evil is to minimize its power, influence, and impact by denying its consequences and ignoring its presence. In a sense, we can take a flippant pose towards it, while denying that it has any real power to impact our lives. We reason that we are intelligent people and the idea of evil is lame in light of the advanced, "tolerant" society we live in.

What most people fail to realize is that evil is not an intellectual issue. Granted, we may have the intelligence to recognize evil, but evil is a moral and spiritual problem. Therefore, it cannot be confronted on an intellectual front. It must be addressed on a spiritual level.

It is not enough to recognize evil; rather, it must be properly confronted and overcome in our personal lives. To overcome evil, one must see the affront it can have on his or her soul, as well as with his or her standing with God.

For me this means I must recognize what I am exposing myself too. I must also choose to not only recognize evil, but I must be quick to depart from it in order to be right before God. This is the only way I can be assured of dwelling in His presence forever.

Prayer: Lord, we can have great ideas of how to serve You, but many times we fail to address the very matters that separate us from You. Cause me to hate evil as Job did so that I can pursue the ways of righteousness like King David. Amen.

June 16

Little children have "big ears" when it comes to what they often overhear from the adults in their world, and some of those things stay with them for their entire life. Such was the case with me, when I was a very young child, listening to a story my grandma's older friends related to my parents during a visit with them.

The story was told to them by a pioneer woman who was no doubt older than they were, but it's a story that totally captured my mind and heart. The story went as follows: Towards the end of the wagon train era that brought settlers out west to homestead the land, a certain pioneer couple in a wagon train happened to look down at a small, shallow grave that lay near the trail. As they drew closer, they were shocked to see movement under the dirt. They halted their wagon, ran over to the grave and began scooping the dirt away. There lay an infant baby girl, still alive! They lifted her up, cared for her, and kept her alive.

There had been another wagon train that had recently gone on before them, so their wagon train hurried to try and catch up with it in order to find the parents of the baby girl, but to no avail. They continued to hunt for the parents of the baby, even for a long time afterwards, but they were never found, so they kept the child and raised her as their own.

The woman who related this story had been the baby who was miraculously saved. She had no way to find her birth parents, so whoever they were, they never knew that their daughter was still alive, and she never knew who she belonged to.

As born-again believers, we can, in a way, relate with that baby. We once were "dead in our sins" and "in darkness, buried under a load of care" with no hope of life until Jesus found us and raised us up into new life in Him. We, too, have been adopted, and our adoption is sure for it is into the family of God, and we know Who we belong to—the Lord Jesus Christ! *"But as many as received him, to them gave he power to become the sons of God, even to them that believe on his name" (John 1:12).*

Finally, no matter what earthly family we may belong to, and no matter what lineage we may have, what matters the most is this truth, *"For the Son of Man has come to seek and to save that which was lost" (Luke 19:10).* The question is, have you been found of Him, or are you still buried under a load of sin? – J. Haley

Prayer: Lord I was buried by sin, left for dead, but You found me, revived the little life that was in me with a new life and now I'm part of a family, an eternal family. Thank You for not leaving me in a barren wilderness of sin and death in an unmarked grave, and adopting me into Your family. Amen.

June 17

To be a great leader, you must be sensitive to not only the people around you, but to the environment in which you must stand, A leader must be distinguished by inner character. No leader can be great unless he or she can be led by that which signifies greatness.

One of the realities I try to keep in mind is that as a Christian what must distinguish me is the presence of the Holy Spirit in my life. The Apostle Paul reminds me of this in such scriptures as *1 Corinthians 3:16, "Know ye not that ye are the temple of God, and that the Spirit of God dwelleth in you?"*

Each believer is a dwelling place for the very presence of God. A. W. Tozer stated that our blunder as Christians is that we have neglected the doctrine of the Spirit to a point where we virtually deny Him His place in the Godhead. He then points out that our formal creed may be sound when it comes to the Spirit, but the breakdown is in our working creed. In essence, there is no practical value or practice when it comes to our Christian walk in regard to the Holy Spirit.

I know if I am to display any real power or leadership in the kingdom of God, the Holy Spirit must not only be present, He must be directing my life. Therefore, I must not settle for a simple understanding of the character or work of the Spirit, I must have the practical experience of being led by His wisdom and gentleness, while walking in His power and anointing.

Prayer: Lord, thank You for Your Spirit. I do not want Him to be rendered into a doctrinal box; rather, I want Him to be an ever-present reality in my life. Give me more of Your Spirit so that I can experience a greater fullness of Your life in me. Amen.

June 18

Psalm 36:2 states, *"For he flattered himself in his own eyes, until his iniquities be found to be hateful"* One of the big challenges Christians have is to neglect their pride. As long as we are in these bodies, pride is present to raise its head in any and all situations to claim some kind of recognition. However, true leadership in the kingdom of God never comes from heights of arrogance but from depths of humility.

That is why it is easy to tell if a person or leader is trustworthy. Does the individual have to flatter him or herself in regard to the person he or she is becoming, which requires those around them to feed their fragile egos to keep them from becoming insulted, touchy, and tyrannical?

I have pondered why people so easily become beset by pride and it is because they have a divided heart and are double-minded. A divided heart has to do with trying to serve two masters, but the double-minded exists because the person cannot bring together the person he or she desires to be with the person he or she really is. Obviously, those who are double-minded cannot and will not accept the reality of an unpleasant matter that reveals wrong motives, self-serving intentions, and a lack of true character.

People who must flatter themselves about the person they are, do so in order to feel good about themselves. If they flatter themselves, they will eventually become hateful to those who do not concur with the deception of their flattery. It is for this reason that we must examine ourselves. We must seek truth to avoid succumbing to self-ascribed flattery.

Prayer: Lord, we have a tendency to flatter ourselves as well as others when we do not like our reality. However, it creates a false way that will set us up for destruction. Give me a love for the truth. Amen.

June 19

There are two things that never change: God in His majesty and man in his pathetic plight. Each generation would like to think that they are the enlightened generation and that they are not subject to the foolishness and crutches of those before them, and yet as Solomon pointed out in *Ecclesiastes*, nothing is new under the sun. The same assumptions and presumptions the religious people made in Jesus' day is still being made today.

Therefore, would it surprise some in the Church to realize: Prejudice would reject John the Baptist today because he didn't look the part or approach them properly. Disillusionment would still crucify Jesus Christ because He failed to perform the way they wanted Him to. Self-righteousness would still criticize the Apostle Paul because he would be considered fanatical and unorthodox.

As we can see, as in Jesus' day, humanity clothed in dead religiously-lettered apparel has the same capacity today as it did twenty centuries ago.

Oh, the arrogance of man! We think we know something when we know nothing. We think we are somebody, when we are nobody. What we know is insignificant but what God shows us is eternal. Yet, we take pride in what we think we know, rather than glorying in God who adds or gives whatever eternal virtues are present in our lives.

As Paul cried out in *Romans 7:24, "O wretched man that I am!"* When am I going to fully realize there is no hope, value, or significance outside of Christ?

Prayer: Lord we think we are so smart, yet we can't properly perceive spiritual matters. We think we would not be like those losers of old, but we fail to realize we have the same tendencies and ways they did. Lord, You gave me Your Spirit so I could rise above the foolishness of self, ascend above the world to soar in Your heights, and take flight in Your promises to endure this age and ultimately finish the course. Amen.

June 20

Psalm 35:7 states, *"For without cause have they hid for me their net in a pit, which without cause they have digged for my soul."* Probably one of the most discouraging realities is the injustice that rules the world we live in. Whether we are unfairly and falsely attacked or accused by those who we thought were our friends or the prevailing injustice around us that rejects true justice, it all proves despairing to the soul.

Wicked leadership clearly creates deep despair by putting judges in place who can be bribed, while promoting their own political agendas, as they mock real justice. Their bench is just a miserable platform (or soap box) and their gavel a mocking slap across the face of all that is sane, moral, and just.

It is easy to forget we live in a world where Satan governs its systems. As believers, our great comfort is that we do not belong to this world and that we are simply passing through. We must remember there is no hope, lasting satisfaction, and purpose in this world and that our spiritual inheritance awaits us in the next world.

The challenging reality for Christians is that we are to walk in the ways of what is right and just. However, this will put us in the sites of such people who will attempt to work grave injustice against us. They will lay snares for us with the intent to bring ruin to our lives in order to bring forth claims against us. We must always remember that God is just and in due time He will judge the world. His justice and righteousness will not only have the ultimate say, but He will rule with just judgments.

Prayer: Lord, it is such a despairing world we live in. But we have the promise of a future kingdom where the knowledge of Who You are will cover the face of the earth, and You will reign in righteousness. Amen.

June 21

"What's so funny?" I asked a friend who was literally doubled over with laughter as I angrily held up my letter for her to see. I failed to find any humor in what I was so mad about. After all, I had paid good money for a mosquito plant, and all I got was an itsy bitsy, wilted, sickly start in the mail. And, within three days it was dead and gone.

To add insult to injury, I figured that by the time that thing would've grown to any decent size, the thick swarms of mosquitoes around us would have bled us to death. Therefore, I wanted a refund and said just that as I Scotch taped the two-inch dry, brown stem to my letter, which stated in part, "Here is your mosquito plant." They did refund part of my money, at least, and I suppose the laughter it caused for her, and eventually myself, was worth it.

On top of that, I recently learned that mosquito plants don't really work all that well, and you have to crush the citronella scent out of it yourself. In other words, it's no work-free, easy fix. We all love "easy fixes" but it seems that there are no "easy fixes" for almost everything in life, especially when it comes to others.

You probably know how that is—those annoying people that, even though you may love them, you want to somehow "fix" them so your world will be better. We think that with just a little "tweak" here and a little "adjustment" there it will make them less of a bother, bummer, or burden.

The problem is, we can't "fix" anybody, especially spiritually. We can pray, be a witness and example, but we can't "save" them. Even though we may bring Scriptural instruction, wisdom, correction, rebuke, or exhortation in the right spirit, people still have to make the right decisions for themselves. The power to truly change a person for eternity belongs to Christ alone. *"Therefore if any man be in Christ, he is a new creature: old things are passed away; behold, all things are become new"* (2 Corinthians 5:17). – J. Haley

Prayer: Lord, we want an easy fix but if we had one every time we had a challenge, we would never have to develop godly virtues, discipline our flesh and learn to trust You. Thank You for causing the different "road bumps" in life to cause us to remember who is able to change the terrain of land, sea, and souls. Amen.

June 22

How our enemies will test us! David cried out, *"Let them be ashamed and brought to confusion together that rejoice at mine hurt. Let them be clothed with shame and dishonor that magnify themselves against me" (Psalm 35:26).* The enemies of God have no boundaries to warn them of their possible consequences. They are lawless as they devise ways around what is moral and lawful. They are hateful; therefore, they want revenge against those who would dare challenge them in their evil state. They will rejoice when failure besieges those they hate, while they secretly plan to dance on their graves when their voices are finally silent.

Such people create an insane world. They have no fear of God or consequences. Not only are they indifferent to the wrath that awaits them, but they are arrogant enough to believe that the end results will not matter.

For me, I am thankful that I am a citizen of another kingdom. Although it is presently unseen, one day it will manifest itself when the King of kings, the righteous Judge comes to earth to set up His everlasting kingdom. Meanwhile I must keep my senses about me by keeping my focus heavenward where righteousness awaits to reveal itself in judgment upon those who hate, reject, and ignore it.

Prayer: Lord, I am thankful that my future does not depend on this present world. Thank You for providing me with a new citizenship. Amen

June 23

Scriptures that cause me to pause and meditate are those that remind me of my great need for the Lord Jesus Christ in my life.

Consider *Psalm 33:15, "There is no king saved by the multitudes of an host: a mighty man is not delivered by much strength."*

Every time I come upon the matters of life I am faced with my need for intervention. If a king cannot save himself with the strength of a host or the mighty man with his strength, how can I save myself? It is clear that I am weak and vulnerable in my present state. I have no means to change my circumstances or my miserable plight. Therefore, I am always in need of God's mercy, desirous of His grace, and a candidate for His ongoing work of salvation.

It has taken many years of failures, detours, and hard lessons to realize that my self-sufficiency lies at the core of all of my folly. It is arrogant about its abilities, deluded about its strength, and foolish about its ways.

The wisdom from above will always remind me of my need for God's constant intervention. I need to know His hand is upon all situations. My prayer is that I will feel its firmness when I start to go my own way, know its gentleness when I need comfort, its pressure when I need to move, its restraint when I need to stop, and its protection when the darkness enfolds me.

Prayer: Lord, every day I become more and more aware of how You are my strength and hope. I cannot depend on this world, nor can I imagine what it would be like to walk in my own strength as I face each new challenge. Amen.

June 24

When I read such scriptures as *Psalm 37:9, "For evildoers shall be cut off: but those that wait upon the LORD, they shall inherit the earth,"* I am reminded that the way to life in Christ is a narrow way. The problem is that even in wickedness a person can be blessed but eventually, they will be cut off from life, hope, and promises.

There is an easy way to discern what side of eternity a person is on even when people wear the religious garb and talk the talk. The wicked are often striving to rob, kill, and steal any worldly inheritance or legacy of the righteous. They are forever trying to gain control in order to serve as little gods. Their goal is to make a personal memorial of themselves by establishing some type of dynasty for their future descendants as a means to rise above the inevitable.

The inevitable that all wicked despots and tyrants try to avoid is judgment. They do not want their memorial or legacy to be wiped out. However, history clearly reveals that all wicked leaders will be cut off. Their names become bywords that are often spit out, while their descendants become part of the masses, and their memorials are eventually ground into dust to serve as mounds in which others establish their own memorials or legacies.

It is clear there is a just God. The wicked will reap what they sow, and those who fear the Lord will inherit a new earth and a new heaven.

Prayer: Lord, I look forward to realizing the fullness of my inheritance. Thank You for securing it on the cross. Amen.

June 25

I love the promises of God. Meditate on *Psalm 36:9, "For with thee is the fountain of life, in thy light shall we see light."*

As the darkness of the world encloses around us, we as believers, must remember that the great light that penetrated our souls, bringing us salvation, is also the great light that resides in our inner being to guide us. That great light is the life of Christ that lights the way in which the Holy Spirit will lead each of us through the darkness.

My need for God in the barren wilderness of this present world becomes more apparent as the times we live in causes leanness and vexation in my spirit. In such times I realize I do indeed need to come to the fountain of life, Jesus Christ.

I enjoy the beauty of fountains. They not only add beauty to the landscape, but they imply perpetual movement. They give the impression that they are operating according to an unlimited source, when in reality they are often constructed to use the same water over and over.

As Christians, we have a fountain that does not reuse water, but instead finds its source in that which is eternal. This water will refresh, revive, and bring forth new and lasting life.

We know that this life serves as the light of men. It is connected to the throne of heaven where all wisdom and enlightenment flows. In this heavenly water is the salve of healing balm that will take away the blinders, enabling us to see into the unseen and the eternal.

Prayer: Lord, we thank You for being the fountain of living water that even though unseen, flows freely and is eternal. Amen.

June 26

The geranium was picture perfect! So perfect, in fact, that people touch their lovely peach petals to see if they're real. After working hard all summer to get a few pots of struggling geraniums to live and at least do something, three of them suddenly have taken "center stage."

Their perfection speaks to my swirling emotions as I grapple with recollections of past failures that, like weeds, mar the landscape of my mind. Perhaps the message of the perfect geraniums is that GOD IS, and all He created was "good."

We cannot create anything out of nothing, and we certainly cannot work or earn our way to perfection in the sight of God. But regardless of what we, or others, conclude about the "real us" because we've miserably failed according to standards and expectations, we must trust His Word that reassures us that a "perfect heart" is one that has been cleansed by the blood of Jesus, one that is made new in love, pure in thought, word and deed; is upright and righteous, hating evil as Job did.

Therefore, my friends, never give up but continually press into God, His ways, and His will through His Word and prayer, becoming "like a little child" in simple, yet powerful faith, knowing that our short journey in this world is about daily faithfulness in the little things because perfection in the little things leads to greater glory in the great things of heaven and eternity. *"Not as though I had already attained, either were already perfect: but I follow after, if that I may apprehend that for which also I am apprehended of Christ Jesus" (Philippians 3:1).*

"For by one offering he hath perfected for ever them that are sanctified" (Hebrews 10:14). "But let patience have her perfect work, that ye may be perfect and entire, wanting nothing" (James 1:4). – J. Haley

Prayer: Lord, we so appreciate Your faithfulness to us. We can waver, fall, and stay in the mud for a while, but You remain true to us and may I prove to be a child in disposition that is quick to believe and see that it is a great privilege to obey You. Amen.

June 27

I have been pondering lately much about how to survive the great spiritual darkness that is engulfing the world. When I think of darkness of this manner, I think of Paul when he was Saul. *"And Saul arose from the earth; and when his eyes were opened, he saw no man: but they led him by the hand, and brought him into Damascus"* (Acts 8:8).

Sometimes it is in the darkest times of our lives that we are able to see the most accurately as to our personal spiritual condition. In *Acts 9*, the man from Tarsus, Saul discovered this truth when he was blinded on the road to Damascus. It was because he encountered the bright light of heaven that he lost his physical sight. What light did he see? He saw Jesus. Light is meant to bring contrast as to how great darkness is.

For the zealous, religious Saul, the intense light of Christ revealed the great darkness of his soul. This is the reason most people flee from the light of Christ. They do not want to see the darkness of their own souls.

To survive the ensuing darkness, we must risk personal blindness and run to the light to ensure that we will ultimately be able to see our way through the darkness. Granted, we might be initially blinded by the light as we face the darkness of our own souls, but if we humble ourselves, we may end up clearly seeing our spiritual plight and experience the healing balm of heaven.

Saul's physical sight was restored, but what he had seen in relationship to Jesus and his spiritual condition forever changed his direction and course.

Prayer: Lord, do I need to personally encounter You to ensure that I have been spiritually healed, restored, and am walking in the right direction? If so, do what You need to do so that I can see You in Your transparent light of glory. Amen.

June 28

After sin entered into Eden, our first parents showed the end result, *"And they heard the voice of the LORD God walking in the garden in the cool of the day: and Adam and his wife hid themselves from the presence of the LORD God amongst the trees of the garden" (Genesis 3:8).*

It is not unusual for people to hide from the penetrating light of God. One of the popular games children play is hide-and-seek. However, that is a game that ends with the last child being found (or he or she coming out of hiding) to claim victory. However, hiding from God is not a game. Those who remain hidden from God illustrate the sober reality of how lost they are. In many cases, such individuals do not want to be found.

Sadly, we all start out unknowingly hiding from God because we are afraid to face the wretchedness of our own spiritual condition. In the darkness of deception, we all think we are a certain way when in reality we have no idea as to the darkness that engulfs our souls and blinds us to our need to be saved. Granted, we may sense there is something terribly amiss in our lives, but in darkness we have a tendency to believe such a condition will eventually pass. However, the darkness consuming our souls will not pass. This darkness must be extinguished by the dawning of the bright and morning star of Jesus arising in our souls with the truth of His salvation, reconciliation, and restoration.

Has the light of heaven graced your dark soul with the hope of life?

Prayer: Lord, I have hid from You, but You found me. Thank You, that I cannot hide from Your Spirit and Your glorious light of truth. Amen.

June 29

I think one of the saddest Scriptures is Genesis 3:9, *"And the LORD God called unto Adam, and said unto him, Where art thou?"* The rebellion of our first parents brought a separation between their creator and them. From that point, they hid from God, becoming lost to His light.

Why do we hide from the penetrating light of God? We see Adam and Eve hiding from God because of shame. They stood naked before Him because their rebellion had stripped all innocence and its glory away from them. They knew that in such a state, they would stand exposed before a holy God. They had fallen away from the center of righteousness into the grave darkness of separation.

It is because of the fallen state that we have inherited from Adam the natural tendency of attempting to hide from God, hoping His light will never find us in our present condition. We may even try to reform ourselves enough to think that we will be able to at least face Him. After all, the concept of facing a holy God can be unnerving to any sound thinking individual.

The real reason we usually start out hiding is because we are afraid to face our wretched state and God's penetrating light that will strip us of any self-delusion we may have about our so-called "goodness." We all think we are a certain way, but we are deluding ourselves, and the light of God will reveal the real truth about who we are becoming because of the darkness that is reigning in our own souls.

Prayer: Lord, I spent many years hiding from You behind silly garbs of religion, excuses, and rights to justify myself in my pathetic plight. To me it might have been a clever game, but it revealed how foolish I was in my delusion. Lord, You found me when I least expected it. I praise You for Your penetrating light that seeks and finds those who are lost and seeking an answer. Amen.

June 30

Compared to all the other Montana grasshoppers, the one I captured as a little kid just had to be a giant. Chasing grasshoppers when visiting my paternal grandmother in Montana was a pastime that kept me temporarily occupied, and everything was going well until my dad spotted that huge grasshopper in the jar that I was carrying around with me. That's when the raucous began.

You see, Dad was also collecting grasshoppers, or trying to, because he had plans to go fishing (his favorite sport), so when he saw my prize grasshopper, he decided it would do very nicely on the end of his fishhook. Those of you who know me, know that there was just no way that my grasshopper, that I caught by myself, and who in a very short time became a temporary pet for the day, was going to be sacrificed so he could use it to catch a whopper of a fish!

Thankfully, my mother heard my loud protesting to Dad's insistence that I hand over Mr. Grasshopper. She swept in like a professional wrestling umpire to defend me, and told him to go find his own grasshoppers. So, the end result? My dad was not happy, but I was, and Mr. Grasshopper was especially glad when I turned him loose that evening.

This simple little story can serve as an illustration of some of the shameful shenanigans that often take place in churches when one or more people envy, or covet the calling, spiritual gifts, or "oil" of others who have "paid the price" by taking up their cross, walked their faith out in humble obedience, made the right decisions, developed godly character and are prepared to meet the bridegroom when He appears. *"And the foolish said unto the wise,*

Give us of your oil; for our lamps are gone out. But the wise answered, saying, Not so; lest there be not enough for us and you: but go ye rather to them that sell, and buy for yourselves" *(Matthew 25:8, 9).* – J. Haley

Prayer: Lord, keep me from petty jealousies and give me the willingness, desire, and courage it takes to possess You no matter the personal cost. Amen.

July

July 1

Hiding speaks of fear or dread of something. David knew the solution to all of his fears, *"I sought the LORD, and he heard me, and delivered me from all my fears" (Psalm 34:4).* The truth of the matter is, when we are hiding from what we fear, we do not want our location or deeds to be discovered. It is important to remember that if I feel the need to hide from God, it is because I have something unpleasant to hide from Him as to my attitude or conduct.

There are other reasons that fear reigns besides the presence of sin. But what I need to recognize is that fear is the greatest enemy of active, effective faith. It either paralyzes or drives. For me, it closes me down as I choose to ignore the storms gathering on the horizon. It makes me complacent in my attitude as I live in denial about the tsunami that is gaining momentum in the far distant horizon. Eventually the great wave will broadside me, leaving failure and destruction in its wake.

The truth is, I must confront my fear. I cannot worship it or let it dictate to me. I must cease to give it power by looking to the One who has all power over the challenges and storms of life. The only way I can look to the Lord when fear is oppressing me is that His desire is not to meet me in judgement because the fearful will not make it into His kingdom, but to restore me out of love, grace, and mercy.

Prayer: Lord, You know how to enable me to overcome my fear. Help me to look up to take Your hand, knowing that You will help me walk through the darkness that encases my soul when fear is taking center stage. Amen.

July 2

In yesterday's meditation I was pondering fear that paralyzes and drives, but there is a fear that can create the right attitude and conduct in me. *Psalm 34:9* reveals that acceptable fear, *"O fear the LORD, ye his saints: for there is no want to them that fear him."*

The fear of the Lord is often made out to be anything but fear of God. However, the fear of the Lord points to having a healthy and right attitude about God and His ways. It is true, fear can be natural or it can be a spirit that is associated with the world. Such a spirit will strip a person of power to overcome, rob one of the perfect love that can cast it aside, and cause confusion and double-mindedness.

However, the fear of the Lord will not be defeating or destructive. It finds its origins in love for God, and is sensitive of who He is. Godly fear does not hide from God, live in denial of darkness, or drive one into utter torment and despair. It actually leads to righteousness because it hates the ways and consequences of evil. It ends in life because it dreads to displease the Lord.

Because of the different fears that are in operation in this world, I have realized I have a choice as to which fear will influence my life, as well as what environment I expose myself to and the attitude I take on. It will also be obvious as to what fear I allow to become a point of my inspiration. Either a person will fear being found out by God, or he or she will fear not pleasing God. For me, I choose the latter.

Prayer: Lord, I do prefer to fear You. This fear does not make me feel the need to hide from You; rather, it causes me to dread meeting You on any other ground than that which believes, honors, and pleases You. Amen.

July 3

Imagine my surprise when, after I showed a close friend a new "volunteer" flower, she carefully stepped towards it, quickly grabbed its slender stem and yanked it out! I had explained to her that this particular plant with its single orange flower had simply shown up, and while it didn't "match" my general color scheme of various shades of pink and purple, with some white, and a few splashes of yellow, it seemed pretty and harmless enough.

As it turns out, she recognized it as being a noxious weed. To be honest, real friends will not only pull a noxious weed out of your flowerbed, they will also faithfully point out any "spiritual weeds" that may be taking root in the garden of your soul.

There is a time to speak, and a time to remain silent; but when the LORD uses someone you love and trust to warn you of "danger ahead," the wise thing to do is to "stop, look and listen" and ask the LORD to show you your own heart. *Proverbs 27:6* tells us, *"Faithful are the wounds of a friend; but the kisses of an enemy are deceitful."* – J. Haley

Prayer: Lord, sometimes You use my closest friend to shake up my comfortable world but You do so knowing that a friend only wants the best for me. Thanks for my faithful friends, and thank You for being my Friend. Amen.

July 4

What does it mean to be free? We supposedly live in a free country but if there is grave oppression present, such freedom is nothing but a façade. Real freedom does not depend on outward environment because if you are oppressed, you can't begin to understand or enjoy it. The reality behind freedom is best summarized in *John 8:36, "If the Son therefore shall make you free, ye shall be free indeed."*

Real freedom is an inward freedom of the spirit and soul because of the great work of redemption wrought by Jesus. If there is oppression in the environment but real freedom is present in the inner being, the spirit is still able to soar in worship and the soul will know the peace of God that passes all worldly understanding.

The one reality I must constantly confront is that my take on life may fall short of truth. Jesus is THE TRUTH, and there is power in His truth, but if I insist on my own reality, I will never know the liberating ways of truth. Granted, truth is sharp enough to cut through the fog of confusion, but it will offend, and not liberate me if I do not desire it. It is penetrating, but such penetration will cause repulsion in me instead of acceptance if I do not prefer it to my personal conclusions.

Truth brings me to the revelation of Jesus Christ. If I do not love truth, I will choose to hide from it, rather than embrace it as my reality.

The truth of the matter is that the reality around us is meant to bring us to three wise conclusions. 1) We are not God, 2) we need God, and 3) nothing makes sense in this world except God. The reality around us can prove to be shocking and unbearable, but as believers we must remember that it constantly reminds us that our hope is not in this present world, but in Christ Jesus who is coming back to set all matters right.

Prayer: Lord, You are the only one that can ensure a sound mind and bring order to that which is confusing, and newness to that which is old and unsavory. We commit everything to You as we wait upon You to translate us into that which is ordained by You. Amen.

July 5

We love to read and quote *John 3:16* but how many of us venture past it to consider the rest of Jesus' statements? For instance, consider *John 3:19, "And this is the condemnation, that light is come into the world, and men loved darkness rather than light; because their deeds were evil."*

This scripture tells us the main reason people hide from the light of God is because they do not want their deeds to be exposed for how wicked and unacceptable they are. In their delusion they want to believe that at the base of their deeds is something that can be considered good and acceptable, but the truth is that to a holy God it is humanistic and nothing more than filthy rags. Clearly, the reason for man to play hide and seek with God is due to shame caused by sin.

What we easily fail to realize in our fallen state is that it does not matter how well we think we are hiding our true condition, it's nothing but fig leaves when it comes to God's penetrating light of truth. Like our first parents, we stand guilty as charged by our shame. However, the beauty of God is that because of His great love He has never ceased to seek out the lost sheep that desires to not only come under the penetrating light of truth, but to be set free from the guilt of their shame by His work that was displayed through Christ's work of redemption on the cross.

I, for one, know the liberating light of His truth. I was in complete spiritual darkness, groping for some branch of hope that would allow me to hold on until the light penetrated my dark soul of sin and despair. Faithful to His promise, Jesus found this lost sheep and translated me from the kingdom of darkness into His precious light.

Are you willing for your deeds to be brought to the light so you can walk in truth?

Prayer: Lord, I hate my dirty laundry being aired for others to see, but the truth is You can see it; therefore, how can I convince myself I am truly hiding it? Lord, bring my laundry to the light in order to sanitize my life with Your Spirit and Word. Amen.

July 6

How many ways could you spend a dime back when ten cents was actually worth ten cents? I figured I was the smartest kid on the block when a bunch of us would head for the Five and Dime store after we were given our weekly allowance of a whole dime. That's because I looked for the best deal in penny candy, bought five of them and then was the only kid that had five cents left. With that much money I could save it towards a ten-cent comic book, or put it in my piggy bank.

But my favorite purchases were when the boy I palled around with and I walked up the hill to where the real treasure stood, in the form of a gumball and trinket machine! We'd ooh and ahh at the myriad of colorful charms and trinkets mixed in with gumballs, and picked out the ones we hoped would be released into our eager hands. As our collections grew, we'd trade them back and forth, and even buried a few in an envelope in my front yard to "discover" in a couple of weeks as "real treasure."

There's something alluring about hunting for hidden treasure that captivates both young and old. Even today we follow the television series about the buried treasure on Oak Island, and tune in to other historical treasure mysteries.

The truth is, however, earth's trinkets and treasures, exciting as they may be, are only temporary and can add nothing to a person's eternal destiny. But the indescribably beautiful truth is, born again, obedient Christians have an eternal treasure, a treasure reserved in heaven (*Luke 12:33; 18:22*). *2 Corinthians 4:7* assures us, *"But we have this treasure in earthen vessels, that the excellency of the power may be of God, and not of us."* Praise the Lord! – J. Haley

Prayer: Lord, remind us our real treasure will never be found in this world but the next one. We will get glimpses into these treasures and occasionally taste them, but we will experience all of their beauty, grace and worth in heaven. Amen.

July 7

"For ye were sometimes darkness, but now are ye light in the Lord: walk as children of light" (Ephesians 5:8). One problem I had as a new Christian is that I did not understand the extent of the darkness that was enfolding my soul because it seemed like light to me. I thought I was perceiving, comprehending, and understanding what was going on around me, when in fact I was being blinded by it.

Experience in time taught me that if you are going to understand the extent of darkness, you must come to terms with the light that has been given which can penetrate the darkness. For instance, there are different types of darkness. There is the darkness of the night, the darkness of the age we live in, and the dark night of the soul. But God has provided the light in which we can see what we need to see to walk through each type of darkness.

For example, the world we live in has its own natural darkness. However, God has provided the light of the moon and stars to shine through the natural darkness of night to highlight the landscape around us. In the age we live in the darkness is caused by sin and death, but God has provided His Son to penetrate the darkness of this present age with His light of truth. In the dark night of the soul, He has provided His Spirit to bring comfort and His Word to guide our steps.

As Christians, we have the abiding light with us at all times. However, in order to see we must let the Lord provide the type of light we need by seeking Him in the times of darkness.

Prayer: Lord, there may be reasons why Your light is not shining, but I can trust it is shining and if I seek You, I will find that light shining forth from You. Open the eyes of my heart so that I can see the path that leads to You in all of Your splendor and glory. Amen.

July 8

"This then is the message which we have heard of him, and declare unto you, that God is light, and in him is no darkness at all" (1 John 1:5). God has provided the light that we have need of to walk in sweet fellowship with Him. Clearly, as believers there is no need to grope, stumble, and fall into some pit or abyss where destruction or death awaits us.

We indeed possess the true light of the soul. We also have the means to walk according to the light that penetrates spiritual darkness, and we are quite aware of the fickleness and changing lights of the natural world around us. It is obvious that the real issue comes down to the type of light we are able to see. Most are able to see because of a natural light, but when it comes to the light of God, the number of those who possess the inward light of Christ dwindles greatly.

I must honestly examine if I possess the eyesight and light that is able to guide me through the darkness that is now engulfing the world I live in to avoid its traps of spiritual destruction and ruin.

Prayer: Lord, upon my spiritual birth You gave me the light I needed in order to walk through the grave darkness of this world. However, it occasionally becomes dim. Revive the passion of my life so that I can walk through this world with boldness. Amen.

July 9

"But if thine eye be evil, thy whole body shall be full of darkness. If therefore the light that is in thee be darkness, how great is that darkness" (Matthew 6:23). To think that my darkness is my light is very disconcerting to my perception of my wisdom, intelligence, and ability to rationalize something to a proper conclusion. The truth is we all start out blind in some way.

Some are actually physically blind. They cannot see the physical world they live in. Some are blinded by their own prideful judgments and ways. They refuse to deal in reality, preventing them from seeing what is really happening around them, creating a tidal wave of destruction that will eventually consume them. Since we are born with an Adamic disposition, we all start out spiritually blind, causing us to be lost in a world of sin, darkness, and death.

Obviously, we must have the means to see if we are going to survive. For those who are physically blind, they learn to use their other senses to guide them. Individuals, who are blinded by their personal take on life, must be willing to step outside of their narrow perspective to see what is really happening so they can address or avoid the tidal wave that is gaining momentum. In addition, those who are spiritually blinded need the healing salve of Jesus' redemption to open up the eyes of their heart so they can see His salvation and truth, as well as avoid the abyss of damnation.

Again, I must examine myself to see if I possess such eyes or if my heart is dull and unreceptive towards that which is spiritual and eternal.

Prayer: Lord, blindness is all around me. You are the great physician, please heal the eyes of my heart, the seeing eye of my perception, and the physical eyes of my body. May I only see that which is eternal, truthful, and real. Amen.

July 10

The Apostle Paul tells us what it will mean to evaluate a matter in *1 Thessalonians 5:8, "But let us, who are of the day, be sober, putting on the breastplate of faith and love; and for an helmet, the hope of salvation."* I have often noticed that people see matters differently. You may have two individuals witness the same event, but when you ask them what they witnessed, it usually sounds like two distinct happenings.

What many people fail to realize is that eyesight is one of the most untrustworthy senses when it comes to witnessing a matter. There are three problems when it comes to our physical eyesight. The first problem is we often don't know what we are looking for or at. There are so many things to focus on that unless something catches our full attention for more than a glance or just a second, we are unable to give a viable record of what was going on around us. It is for this reason that many people cannot give the same type of description or record of a traumatic event. And, it is also for this reason that people must be trained to be able to note what they are seeing when they witness something.

The Apostle Paul tells us what it will mean for us to see correctly. We must be sober by putting on the breastplate of faith and love and the helmet of hope. We must look at things from a realistic perspective that insists that all matters begin and end with God's Word of truth.

Prayer: Lord, in my present state I see things according to the light I have, but I want to make sure that ultimately, I see a matter the same way as You. Give me Your attitude so that I can approach and process information properly. Amen.

July 11

I was meditating on how the people during Jesus' day viewed Him. *John 1:1* tells us, *"He came unto His own, and his own received him not."* The people of Jesus' day had an idea of what they were looking for and were even waiting for His entrance into their midst, but when Jesus walked among them, what did they see? Did they understand what they were looking at?

This was the problem the people had when Jesus came into the midst of humanity the first time and still exists today. In fact, I recently talked to a couple of young men who were on a mission, explaining we do not have the same Jesus, and the Jesus I know is the only One who can save us.

Like the people of Jesus day, even though we have the witness of prophesy as the Jews, many either have no idea who they were seeing when Jesus was presented to them or they refused to see. Some are focused on what they consider to be more pressing events, while others have their attention directed towards the demands of life, and some simply regard Him as a troublemaker because He does not fit into their religious understanding.

Clearly, the key is that we must not only see Jesus, we must know who we are looking for and at if He is going to have the type of impact on us that will enable us to walk through the darkness of this age.

Prayer: Lord, I do become concerned about what I see when I consider You. I must allow You to be who You are if I am going to recognize You. Strip away false notions, immature ideas, and foolish conclusions about You, so I can truly see You. Amen.

July 12

Nicknames can be very interesting—some are endearing, others caustic, and many humorous. I never had an "official nickname" although sometimes my mother would call me "Susie Q" or "Kertinka."

My dad, on the other hand, strongly suggested that "Yabut" would be a fitting nickname for me because it seemed that every time I was given some instruction, or told what to do, I'd respond with "Yeah, BUT" which meant "Yeah, sure, I get it, but I have other ideas and I don't agree with you." I'll never know how many times "Yeah-but" flew out of my mouth, irritating and exhausting my parents, but I do know that God's Word has plenty to say about "Yabut" "Christians" who give lip service to the LORD when all the while their hearts are far from Him.

Jesus said, "*Ye hypocrites, well did Esaias prophesy of you, saying, This people draweth night unto me with their mouth, and honoureth me with their lips; but their heart is far from me. But in vain they do worship me, teaching for doctrines the commandments of men*" *(Matthew 15:7-9)*. Let us take heed before we say "Yabut" to the LORD instead of "Thy will be done," and remember *1 Samuel 15:22, "And Samuel said, Hath the LORD as great delight in burnt offerings and sacrifices, as in obeying the voice of the LORD? Behold, to obey is better than sacrifice, and to hearken than the fat of rams."*

The bottom line is, if God says, "Do it," then do it! – J. Haley

Prayer: Lord, we always have our" Yabut," in our responses towards You but any "yes" with a but attached to it just a way of saying Your will is not my will and Your way is not my priority. Forgive me for my rebellious attitude and ways and cause Your hand to become heavy on me until I do what is right. Amen.

July 13

Every time I come to *Luke 8:18*, I stop and consider what spirit I am in when I hear matters that I may not agree with. After all, it was a sober warning from Jesus, *"Take heed therefore how ye hear: for whosoever hath, to him shall be given: and whosoever hath not, from him shall be taken even that which he seemeth to have" (Luke 8:18).*

In my last meditation I was thinking about the untrustworthiness of our physical sight. The first reason sight proves to be untrustworthy is that we do not always know what we are looking for; therefore, we cannot always recognize what we are looking at. This is why we often overlook an object that we are trying to find. We have a certain idea of what we are going to see, but when an object is in obscurity, it will not look the same way we perceive it should look. It is for this reason that lost objects remain lost until the right light or circumstances illuminate them in a way that we will be able to personally identify them.

Jesus also warned that we must beware of how we hear a matter. I have learned that the way I see a matter is going to affect how I hear about it.

My eyes often limit what I will hear by the conclusions I draw according to what I have seen. I realize that after reading these simple truths that it is a miracle that we humans get anything right. It clearly takes the penetrating light of Jesus to illuminate those things that are hidden from our understanding in order to bring clarity to our way of seeing and thinking.

Prayer: Lord, it is foolishness to cling to my take on things, stupid to insist on it, and suicidal if You give it to me. Help me to cease from foolishness, flee the stupid ways of self, and bow out of committing spiritual suicide over nothing more than the vanity of the world. Amen.

July 14

The Bible tells us in *2 Corinthians 2:11* that we must not be ignorant of the devices of Satan. He uses three effective avenues to take us captive: Lust, pride, and dissatisfaction, often sending us on endless and despairing rabbit trails, detours that leave us weary, and into extremes that border on insanity. In considering some of the members of the Church, I could see how it would be natural for them to operate in extremes.

1) If they are ignorant about righteousness, they can prove to be ridiculous in their causes.
2) If they aren't complacent towards the matters of God, they can become fanatics.
3) If they aren't asleep in the pews, they are flying from one unrealistic limb of heresy to the next.

The major problem in the visible Church is that people have not been properly trained or discipled. As a result, they do not know how to discern the enemy.

There are three main enemies of the cross: the flesh, the world, and Satan.

1) The flesh entices and leads to death.
2) The world entangles and chokes out the Word of God.
3) Satan enslaves in order to destroy.

Sadly, many do not know how to discern the different enemies of the cross because each one requires a different response.

1) We must repent of the works of the flesh (crucify them).
2) We must flee the activities of the world (become separate).

3) We must take authority over Satan.

What I often see is people repenting of Satan's work in their life, trying to take authority over their world to control it, and fleeing from taking responsibility for giving in to the dictates of the flesh.

No wonder why Christians often live defeated lives in a world that highlights destructive avenues, makes the enemies attractive and desirable, and causes some to believe gaining Jesus is not worthy of suffering any loss, sacrifice or possibilities where the world is concerned.

Prayer: Lord there is much against us in this world, but the Bible is clear if You are for us, we have nothing to worry about because we live in light of Your Word and promises. As a result, we are assured that we are on the winning side of heaven which will prove victory over the darkness of the age we live in. Amen.

July 15

One Scripture that states there is more than knowing about Jesus, we must also sense His presence, discern His works, and know what it means to truly interact with Him in Spirit and truth. *Acts 17:27* tells us, *"That they should seek the Lord, if peradventure they might feel after him and find him, though he is not far from every one of us."* In essence, we must experience Him.

It is amazing to think our physical eyesight is not trustworthy because we start out with a perception of how it will look when we see it. This brings us to the second reason our physical eyes serve as untrustworthy witnesses to a matter. What many people fail to realize is that we interpret what we are seeing before we can begin to understand what we are actually looking at.

If something is interpreted as being insignificant up front, we will not take note of it. It simply becomes a blur that is never really recorded. It is only when we are personally impacted that we begin to give something any real consideration. However, when something impacts us, we will also view it according to our bias or prejudices.

For example, we do not take note of what we are seeing at the moment we are being impacted; rather, we immediately interpret why something is making us feel the way we are feeling. It is from the premise of the type of impact it makes on us that we will interpret what we think we have witnessed.

Since people are impacted in different ways, they will present a different take on an event. It is for this reason that the Apostle Paul made the statement he did in *Acts 17:27.* Notice how he used the words *"feel after Him."*

Prayer: Lord, we need to see You, but we must first seek after You. We must feel our way through the roller coaster of the fickleness of emotions and properly discern Your presence and ways in the midst of uncertainty and confusion. Amen.

July 16

"And ye shall know the truth, and the truth shall make you free" *(John 8:32).* Most people believe they possess all the truth they need to know. However, unless we possess the Jesus of the Bible, we at best possess bits of truth and pieces of delusion, that end up being a lie.

Why do we refuse to see the truth? As I have pointed out, our physical sight does not necessarily make us reliable witnesses because much that we see is inspired by the unseen realm. Unless we are focusing on something, we really do not see what is happening around us. Most matters either remain unknown to us or they become a blur at best.

The reason for such a state is unless we see it, we tend to ignore it and even when we do, we can't discern what we are really seeing. For this reason, it is the impact that an occurrence makes on us emotionally that leaves its lasting impression.

This brings us to the third reason why our physical sight is not very trustworthy. We have a tendency to see only what we want to see. In short, we operate from a biased premise or select memory.

Our tendency is to justify our present understanding about a matter in order to avoid facing it so we can come to realistic terms with it. One of the emotional mechanisms that protects man from the initial devastating impact of trauma is shock, but the shock must give way to the reality of something before we can honestly address it.

It is true that truth can be very shocking to our fragile realities, but it is the only virtue that will set us free to face what is shocking. Truth is a two-edged sword. The initial situation when the sword penetrates our reality will shock us, but the second swipe will reveal the hope of Jesus, bringing sanity and comfort back into our lives.

Prayer: Lord, thanks for Your abiding hand upon each of our lives. You will never leave nor forsake us when it feels like we are drowning in a cesspool of hopelessness and despair. You are able to bring comfort to our lives by unveiling Your love and mercy to us. Amen.

July 17

Great-grandma used to say, "You don't miss the water 'til the well runs dry." How true that is! In our case, it's not so much that the community well runs dry, but the fact that proper equipment and diligent maintenance have been sorely neglected.

Needless to say, after struggling through nine years of either no water at all, or such low water pressure that household appliances can't function properly, along with all the hassles of daily living because of it, a person can begin to unravel.

As I thought about the "iffy" water pressure at our house, and the plight of a neighbor who has had mere "drips and drops," I was reminded of weak, dry, dead "Christians." There may be a "form of godliness" outwardly, but no evidence of the power, presence and Person of the Holy Spirit inwardly. *Jeremiah 2:13* says *"For my people have committed two evils; they have forsaken me the fountain of living waters, and hewed them out cisterns, broken cisterns, that can hold no water."*

Jesus declared to the woman at the well, *"But whosoever drinketh of the water that I shall give him shall never thirst; but the water that I shall give him shall be in him a well of water springing up into everlasting life" John 4:14*.

In *John 7:38* Jesus said, *"He that believeth on me, as the scripture hath said, out of his belly shall flow rivers of living water."* If we find ourselves spiritually thirsty and dry, the question is, when did we forsake the Lord who gives us living water because we really do prefer to do things our own way? – J. Haley

Prayer: Lord, there is only one source of lasting water and that is You. There are days I know You are there, days that I know I have need of You, days that I am thirsty for Your water that revives, and days I desperately need You. The truth is I need You at all times, but I must be made desperate to seek out Your water. Create a thirst in my soul that will not settle for anything less than my spirit overflowing with Your water. Amen.

July 18

Luke 16:10 states, *"He that is faithful in that which is least is faithful also in much: and he that is unjust in the least is unjust, also in much."*

As many know, I have written books and now self-publish them for various reasons. Some have been promoted in the past and in one incident the particular promoter of one of my books became frustrated with me because I would not respond to his sales pitch about one of the publisher's promotions in making my book "well-known". His attitude and mocking statement basically were, "Why write a book if you don't intend for it to be a best seller so you can make money off of it."

I understood his secular, worldly attitude, but I have to admit I didn't appreciate it, but it caused me to examine my motive for writing books. First of all, I realistically know my books are not for everyone because 1) they are Christian teachings meant to challenge the believer to come higher in their relationship with the Lord so He can be glorified, and 2) without a known name, people have a tendency to ignore independent writers even in the Christian realm, who are unable to break through the agendas, politics, and ceilings of the well-known publishing companies.

As I examined my motives, I realized I wrote books for two reasons: Number one reason is my books for the most part are based on Bible Studies I have taught. Those attending the study would ask me for notes, but all I operate from are outlines. My solution for them, as well as for me to preserve spiritual treasures and revelation, was to write books.

The second reason is based on an important lesson that I had learned during a time of great spiritual growth. The lesson is, "If you don't give away what you have received from the hand of God, He will not entrust you with more." Every time I was given spiritual insight, I knew it was not mine to bury, hold close to my heart, or lock away for some rainy day to bring out as a point of personal inspiration. I would look for the opportunity to share the spiritual treasure so, in turn, I could go back to His banquet table of fellowship to receive more from His Spirit. I realized books were the way I could give away what He had so graciously and abundantly imparted to me. As you can see, I do much for selfish reasons because I so covet His heavenly insights.

This lesson of wisely giving away what God has given is brought out constantly in Scripture. For example, the little boy giving his lunch away fed over five thousand people. However, our greatest example is that God gave His Son to provide the solution, and His Son gave His life to ensure greater fruit in light of blood-bought, saved souls.

Prayer: Lord, we gauge success according to the world's way of counting numbers and dollars, but You count such things as faithfulness, obedience out of love, and walking out the Christian life by faith. Thank You Lord because You provide the real riches we can afford to give away because they are from Your eternal storehouse. Amen.

July 19

How many times has someone used *Matthew 7:1, "Judge not, that ye be not judged,"* when you have been discerning that something is not right. We naturally will judge a matter based on our personal understanding and feelings which are fleshly and not spiritual. As a result, as a believer, I must be realistic about how I perceive matters in order to honestly face what is going on around me. I will not be able to live in ignorance, denial, or according to wishful thinking, for the harsh tide of reality is never far behind me.

I must remember that if I am not willing to face the failures of the past and the harsh realities of the present, that my former experiences dictate that I will eventually be blindsided in the future by the tidal wave that is about to crash against my present understanding. Granted, I must be aware of areas where I cannot see because of some limitation or obstruction.

Even though I know these areas exist, I often assume that I know what is going on in each arena. As a result, I end up making judgment calls based on assumptions rather than on the present reality. These judgments become "beams" of presumptions that will create a blind side in my understanding or perception when it comes to rightly judging or discerning the actual events that are resonating around me.

How we need God's perspective in all matters!

Prayer: Lord, I am weak in so many areas, but those are the areas where You can become strong. Lord, I need to be made weak and humble before You and others at all times to properly, righteously judge a matter according to Your Word and discern the spirit behind it. Amen.

July 20

Have you ever noticed how people want to feel good about themselves, but really feel bad about who they are? They so much want to change and yet there are trigger points that sets them off, unfair situations that leave them angry, reactions that make them feel defeated, and results that cause them to despair about their lives.

The Apostle Paul stated in *Romans 7:19, "For the good that I would I do not; but the evil which I would not, that I do."* Paul clearly understood that one may take some important steps forward in certain matters, but find themselves taking many more backwards because of the state of man.

Due to the inward state of man, Paul recognized there was nothing good that could come from the flesh, and understood the battle often raging within man. There is the war with pride, guilty conscience, the Spirit, and rigid standards. What seems so right turns out wrong. What seems wrong seems to come out on top, and what is mundane seems to win the focus of the day.

We often wonder why the inward struggle is so intense because Paul went to great lengths to describe it. The answer is simple: To overcome, one must be broken over their sin. This brokenness begins by recognizing that Jesus had to die in our place for the sin that besets us and holds us captive to condemnation, misery and despair.

Sin will often break us, but if it is because of consequences and its wages, and not in light of the great price Jesus paid on the cross for it. As a result, people can become hard of heart and bitter in their soul. Even Christians have a hard time finding victory over destructive cycles, and it is because they have not been broken at the point of pride that refuses to be wrong, and independence that hides behind rights that justify wrong attitudes and conduct.

Often, these individuals hide behind such things as religious cloaks and platitudes that speak of God's love, grace, and the good deeds they do to justify or water-down any iniquity. Ultimately, they end up hiding or running from the light of God's holiness that would reveal the secret sins that would leave them broken, repentant, seeking His mercy, and restoration.

When you study Scripture and understand that a defiled clay vessel, (which we all start out as) must first be broken in order to be cleansed by the water of the Spirit and the Word, and be reshaped by the great Potter as a means to put it in the fire to be established, you will not ask for such brokenness to occur in your life. Until you do, you will be broken by everything else but your sin.

Prayer: Lord, have your way, break me and make me pliable in Your hands, shape me to be used by You, and establish me in my faith so I will overcome and You will be glorified. Amen.

July 21

It's a fearful thing, at least it is to me, to be given anesthesia for any procedure, but back when I was around 19 or so, impacted wisdom teeth made it necessary for me to be "put out." I had heard that Sodium Pentothal caused people to talk in recovery, and the last thing I wanted to do was blab something unbecoming or discrediting to the Lord.

I remember when I finally "woke up" seeing my mother patiently sitting in the room with me. She had a rather serious look on her face. Then she told me that I had said, "Jesus is coming soon, and I want you to be there!" When I asked her how the attending nurse had reacted, she stated, "She ran out of the room and hasn't been back."

Isn't it wonderful how our great LORD and Savior works in and through our lives, even when we're not aware of it? Our part is to live by the Word of God, and obey *Proverbs 4:23* which says *"Keep thy heart with all diligence; for out of it are the issues of life."* Jesus said that out of the abundance of the heart, the mouth speaks (see *Luke 6:45*.)

The truth is, when we receive (not "accept") Jesus into our heart, then we receive a new heart (disposition and identity). "But as many as received him, to them gave he power to become the sons of God, even to them that believe on his name" *John 1:12*. *"For it is God which worketh in you both to will and to do of his good pleasure"* as stated by *Philippians 2:13*, and that means whether we're conscious or not. Praise the Lord! – J. Haley

Prayer: Lord, as believers You have given us a new heart towards You, a heart that desires to please You. In that heart is life and truth and we can trust that out of it will flow that which honors Your truth and glorifies You. Amen.

July 22

We are in a battle, but what many fail to realize is the enemy is subtle and therefore, he must be properly discerned. His subtlety will confuse or hide the real challenge. King David made mention of this, *"For lo, they lie in wait for my soul: the mighty are gathered against me; not for my transgression, nor for my sin O LORD"* *(Psalm 59:3).*

The light of God enables me to honestly face myself and the world I live in. The greatest aspect that I must face about myself is my spiritual condition in relationship to my Creator. I have realized that people have a tendency to live in the darkness of denial, delusion, and wishful thinking when it comes to their spiritual life. As a result, many have turned their backs on God and are walking in darkness towards spiritual ruin and chaos.

As God's people, we each must always strive to get our spiritual bearings according to God's truth if we are going to survive the darkness and evil that is enveloping the whole world. However, if we are hiding from, living in denial of, walking away from, running, or fleeing from the penetrating light of Christ, we will simply end up heading into the utter darkness of debauchery and straight into the mouths of predators who can be disguised as sheep. We will not only be consumed by darkness, but we will be devoured by the predators of our souls.

Prayer: Lord, You are my strength and my hope. The things of the world are insignificant compared to the matters of heaven. My enemies are powerless compared to Your abiding protection on my life. Help me keep my vision towards heaven pure and straight so I can discern the advancements of the enemies on all fronts. Amen.

July 23

The Apostle Paul left us a warning about the times we live in, *"And with all deceivableness of unrighteousness in them that perish; because they received not the love of the truth, that they might be saved"* (2 Thessalonians 2:10). We may be living in a time of grace, but we also live in the midst of great deception.

The great delusion that persists around us should be a reminder that we are indeed living in serious times which call for sober evaluation and honesty on our part as to our lives before God in light of Christ and according to the power of His Spirit. We must not just consider the truth; we must love it and embrace it as our only hope to spiritually survive the twisted, destructive propaganda of the present age we live in.

We are told that God is sending a delusion to test the hearts of people *(2 Thessalonians 2:11)*. This delusion will look like the real, religious thing, but it will be a counterfeit. Only those who love the truth will be able to discern the destructive spirit behind it.

Due to our fallen condition, we can have an aversion to God's truth. It is the only sharp instrument that will cut away every blinder, cloak, mask, and façade to give us a realistic perspective as to what is going on around us.

The question I must answer is, do I love the truth enough to allow it to serve as the gauge that will line me on the foundation and up to the cornerstone of Jesus Christ in order to get my spiritual bearings?

Prayer: Lord, the neglect of our spiritual lives and the Word can cause so much damage. Forgive me for my complacency towards spiritual matters. Stir me up to love You more, pursue You in truth and holiness, and to become more pliable in Your hands. Amen.

July 24

In an upside-down world, you will encounter nothing more than an upside-down value system that defies what is right and acceptable. I use *Isaiah 5:20-21* to confirm this upside-down reality is nothing new, *"Woe unto them who call evil, good, and good, evil; who put darkness for light, and light for darkness; who put bitter for sweet, and sweet for bitter. Woe unto them who are wise in their own eyes, and prudent in their own sight."* As you study this reality, you realize that a people, or nation, that comes to this point of morally being upside-down is doomed and close to collapsing in on itself.

The prophet Isaiah describes these individuals in *Isaiah 5:18-21.* He used the word "woe" to describe their ultimate fate. The word "woe" points to the anguish and grief these individuals will ultimately experience because of their wickedness. Consider the end of such people: the Lord's anger will be kindled against them and He will stretch forth His hand to smite them *(Isaiah 5:25).* It is from this perspective that we must decide what side we are going to be on.

The righteous side might cost us our place in the world, but the wrong side will cost us our souls. The Bible reminds us we must "count the cost." We cannot possess the world without selling our souls. We cannot properly possess our souls without letting go of the world. This is the reality of the decision that must and will be made by each of us as we come to this time in our lives and in the history we leave behind.

Prayer: Lord, renew my vision. I must see You if I am going to fulfill my calling and finish my course in this present age of darkness. Amen.

July 25

KER-PLOP! Awakened from a sound sleep, my parent's surprised, but hushed, voices failed to fully awaken me as I lay face down on the floor of the dark motel room. After all, I was just a little kid, and the long road trip on a two-lane highway from Seattle to the Bitterroot Valley, MT, was long and tiring.

"What was that noise?" My dad probably had his pistol out and ready to use, just in case, but my mother squelched any wild west ideas he may have had when she said, "It's just the kid. She fell out of bed, and her face is in her shoes."

About that time our black cocker spaniel found me and began licking my face. It seems awfully funny now, looking back on it, but at the time my parents were more than a little annoyed at the surprise interruption and loss of sleep. After getting me back into the unfamiliar bed, I was admonished to stay in the middle of the bed and not fall out of it again.

You know, we can't help what we may do when we're physically sound asleep, but if we have made a conscious decision to close our eyes to any of God's truth as revealed in His Word, our downfall is going to be a lot more serious than plopping face down into a pile of shoes next to the bed. *"Wherefore he saith, Awake thou that sleepest, and arise from the dead, and Christ shall give thee light" (Ephesians 5:14). "Therefore let us not sleep, as do others; but let us watch and be sober" (1 Thessalonians 5:6).* – J. Haley

Prayer: You are the light and we are children of the light. It is clear we must walk in it to expose any darkness in us, around us, and about us. We must not close our eyes to any darkness, but ever be ready to bring it to the light to address it. Lord, help me to boldly walk in the light of Your Word and Ways. Amen.

July 26

One of the Scriptures that always stands out to me when I read it is *Joel 3:14, "Multitudes, multitudes in the valley of decision; for the day of the LORD is near in the valley of decision."* Everything associated with God and His Word is to bring each of us to the valley of decision as to what we are going to do with Jesus, His truth, and His work of redemption.

People often stand between two opinions, waiting to see which side will serve them best *(1 Kings 18:21)*. They often perceive that the middle ground is the safest place there is, when in reality it is the most dangerous ground.

It is in this state that the Lord will spit a person out because he or she is spiritually lukewarm towards Him *(Revelation 3:14-19)*. Instead of displaying godly wisdom, such people are displaying worldly logic and foolishness. Such individuals have failed to recognize no decision is a decision.

The people of Elijah's day had an altar for God, but it was neglected and lay in ruin. Their attitude clearly revealed that they were choosing and preferring their idols to Jehovah God. They were prostituting themselves with these silent, powerless, and lifeless idols while giving some sick semblance of maintaining their identification with their Creator and Maker.

Elijah asked the people how long would they insist on their ridiculous front. They needed to choose. The main reason people avoid choosing is because they know they will have to pay some type of price. If they choose their God, they will have to pay the price of their association with the world, but if they choose the world, they will have to pay the price of their soul *(Matthew 16:26)*. The prophet Joel best described this place as the valley of decision.

What do my decisions say about my life in Christ?

Prayer: Lord, every soul will prove to be a test to my virtue, and every soul will be tested with the truth. You are always bringing us to the valley of decision to decide what we are going to do with You and Your Word. We will either believe or we will go the way of unbelief. I choose to believe Your Word of truth. Amen.

July 27

In the last meditation I mentioned how Joel spoke of the valley of decision. He declared that multitudes are in this valley for the day of the Lord is near. We are constantly being reminded as to the choices we have when it comes to this world in such Scriptures as *Matthew 13:38-39, "The field is the world; the good seed are the children of the kingdom; but the tares are the children of the wicked one; The enemy that sowed them is the devil; the harvest is the end of the world; and the reapers are the angels".*

We know the day of the Lord points to the judgment that will take place at the end of this age. It will be a time when the sickle will be put to the harvest, and the tares will be separated from the wheat.

I am once again reminded that a distinction will be made between light and darkness. Light points to those who walk in the ways of righteousness, but darkness is in reference to those who insist on the ways of wickedness. These individuals will arrogantly perceive that their darkness is the true light and that those who refuse to go along with their wave of destruction are insipid fools who are dispensable.

As a believer, I must remember that I belong to the Lord's everlasting kingdom. One day the harvest will be reaped, and I will be reaped unto everlasting life.

Prayer: Lord, I have found myself in the valley of decision. Am I going to believe and obey You, or am I going to go in the way of the world, and rebellion. Lord, I desire to choose Your way. Put short reins on me and keep me on Your narrow path. Amen.

July 28

Matthew tells us the sorrow of the end times will include, *"For nation shall rise against nation, and kingdom against kingdom: and there shall be famines, and pestilences, and earthquakes, in divers places" (Mathew 24:7).* When wickedness reigns, famine will ravage the land.

The reason for this is because wickedness has no moral fiber in which to develop genuine compassion or care for others. Granted, there are wicked people who do good, but it is to make themselves feel good about their own wretchedness and to throw any real suspicion off of their wicked activities of destruction. Such people are the ones who often cause grinding poverty by their base ways so that they can become the saviors who address the ills of society with their humanistic, godless philosophies and practices.

The gospel these deluded, doomed souls promote is a social gospel. They believe it is through social services that people's lives can be made better. However, the souls of needy people are thrown under the bus, while these wicked individuals play tunes of praise about their contribution to the throes of humanity.

In the end the deeds of these people will result in complete spiritual bankruptcy and ruin. Everything they touch will fall into chaos and disrepair.

As a believer, I must not succumb to the environment of famine caused by wickedness or spiritual indifference. I must keep sharp by the Word of God and remember that I do not live by bread alone, but by every word that proceeds out of the mouth of God.

Prayer: Lord, I see famine growing, and many are dying of hunger including spiritual famine. This could have been avoided if righteousness reigned, but man prefers the dark ways of wickedness so he can live in a state of independence from You, and in rebellion to Your ways that makes us wretched and poor before You. Forgive us for our insipid, foolish ways. Amen.

July 29

I can't tell you how many times I have pondered *Amos 8:11-12*, *"Behold, the days come, saith the Lord GOD, that I will send a famine in the land, not a famine of bread, nor a thirst for water, but of hearing the words of the LORD: And they shall wander from sea to sea, and from the north even to the east, they shall run to and fro to seek the word of the LORD, and shall not find it"*

When the wicked reign, the greatest famine that will occur has to do with the Word of God. In such an environment if the Word has not already been outlawed by those in power, it will have been made common by the attitude of complacency among God's people. If it has not been watered-down by the religious, it will have been deemed obsolete by the intellectual skeptics who teach in our Bible colleges and stand behind the pulpit with various degrees attached to their chest. If it has not been classified by the unbelieving to be made up as fables, it has been stripped of its authority by those who operate from the insipid pinnacle of higher criticism.

Sadly, we live in a nation that is beginning to show the effects of such a famine. It is hard to find people who actually tremble before His Word, and where it is being preached and taught in its unadulterated form to ensure anointing and power.

Thank the Lord, He has been gracious enough to teach me how to feed myself, but there are so many precious sheep running to and fro to find clean waters, healthy pastures, and committed shepherds.

Prayer: Lord, have mercy on Your poor sheep. They desire what is pure but are plagued with hireling shepherds and wolves who do not care for their souls. Revive them with the pure water of Your Spirit and feed them with Your life-sustaining Word. Amen.

July 30

I have been talking about famine but I am not concerned because of what *Psalm 37:18-19* states, *"The LORD knoweth the days of the upright: and their inheritance shall be forever. They shall not be ashamed in the evil time: and in the days of famine they shall be satisfied."*

I love the promises of the Bible. They tell you the conditions that need to be present in our lives to benefit from God's eternal blessings.

There is much famine in the world that is not only of a physical nature, but, as already pointed out, is a spiritual famine. Due to idolatry, wickedness, and abominations, the world is plagued by famine. In fact, there is a prediction of world-wide famine thanks to the wicked ways of governments, kingdoms, and leaders.

The promise for the upright is that the inheritance they receive will be everlasting, and that in the days of famine they will know the satisfaction of what it means to possess the fullness of God's abiding presence in and upon their lives. After all, God is our great provider, regardless of how lean the times are that we live in.

God is not only our provider, but He is our all in all. The life He gives is not only eternal, but it is abundant in its virtues and overflowing in its ways.

Prayer: Lord, thank You for giving me a love for Your Word. I know that the source of that love comes from You. I love Your Word because I love You. Amen.

July 31

In the times of famine, we can only cry out to our great Provider like David did in *Psalm 33:19* on behalf of His people, *"To deliver their soul from death, and to keep them alive in famine."* God indeed is the only One who can deliver my soul and keep me alive in the midst of famine. However, I have learned through the years that there are different types of famine.

There is a personal famine where nothing in life is satisfying. As a result, there is a tormenting vacuum that leaves one feeling empty in every activity. What is lacking in this case is righteous character.

There is physical famine. This is where the body is being deprived of food. However, you can be surrounded by food and still be suffering the effects of famine. What is lacking in this situation is good nutrition.

There is of course the spiritual famine. It is a famine created by deception. Truth has practically become extinct, while people are being conditioned by useless, nonsensical watered-down versions of the gospel. Such gospels are worldly in emphasis, man-centered, hinge on good deeds, and promote nothing more than a humanistic philosophy. What is missing in this environment is the true Jesus.

Only God can work character in us and He is the One who must provide the necessary "nutrition" for us to stay alive through His Word. He is the only one who can unveil the real light of the Gospel, Jesus Christ to our barren souls and thirsty spirits. He is the only one who can save us when famine rages around us.

Prayer: Lord, we have great notions about our abilities to preserve our lives, but famine represents how inept we are to save ourselves. Have mercy on us, and save us from whatever famine is ravaging in our midst. Amen.

August

August 1

Have you ever noticed how the social gospel is trying to alleviate the poor from this world when Jesus made it clear in *John 12:8*, *"For the poor always ye have with you; but me ye have not always."* Poverty comes in different forms. What the world wants to alleviate when it comes to the poor is the poor themselves. They serve as a type of conscience and contrast. The truth is the poor are a test to those who have, as well as bringing a contrast to the rich. The greatest contrast they bring is how poor of character, faith, and valueless the rich often are.

Poverty is really brought out at a time of "giving" in crises and during certain holidays. It is clearly found in people's way of thinking, doing, and being. This is why everyone is looking for a good deal when they go shopping.

Although America is considered one of the richest countries in the world, it is in all essence once of the poorest. In many ways we have squandered what made us rich. We have squandered our rich heritage established by those who knew that what was important was the freedom to worship God according to conscience. We have devalued personal relationships by valuing things that ultimately lose all value. We end up pursuing after things that have no value and will leave us empty.

True poverty leaves one empty, while being rich in the matters of heaven leaves one satisfied in whatever lot they are in. As Christians we should know that godliness with contentment is great gain (*1 Timothy 6:6*).

Prayer: Lord, man is born into slavery and is often rendered into a cringing beggar when it comes to the eternal, and is brought to utter spiritual bankruptcy because he remains outside of the life and treasures of heaven. Lord, You are our prize, the crown of righteousness our reward, and heaven our glorious finish line. Like Paul, I reach forward to obtain You, knowing by Your Spirit, grace, and truth I can possess You. Amen.

August 2

Last night I had a two-part dream that left me pondering because, for the most part I do not remember dreams and when I do, I ask the Lord if He is trying to reveal something to me. I have been wrestling with some of my past. It is not that I want to look back or am all that tempted to look back, but your past can have certain claims and attachments on you. These attachments can have unknown affects on you. I wanted to make sure there were no such claims hanging onto me.

In the first part of my dream, I encountered someone from my past. I expected the individual to have some reaction in seeing me, but they didn't even seem to recognize me. I was a bit surprised, but then I remembered that the life and work of God is to make His saints into new creations where the old passes away and everything becomes new (2 Corinthians 5:17). It dawned on me that my old life would not recognize me due to the new creation the Lord has been shaping my life into.

I had to marvel at the concept of it, but then I had to ask a simple question, "How much of my old life would recognize me because I have not let God have His way in me?" We are not to look back in longing for our past because our past often proves to be an enemy of preparing for the present to be ready for the future, but sometimes God prepares a table in the presence of our past to show us how far He has brought us.

If you came face to face with your past, would it recognize you? I am not talking about facial recognition, but recognition brought about by inward change of heart, mind, and character. Granted, grave transgression will make one unrecognizable, but as a Christian, if you have truly been transformed in your mind by the Spirit and inwardly conformed to the image of Jesus, the old will not only fail to recognize you, but it will have no real claims on you.

Prayer: Lord the past at different times will try to reclaim us but it has no claims for we are Your adopted children and part of your eternal legacy. Thank You for working the new life in me, knowing that it will make me into a new creation. Amen.

August 3

As mentioned yesterday, I had a two-part dream. The other one took place in a religious environment where the old ways were represented by older people and the new by a zealous pastor. In the dream I was aware that I had shared some of my testimony with the older women and they encouraged me to share more, but I was aware that the pastor had his own program planned.

I realized I needed to leave as I suspected that the pastor would probably take a bit of time so I went out to the parking lot to discover that every vehicle was covered in pure white paint and I had no way of recognizing mine. To my surprise the service ended quickly and people started coming out to the parking lot. I figured I would wait until the parking lot cleared out to identify my vehicle. Finally, one of the ladies asked why I was there and I told her I could not properly recognize my car. She asked me if I had the key to the car and I said yes. I took it out of my purse and immediately the white paint came off of my vehicle. Instead of being a perfect car, it turned out to have all kinds of marks and dents in it. I thought to myself, "Now that is my car."

You might wonder what this dream was all about. Today people are trying to bring sense to the problems confronting the church by using old methods in the midst of new ones that often prove worldly, and as the Bible points out in *Matthew 9:16-17*, the two will not mix and will cause conflict and separation.

The white cars represented an old trick of the religious trade, whitewashing the ineffective mixture in order to cover what really ails the church (*Matthew 23:27-29*). The key that will enable us to move forward by unveiling what really lies beneath all attempts of whitewashing is the truth.

The Lord instructed me to "Preach the unadulterated truth." Jesus is coming back for a church without spot, blemish, or wrinkle. We can use the old to try to regain what we once had, or get caught up with the new that has mixed worldly methods in with bits of truths to attract the world to gain numbers. However, God sees beneath all attempts that what ails the church is not a lack of methods, but that there are spots, blemishes and wrinkles that are not being exposed by truth that confronts the present, addressed with repentance, and confessed to God.

I don't know about you, but if Paul states Jesus is coming back for a church without spot, wrinkle, or blemish, then He will bring the church to that state with the sanctifying work of His Spirit and the sharp edge of His truth. However, I must recognize truth is the only key that will set me free from the stifling old ways of religion and the unholy mixture of the new.

Prayer: Lord we can create our own religious reality about what is acceptable and godly to You, but as long as it hides any "dents" because of the blemishes of compromise, marks left due to sin, and spots where the tarnish of righteousness has long faded, I am not really ready to stand before You. Take Your truth and use it to have Your way Lord. Amen.

August 4

How many times have you heard *Luke 21:28, "And when these things begin to come to pass, then look up, and lift up your heads; for your redemption draweth nigh."* What will I see and what will I not see when it comes to the end days? It is clear that when I see that which is prophetic, I am to discern it, spiritually prepare for it by seeking the Lord, standing on what is true, and trust what has been promised.

However, I must admit that at times I'm amazed to see prophecy being fulfilled. It's not that I do not believe the Bible is true, it's that such events send shock waves into my reality. In essence, I find myself coming in and out of a state of shock. Even though I know the ending, I also know that there will be much carnage left behind. Everything will begin to die in this destructive environment that is being conceived by wickedness, and I hope I will be spared from seeing any of it, but I must admit death is prevalent right now.

Is this present age winding down to a climatic event? The Bible speaks of such an event. It is known as the Battle of Armageddon. As we watch everything escalate on the national and international fronts, it would not take much to see that something is looming in the future that will not fare well for those who live during this time.

For Christians, we know that if our lives are not hidden in Christ, there will be no place of protection, safety, or deliverance from what is coming upon the face of the world. Our hope is not in this present age, but in the next one that will be ushered in after a time of great tribulation. These days call for us to look up, knowing that our redemption is at hand.

The question is, am I ready to face the Lord?

Prayer: Lord, You are my place of rest. I can rest and occupy while waiting for You to move. I must trust that You will open the gate at the right time and send forth Your invitation to come to You to be ushered into the place You have prepared for me. Amen.

August 5

What should have been a cute and innocent cartoon movie for children ended up traumatizing scores of young hearts, including mine. And if it wasn't bad enough that Bambi lost his beautiful mother, the famous saying of that endearing rabbit, Thumper, was repeated so often throughout my growing up years by my parents that, (even though I loved Thumper) I sorely wished he had never, ever said, "If you can't say something nice, don't say anything at all."

I do believe in order to comply with that monumental order I simply would've had to pretty much give up talking, period. Fast-forward seven decades, and I wish I could announce to a weary world that my wayward tongue is totally under control, that now there can be world peace (well, at least in my world) and that I've achieved what no man can achieve—taming the tongue! (See *James 3:8*.)

What a headache this human trait must be to the satanic powers that want to strip all freedoms from the people, including our God-given right to "freedom of speech." But that is a whole other matter. As for those of us who are disciples of Christ, there is always hope for victory in Him as we embrace and rely on these beautiful words of wisdom from our God such as: *Proverbs 21:23, "Whoso keepeth his mouth and his tongue keepeth his soul from troubles." Proverbs 17:28 "Even a fool, when he holdeth his peace, is counted wise: and he that shutteth his lips is esteemed a man of understanding." Proverbs 25:11, "A word fitly spoken is like apples of gold in pictures of silver."*

Thus, when we ask for wisdom, let us also pray as King David, *"Set a watch, O LORD, before my mouth; keep the door of my lips" (Psalm 141:3)*. And by the power of the Holy Spirit, He will do it. – J. Haley

Prayer: Lord, You know all about my struggles with my mouth. Things come through my lips out of frustration that proves at times I am void of a proper attitude. The key is do my words come from my heart for that will prove the caliber of my Christian walk. Please do keep a guard on my heart in order to control the door of my lips. Amen.

August 6

You might have heard the term the "Day of the Lord." As you study this term in the Bible, it points to a time of judgment and wrath. We are somewhat given insight into time when it comes to God's economy.

Remember we are subject to time, but in eternity there is no such time. That is why *2 Peter 3:8* gives us this insight, *"But, beloved, be not ignorant of this one thing, that one day is with the Lord as a thousand years, and a thousand years as one day,"* For us a day is a 24-hour period, but in God's terminology, it can represent a thousand years, a season, a space of time, or an allotted time in which an event will be carried out to its fruition.

When we consider how long a day is to the Lord, I do not believe the "Day of the Lord" represents a thousand years, but I do perceive that it will be a season of judgment, a time of grave shaking, a space of time in which God will express His wrath against those who walk in total rebellion and arrogance against His authority and choose to reject the message of His Gospel. It will be an allotted time in which He will set up the environment to bring about His future thousand-year reign. Meanwhile, what do we need to understand about this occasion?

We need to discern the time we are living in and prepare for the darkness that will ensue. As believers we will not be subject to God's wrath, but we have been warned of tribulation and must be sober, watchful, ready, and praying as the Bible instructs. We do not want to be caught off guard like the five foolish virgins who assumed since they had the lamp for the light (Christ) that they were okay, but they had not taken the time to obtain the oil (Holy Spirit).

We must take courage and comfort to know that whatever tribulation comes our way, it will be for a season, a particular time in which God will dictate, rather than wicked men and governments.

Prayer: Lord, You are my refuge in the time of trouble. You will defend that which is of You. The wrong of a matter will be exposed as being so, and enemies will be silenced in their false accusations towards Your servants as You begin to judge the secret thoughts of the hearts, as well as the actions of mankind. Amen.

August 7

Jesus had many confrontations with the religious people of His day. We find one such confrontation in *Matthew 16:2-3, "He answered and said unto them. When it is evening, ye say, it will be fair weather: for the sky is red: And in the morning, It will be foul weather to day: for the sky is red and lowering. O ye hypocrites, ye can discern the face of the sky; but can ye not discern the signs of the times."*

These religious leaders wanted a sign from above to consider whether Jesus was the Promised Messiah. Notice, I said "consider" because they had no intention of believing or accepting who He was. After all, they had the prophecies to confirm His identity, but still would not believe them and asked for some sign from above.

It is so easy to become frightened by the events that seem to be continually unfolding before our eyes. We can ignore them, wish them away, or assume everything will turn out alright. However, as the darkness becomes more foreboding, it will be hard to ignore the inevitable.

The Bible has told us what will happen at the end of this age. Since the Bible has declared it as so, it will be so. As a result, we must walk in faith towards it regardless of how despairing it may prove to be to our own reality.

The Bible is clear that we must be prepared, ready, and aware of the days we are living in. After all, we prepare according to seasons that are upon us. Clearly, if we are going to survive the spiritual season that is now upon us, we must recognize what period of time it is and begin to prayerfully, soberly, and wisely prepare spiritually for it. Otherwise, it will come upon us as a thief in the night that will possibly rob us of our resolve to stand, kill any faith in us, and destroy any future hope of glory that might be awaiting us, for we are told that those who endure to the end shall be saved (*Matthew 24:13*).

The question is, am I spiritually discerning the times and preparing myself to stand by faith in them?

Prayer: Lord, I thank You that You have always instructed us to be ready to meet You. I feel I fail at times, but I can stand in confidence that when I am found to be faithless, You remain faithful and longsuffering towards me. Amen.

August 8

Meditate on Jesus' words, *"Greater love hath no man than this, that a man lay down his life for his friends." (John 15:13).* Jesus came to be a friend and He showed that friendship by giving His life on our behalf.

We would like to all think we have the means to be that type of friend especially to Jesus, but the courage to stand for what is right reveals that we often lack the necessary substance to be part of such a friendship. When challenged and exposed, we discover that there are elements in our fallen disposition that will cut across all common sense and inward strength that reveals the real truth about human nature.

The truth of the matter is, man is fickle and unpredictable unless he has learned to value that which has substance and is more worthy and greater than his present life. The problem with man is he has become the center focus of his world rather than possessing that which possesses worth and character. Without substance, man has no means to recognize that which is worthy and greater. Without such contrast he will see no need to sacrifice the inferior or nominal ways of life to secure that which will prove of greater worth, not only where he is concerned, but for the sake of others.

Jesus gave us insight as to the what type of muscle is needed to possess godliness in *John 15:13.* Godly love is what serves as the point of strength that will allow us to value that which is more worthy and honorable than our own life. Clearly, to survive the darkness of this time we must possess the type of love that chooses to value what is excellent and will be willing to sacrifice all to possess it for ourselves.

Prayer: Lord, we have great notions about ourselves, but unless such notions are brought down before You, we will never develop the love to see that You alone are worthy of all consideration and sacrifice. Forgive me for my idolatrous notions. I need to see You. Amen.

August 9

Psalm 19:14 states, *"Let the words of my mouth, and the meditation of my heart, be acceptable in thy sight, O LORD, my strength, and my redeemer."* It is vital that I meditate on the things of God, but I must make sure such meditations are acceptable to the Lord. Before I can do this I first must still my spirit and calm my soul. I must then meditate on the truths and ways of God. Clearly, I must grasp the real intent and purpose of God's truth in my heart before they become a reality to me.

Jesus stated that whatever is in your heart, will eventually make itself known by what you speak. It is clear that for my words to possess and proclaim life I must ensure life is deeply rooted in my heart. I must assimilate the life from above in all I do. However, to properly assimilate His truths, I must consider, regard, or meditate on what such truths will mean for my life. These truths must not just be a matter of intellectual understanding, but they must become part of my very person. In essence, they must become part of the landscape of who I am.

Prayer: Lord, You gave the gift of life to me. Forgive me for the times I have abused it or taken it for granted because of the influence of sin and selfishness upon my soul. Enable me to embrace and assimilate the fullness of the life You have ordained for me. Amen.

August 10

"It's just a quarter of an inch here on the map" I said to my husband who was driving our motorhome. This was back in the 1980's while traveling in New Mexico to Taos to visit an art gallery where some of my paintings were exhibited. "I don't think this road is going anywhere," he grumbled, to which I emphatically replied, "Well, it's right here on the map!"

True, the road was becoming narrower and rougher, but it seemed to be a notable shortcut on the map. I love studying maps, and even dictionaries can make for interesting reading too. At least my grandma thought so.

Anyway, imagine my surprise when all of a sudden, the narrow dirt road ended and we found ourselves in a huge field. No signs, no fences, no anything! Not even a cow. At least there was ample space in which to turn around and backtrack.

I suppose I could've tried to justify myself by blaming the mapmakers, but the truth is, I was just plain wrong. Not intentionally, of course, but there was no one else to blame.

There's another "map" that people can read and completely misinterpret and it's called the Holy Bible, the Word of God. Many "read this map wrongly" and think that the destination is heaven, and the road is broad and easy as long as you have some sort of a mental idea that God loves you. The truth is, the real destination is reconciliation with God, through His Son the LORD Jesus Christ who is "the way, the truth and the life."

Jesus said this about the way we are to go in *Matthew 7:13, 14, "Enter ye in at the strait gate; for wide is the gate, and broad is the way, that leadeth to destruction, and many there be which go in thereat. Because strait is the gate, and narrow is the way, which leadeth unto life, and few there be that find it."* Jesus is the only way to the Father, and if we miss that fact, we'll end up far worse and more than lost in the middle of nowhere! – J. Haley

248

Prayer: Lord, due to our pride we hate being wrong and Your Word will not change the reality that man begins wrong and will end wrong if he fails to realize how wrong he is before You. Give me the humility to admit when I am wrong, and the wisdom to seek You in forgiveness until it is made right. Amen.

August 11

"His glory is great in thy salvation: honour and majesty hast thou laid upon him" (Psalm 21:5). I just love finding little nuggets in Scripture such as I found in *Psalm 21:5.* I had to ask up front, "Whose glory is great?" "Glory" has to do with what distinguishes something from that which surrounds it. We know God is great.

In fact, if He is presented in the right light, He clearly stands distinct from all of His creation. There is nothing in heaven, on earth, or in the bowels of hell that could hold a candle to His glory.

Sadly, man is forever demeaning God in his mind. He is either trying to humble God to his way of thinking and doing, or he is trying to exalt himself by humanizing God as a means to control his understanding about Him. However, God in His sovereignty makes Him incomprehensible to the carnal mind and would cause a man to lose his mind altogether if he could rationalize out God.

When it comes to God's full glory, flesh would be consumed by His holiness, and in His power man could never stand long enough to even face Him, and for man to try to demean God or deify himself to make God understandable, or man equal to Him in some way, reveals the sorry state of lost, independent man.

Twenty centuries ago, God took on the form of man. Glory from above came to rest on Him, majesty manifested itself through His miracles and deeds, and honor was expressed when He received due worship. That man was Christ, the Son of the Living God. To know Jesus as the God-Man takes revelation from above that is imparted by the Holy Spirit. Yes, we approach the Bible to believe that what it says is true, but it takes the Holy Spirit to reveal the identity of Jesus to our spirit, where it is not just a matter of choosing to believe it because the Bible states it, but knowing it is so in the spirit because it has been unveiled to us by heaven itself.

Prayer: Lord, thank You for putting nuggets about You in Your Written Word. Give me the heart to seek out such treasures and the eyes to see their incredible value. Amen.

August 12

"But thou art holy, O thou that inhabitest the praises of Israel" *(Psalm 22:3)*. I have to admit one of my favorite Scriptures is *Psalm 22:3*. This Scripture is comprised of very few words, but it speaks volumes. First of all, it gives us insight into the One we are to praise—He is holy.

What does "holy" mean? It seems in certain camps the concept of holiness is non-existence. How do I know this: because there is no fear of the Lord. In other camps it means "pious living" and "stoic countenances", but yet there is no life or joy present to imply salvation has taken root in these people's souls. There are other camps that speak of holiness, but hide inconsistencies behind robes and masks of hypocrisy.

God is holy and He alone is the standard of it. He is pure with no deviation in His character, transparent with no darkness present in all He does, and a consuming fire to all that is contrary to it. It is in light of who He is that acceptable praise will come forth.

Praise points to life, joy, and delight that was and is inspired by the Holy Spirit, and is being directed back to God in utter recognition and adoration that He alone is God and stands distinct in all of creation. It is in such praise that He is able to inhabit the environment with His presence, ensuring blessed worship and sweet communion.

Prayer: Lord, praise lifts my mind above the present world, while worship opens my heart and brings my spirit into that secret place of communion with You. Lord, You deserve to be praised and You are worthy of all worship. Lord, I humble myself before You in sweet adoration and worship. Amen.

August 13

It is natural to live according to assumptions about spiritual truths, without ever really experiencing the blessings that are attached to them. What does it mean to trust God for deliverance?

Salvation points to deliverance. We need to be delivered from ourselves, the influence of the world, and the oppression of Satan that comes through his lies and world systems. The questions are, do we see our need to be delivered and do we want to be delivered?

King David made this declaration, *"He trusted on the LORD that he would deliver him: let him deliver him, seeing he delighted in him" (Psalm 22:8).* As believers, we know God is the source of all deliverance, bringing liberty to our souls. He saved us by sending His only begotten Son to take our place on the gallows of the cross. We are being saved today by the presence of His Spirit, and He will save us in the future because of the life and resurrection power that is present in us through the born-again experience.

It is God's heart to save those who are lost. He wants people to be reconciled back to Him in a viable, growing relationship. He wants to have that joy present that brings delight to Him because we seek Him for such deliverance as we develop an intimate relationship with Him that is sustained by child-like faith, loving adoration, and sweet worship.

I know for myself that at times when life is overwhelming and hard, that it is hard to think of a Holy God in terms of experiencing joy and delight. However, if the right relationship is present, there is that place where joy serves as an anchor and delight pulsates through sweet fellowship with our Lord, while His holiness serves as our abiding umbrella of protection and peace.

Prayer: God, You are holy, but such an attribute is a sweet blessing. It is out of holiness that excellence continues to manifest itself in the person, work, example, and message of Your Son. Thank You for making my joy complete and Your heavenly delight a reality in my life. Amen.

August 14

"The voice of the LORD is powerful: the voice of the LORD is full of majesty" (Psalm 29:4). It was interesting to read *Psalm 29.* This psalm is all about the voice of the Lord. I know that with His very words He framed all we see in creation. Therefore, it is clear that His voice is powerful, and that what is declared by Him will be brought forth to completion. Clearly, His voice has distinction that should inspire trust, result in obedience, and bring trepidation to my soul if I choose to ignore or disobey it.

I know that the Bible is the recorded voice of God, His Spirit is His still small voice, His Son His living, visible voice, and creation His active voice. The truth of the matter is He is speaking all around us, but how many of us really hear Him? How much do we hear when He does speak through these avenues?

What does it mean to hear the LORD? We do not hear the voice of the Lord with our physical ears, but with the unseen ears of the heart. We may not see the power of His words, but we can sense it. We may not understand them, but they can become the very bread and meat to nourish us with His eternal life.

Prayer: Lord, I want to hear Your voice. It is the only voice that makes sense in this mad world. Thank You for the many ways You speak. Help my soul to grasp Your words, my spirit hears what Your Spirit is saying, my eyes to see the declarations of Your creation, and my heart to discern Your voice. Amen.

August 15

Hot summer days make me wish I was a kid again because way back then summer was fun. Some of you may remember chanting, "No more pencils, no more books; no more teacher's dirty looks." Summer meant games, and play acting "cowboys and Indians" or "good guys and bad guys" scenarios, followed by slices of sweet, cold, juicy watermelon. There was Kool-Aid, popsicles, and sometimes cookies that someone's mom would make, but my mother's were always the best of course.

A favorite activity (when the heat was unbearable to the old folks over thirty) was "running through the hose," as we called it. Mom would set the sprinkler so it was "just right" and then we'd run through it to stay cool. I'm so thankful for all the treasured memories of childhood I have, but the most meaningful ones are priceless in light of eternity, such as, Sunday School and a dedicated, born-again Sunday school teacher who emphasized memorization of Bible verses and hymns.

I'm so thankful that Satan didn't steal my childhood away from me like he's done with so many children of the world today. Truly, who, or what we are today is based in large part upon the decisions we made in the days of our childhood. Therefore, pray for the little ones, and seek for ways to bring them to Jesus! "*But Jesus said, Suffer little children, and forbid them not, to come unto me: for of such is the kingdom of heaven*" (Matthew 19:14). J. Haley

Prayer: Lord, we can remember the good times of our childhood, but how many children don't have such memories. Satan has managed to rob their innocence, kill hope and destroy their lives. Lord, all I can ask in tears is for You to help the children of this terrible world. Amen.

August 16

"O LORD my God, I cried unto thee, and thou hast healed me (Psalm 30:2). In this Psalm, I notice an array of emotions and declarations coming forth. There is so much in this world that affronts my soul. It is clear that challenges can throw me into grave struggles.

I must wrestle with each challenge, confront each hindrance, endure each test, seek the right passageway around each obstacle, climb up the trail of each mountain, and finish the course that is before me. However, in the process of the struggle, my soul can become marred and weary, my spirit can experience a wounding that comes from a hopeless blanket of despair, my heart can be broken by failure, and my body riddled with weakness and uncertainty as my strength ebbs from me.

At this point, I must choose to remember my solution. The Lord is the only One who can heal me. He will become my helper and enable me to endure the night that has come upon my soul. He will turn my mourning into dancing, causing me to replace my sackcloth of repentance and humility with gladness. Therefore, I must remember to look up, knowing the Lord is my great Physician.

Prayer: Lord, You are the only solution in this world. There is no way we can walk through this world without being wounded, but You came to heal us from all that besets and affronts us. Thank You for being the mighty God who knows all and is able to accomplish Your purpose regardless of the hindrances of the age. Amen.

August 17

"O LORD, thou hast brought up my soul from the grave: thou hast kept me alive, that I should not go down to the pit" (Psalm 30:3). Each age of the world carries a big shovel with it. In other words, the world has the ability to bury each of us with it various demands, trap us with its numerous temptations, confuse or delude us with its humanistic philosophies, and cause us to succumb to its deadly ways and lies.

This beautiful psalm reminds me that the grave has no claim on my soul. It is the Lord who keeps my spirit alive with the presence and power of His Spirit. He has equipped me with resurrection power. Even though my physical body will eventually be reduced to dust, I will be raised up in newness of life by His power. Therefore, I need not worry about the pit, whether it is emotional, spiritual, or physical.

My Lord knows how to heal, deliver, and resurrect me to experience His everlasting life, indescribable beauty, and unspeakable glory.

Prayer: Lord, I so thank You for the promise of life. You are the essence of life and resurrection. You not only give life, but You can raise it out of a grave of darkness, hopelessness, and death. Amen.

August 18

Who will deliver me from myself, from the world's destructive ways, the hatred of my enemies, and the wounds of my so-called "friends?" Who will bind up my wounds, heal the painful sores of rejection, the deep cuts of betrayal, and the despairing failures of life? *Psalm 31:7* answers that question, *"In thee, O LORD, do I put my trust: let me never be ashamed: deliver me in thy righteousness" (Psalm 31:7).*

I know the Lord is my great physician, but before He can heal me, I must first put my trust in Him. Faith clearly allows the healing virtues of God to flow into every place of hurtful penetration. When I trust God to put all matters right in light of His eternal work and plan, I ultimately will let Him be God.

It is faith directed towards the Lord that will assure me that I will never be left with a sense of disappointment or shame. It is faith that allows God to reckon me as being in right standing in Him and right standing before Him. This is what it means to be delivered according to His glorious righteousness.

Prayer: Lord, thank You for being my great Physician. You have never failed me in any area of my life. I know in the end Your healing will be complete and everlasting. Amen.

August 19

Psalm 15:5c gives us this promise, *"He that doeth these things shall never be moved."* What will it mean for me to never be moved? As Christians we are told to examine ourselves. How can we honestly discern our own spiritual condition? We must truly consider the fruits of our lives. We must have the integrity to ask ourselves the right questions and honestly answer them.

Psalm 15:1b asks a very important question, *"Who shall dwell in thy holy hill?"* From that point on, the verses that follow answer the question. It would benefit me greatly if I would consider the criteria that would ensure my right standing before the Lord.

As I consider the criteria, it deals with personal conduct, the light that serves as our conscience, the use of our tongue, the attitude we have towards others and the Lord, and keeping our vows.

Personally, I want to be assured that I will forever abide in that place with God. Such abiding will cause me to stand in confidence that I will never be moved from the Rock of the Lord, regardless of the challenges and temptations.

Prayer: Lord, I do not want to simply dwell with You for eternity in order to avoid hell. I want to learn what it means to abide with You here before I enter eternity. I want to be conditioned in Your ways, develop Your attitude, and walk according to Your righteousness. Amen.

August 20

From the posts you've read and the paintings you've seen so far on my Facebook page, you probably have a pretty good idea of where my heart is when it comes to a "satisfied, or fulfilled soul" in this short life, for out of the heart, not only does the mouth speak, but what we produce or gravitate to in the three important "God-given" avenues of creativity—art, music and literature—also reveals much about us.

It not only reveals much about us as individuals, but it is also an indicator of the state of the nation we live in. It goes without saying that, as a nation, we have let the lofty, majestic and gloriously inspired music and worshipful hymns fade out of our churches and culture, as well as ignored and stifled appreciation for the masterful and great works of art of the past, and, in addition, have miserably failed to guard the tasteful use of influential language in meaningful literature.

As a nation we have let things slip and slide as the enemy has taken control of just about anything you can think of. But, as long as we have breath and "our being" in this world, we still have a choice as to whom we will worship and serve. God help us to *"endure to the end" (Matthew 24:13).* – J. Haley

Prayer: Lord, keep me from neglecting, squandering, and casting aside the gifts, blessings, and promises You have given me. You are faithful to me and I need Your grace and power to be faithful to You. Amen.

August 21

One of the frightening realities for me is that the Christianity being presented today is not the Christianity of the Bible. The Christianity of today has no prize that must be gained through loss, no depth in which to delve to discover treasures, no heights in which to ascend to gain a heavenly perspective, no personal growth in which to aspire to, no challenge in which to forge character, and no battle in which one is seasoned to endure to the end.

The unrealistic presentation of Christianity is that it is a carefree life where one is going to be constantly blessed. There will be no sorrow brought on by loss. There will be no lamentation brought on by despair, no real challenge brought on by adversity, and no real battle to thwart any advancement in growth or accomplishment. Such a presentation is not only a fantasy, but it is unscriptural. Just consider the following Scripture, *"Many are the afflictions of the righteous; but the LORD delivereth him out of them all" (Psalm 34:19).*

The Word of God is clear that the way of the Christian life is hard. It is the way of the cross (death), the oven of afflictions (suffering), and the fiery tests of faith (preparation) in order to ensure depth, growth, and victory.

Even though many try to flee the narrow, hard way of the Christian life, I personally embrace such a way. I have learned that in the end this is the only way I will gain Christ.

Prayer: Lord, Christianity is the essence of Your life being developed in me. Such development cannot come without adversity and testing. Lord, I desire Your life no matter the cost. Amen.

August 22

What unnecessary burdens are you carrying? Consider *Psalm 38:4, "For mine iniquities are gone over mine head: as an heavy burden they are too heavy for me."* The psalmist acknowledged that some of his burdens were due to his moral deviation. Born in a fallen condition, there is always the burden or sin that can easily beset each of us along the way, but they must be discerned.

There are so many people who are laden down with grave burdens. Some are personal, emotional, and spiritual. There are four types of burdens that people can carry. Following are three of them:

Cares: There are so many cares of the world. These cares cause confusion with one's affections in regard to the world. The responsibility of such cares can weigh a person down as to their loyalties, causing great frustration.

Problems: Unresolved problems can become great burdens to the resolve of a person. It is hard to see them through to the end; therefore, they can cause hopelessness to the soul.

Sins: The next burden that people carry is attached to the heaviness of sin that weighs upon their conscience. They feel condemned, but instead of bringing it to the light they try to cover it under the darkness of excuses. However, they continue to envelop a person into a world of despair.

These three burdens find their foundation in unbelief. Unbelief is the expression of fear running rampant in the imagination of the person. People are afraid to give their cares to the Lord, for they cannot see how problems ever can be resolved to their satisfaction. They actually fear God will reject their plan, keeping them from resolution and peace.

Prayer: Lord, You have told us what to do with our burdens, but we do not trust You with them. We fear that You will not see or do it our way. In such a state we need to repent of our unbelief towards You. Amen.

August 23

I have been meditating on the different types of burdens that people can carry during their journey through this world. In my last meditation I touched on the wrong types of burdens. However, the remaining category of burdens represents righteous burdens. We are told in Galatians 6:5, *"For every man shall bear his own burden."* These burdens are attached to a godly life. They have been ordained by the Lord.

The first burden is that of godly responsibility. Burdens are meant to put enough pressure on us that we will feel compelled to do all we can to ensure that they are lifted from off our shoulders. This is what responsibilities attached to God entail. However, the main motive behind such attitudes and actions is doing what is right and acceptable to God.

The Bible is clear that we are to carry our own burdens in a respectable manner. We even see this in the case of the Jewish High Priest in the Old Testament. Twelve stones with the names of the children of Israel were sown onto the shoulders of his priestly garments. They were equal in weight and was for the most part unnoticeable to him, but nevertheless he carried them daily in his priestly duties.

We are told by Jesus that the burdens we have are light, but nevertheless we are to carry them. The burdens have to do with loving God and others and if we have the love of God in us such burdens prove to be light.

The concept of bearing our own burdens is the acceptable way of avoiding putting unnecessary burdens on others who are already burdened with personal responsibilities of their own. I have been around people who will be glad to let you carry every one of their burdens when it comes to their Christian life.

As a Christian, it has always been my goal to not be a burden to others. However, I am thankful that the heaviest part of the yoke rests upon Jesus but there are times when the burden becomes too great that others, like Simon who helped bear up Jesus' cross, are impressed to come under the yoke as well in order to help you bear it until the mission is accomplished.

Prayer: Lord, thank You for providing the yoke that allows me to walk in step with You and ensures the weight of any burden that may be put upon me will not become too great. You are the One who truly carries the burden. Help me to remain under Your yoke at all times and trust You to send others in when necessary. Amen.

August 24

It just had to be a big, beautiful salmon that had taken the bait and fought so hard. The harder it fought, the more convinced I was that this would be the best catch of the day; especially since neither of my folks had caught anything. How could fishing be so bad when you were in such a great and beautiful location off of Whidbey Island's Deception Pass Bridge?

Finally, the angry fish surfaced, and suddenly the sight of it made me recoil in revulsion, for it was a rat fish! My heart sunk as the ugly fish was cut loose and flopped back into the sea. That was my first encounter with a rat fish, and the last fish I ever caught.

Not that I didn't like fishing, it's just that life for me turned a corner and I haven't had occasion to go fishing. Besides, I prefer salt water fishing to fresh water lakes and streams of the Inland Pacific Northwest where I live.

Jesus certainly knew all about fish and fishing. In *Matthew 4:19* He said to Simon Peter and his brother, Andrew, *"Follow me, and I will make you fishers of men."* Then Jesus called two other brothers, James and John, and they too, left their occupation and their father and followed Him.

I've thought a lot about those fishermen, and the other disciples, who left all behind to follow Jesus and "fish" for the souls of lost people. I do believe their hearts had been prepared by the Holy Spirit, as well as by John the Baptist, to hear His Voice deep within their innermost being and to immediately respond.

How much more valuable are the souls of men than fish? The question is, if you are truly born again, what are you fishing for in this life? If it's not for the souls of men, then whatever "reward" is on your hook can, in the end, only be likened to a worthless and ugly rat fish. – J. Haley

Prayer: Lord, fishing teaches us that there are counterfeits and disappointments. However, there is one type of fishing that, in light of Your kingdom, will never prove useless and that is when we fish for souls. Lord, thank You for catching my soul with the bait of Your love, the hook of Your grace, and the line of redemption. Amen.

August 25

There is much bondage in the world, and yet we are told there is one liberating source and that is truth which comes by way of The Truth, Jesus Christ. When you take the combination of God's love and truth, one will have the liberty to come under legitimate burdens that will not oppress, maim and destroy.

However, sometimes what we consider to be necessary or required burdens due to religious affiliation can prove to be the most oppressive. Consider *Galatians 5:1, "Stand fast therefore in the liberty wherewith Christ hath made us free, and be not entangled again with the yoke of bondage"*

As I consider the Ten Commandments, I realize they are outlining my burden. Scriptural burdens are moral responsibilities or obligations toward God and others that cannot be ignored. These commandments are not a matter of dos and don'ts but of ensuring one has a right attitude towards both God and others to ensure a proper spirit behind all conduct and acts of obedience.

This brings me to another burden and that is liberty. In order to do what is right, I must have the liberty to do so. However, liberty can prove to be frightening. People who are oppressed desire liberty, but once they receive it, they don't know what to do with it.

Before these poor souls experienced liberty, they were in bondage to some type of tyranny. These enslaved souls were told what to think and how to conduct themselves. However, liberty points to the frightening prospect that they are now responsible to think right and do right to ensure uprightness in a matter. Liberty does not mean the freedom to do wrong without consequences, but to do right to ensure the right results.

As I have learned in the past, there can be much bondage associated with religion. However, Christianity possesses liberty to discover what is excellent, and will walk in a right way to discover what true liberation in the spirit and soul is really like.

Prayer: Lord, I know what slavery feels like, but I also know how liberty works. I choose the way of righteousness to ensure the caliber of my journey and life. Amen.

August 26

"Lift up your heads, oh ye gates, and be lift up, ye everlasting doors, and the King of glory shall come in" (Psalm 24:7). As I meditated on this Scripture in *Psalm 24:7*, I realize that everything we must enter into to discover the eternal treasures of heaven comes by way of Jesus.

Jesus is the way I must travel. In essence, I must follow His indelible example. He alone established the narrow way of the gate, via the cross. The narrow way shows me that I can only enter into the things of God by way of death to the old in order to apply and assimilate the new.

Jesus is the door. As His sheep, I must follow the direction of His precious voice to come into places of nourishment and rest. He is the veil that has been parted by redemption to ensure sweet fellowship with God in the most holy places of communion.

Jesus is clearly the way to life. He is the only way. However, it is easy to miss this narrow way because it is not marked by great signs, but by humility wrought by the redemptive act of His sacrifice.

Prayer: Lord, You did leave the people of the world a glorious sign, but many refuse to see it. Thank You for opening my eyes so I can see You lifted up above the world, bidding me to come and receive the gifts and promises attached to Your eternal life. Amen.

August 27

"Not every one that saith unto me, Lord, Lord, shall enter into the kingdom of heaven; but he that doeth the will of my Father which is in heaven" (Matthew 7:21). This Scripture always reminds me how narrow the path to heaven is and how many strive to enter the sole gate of salvation and yet fail to.

I have been thinking about how Christianity is often being presented. In a way, the presentation of the Christian life has brought much mourning to my soul. Some in the church realm make it about doctrine, others about religious affiliation, rituals, or good works, and some even identify it with a church pew that bears their unseen name. However, none of these points of association identify a person as being born again with the life of Christ.

As I think about these different points of identification, I realize that each mark can reveal the type of gospel that people are hiding in. For those who see doctrine as their savior, they are hiding in a gospel that may be decent, but has no life. When it comes to those who are religious, their gospel is one of self-exaltation in personal righteousness. Those who are looking to rituals can end up with an anti-Christ gospel that serves as a substitute for real faith towards God. Those caught up with good works can succumb to a social gospel that will make people comfortable in their doomed state, and for those who see their pew as their ark of safety, they will eventually hear destructive storms slam against the doors of their lives, threatening their well-being.

The one identifying mark upon the lives of God's people is their desire to do His will. In order to do God's will I must believe who He is, trust His intentions towards me, and by faith walk in obedience to His Word.

Prayer: Lord, salvation is clear. It is marked with Your life and the presence of Your Spirit. Thank You for providing an irrefutable witness of Your salvation. Amen.

August 28

Have you ever noticed how dark spots show up so well on a light background? And, it seems, the lighter or brighter the background is, the more "spots" you can see. That's one of the reasons I rarely ever wear white or even pastel colors.

Now that we're continuing the slow-but-sure process of repainting our house in much lighter tones, the easier it is to see those tiny black spots that crawl into position directly across from your line of sight. I'm sure every small, black spider that wants to become a permanent resident in people's houses knows just how to do this. Suddenly, the entire expanse of wall is forgotten as the focal point becomes that annoying black dot. This is how it is with sin.

The "whiter" a person's life is, the easier it is to see and focus on the sin that mars that "whiteness" whether it's in your own life, or in the life of another believer. When it comes to our personal "dark, dirty spots," the only way to be cleansed from them is to quickly turn to Jesus for forgiveness, as *1 John 1:9, 10* tells us. *"If we confess our sins, he is faithful and just to forgive us our sins, and to cleanse us from all unrighteousness. If we say that we have not sinned, we make him a liar, and his word is not in us."*

When it comes to others, Jesus made it clear how careful we must be in trying to "help" others remove their "spots" when we are sporting a huge smudge of pride in our own character and "whiteness." We are all familiar with His admonition, *"Thou hypocrite, first cast out the beam out of thine own eye; and then shalt thou see clearly to cast out the mote out of thy brother's eye"*

(Matthew 7:5). In other words, take care of the sin in your own life before you set out to "help" remove the sin in the lives of others.

It's not that we are to ignore sin, no, not at all. It's about going through the humbling process of examining ourselves, asking the Holy Spirit to reveal our own hearts, denying our-self of the "right" to our self-will, and receiving His forgiveness and cleansing so that we can be Jesus' hand extended in the right Spirit of humility, love, compassion, and truth that sets the captive free. – J. Haley

Prayer: Jesus it is easy to think we have all the right answers, but if we lack a right attitude, we will find ourselves tasting the bitterness of it in due time. Lord, when will we learn that being right before You in our responses is far more important than being right in our minds about Your matters? Amen.

August 29

King David declared in *Psalm 20:6*, "*Now know I that the LORD saveth the anointed; he will hear from his holy heaven with the strength of his right hand.*" Like most people, I am a creature of habit. I am comfortable with what I know, what I believe, and what I understand about matters.

It is for this reason I have my standby Scriptures that I always run to depending on the subject or matter. The problem with my standby Scriptures is that I fail to discover the nuggets in other Scriptures. I must avoid glossing over the less familiar Scriptures and take time to meditate on them.

For example, take *Psalm 20:6*. The million-dollar question is, "What must I do to be saved?" The truth of the matter is the Bible tells us how to be saved, what salvation looks like, and how to make sure it is being worked in and out of our lives.

The real question should be, "Just how serious or desperate am I when it comes to salvation?" Most people embrace the idea of salvation, but not the life or responsibility of it. In this Scripture, we are told that the Lord saves those who are anointed. We know that we are anointed by the Spirit of God according to *1 John 2:27*, and that such anointing comes from above through the life of Christ being established within us.

It has been made obvious that to be saved, I must have the presence of the Holy Spirit in my inner tabernacle, ever cleansing, sanctifying, anointing His work, and setting me apart for the glory of God.

Prayer: Lord, I thank You for the means of feeding my mind with Your Word, disciplining my body with godliness, and nourishing my soul with the ways of righteousness. I praise You for providing an abundant life through the presence and work of Your Spirit. Amen.

August 30

One of the most humbling times in my Christian life was when someone told me that it was commendable that my one great desire was to hear from the Lord, "Well done thou good and faithful servant," but it was in His heart to call me friend. I was reminded of what Jesus said in *John 15:15*, *"Henceforth I call you not servants, for a servant knows not what his Lord doeth but I have called you friend."*

As a believer, I have been aware that I am on a spiritual odyssey, a journey. However, I cannot take a journey unless I have a destination. I cannot venture through this world unless I have landmarks.

As a new Christian, my initial journey began with me heading towards the destination of heaven. However, through the years the different landmarks of experience and the guidelines of the Word of God changed my goal.

Don't get me wrong, heaven is still my destination, but my goal is to discover God, to seek Him in the midst of uncertainty, to find Him in darkness, to know Him in spite of the worldly terrain of deception and ignorance, to serve Him regardless of the lures of other masters, and to love Him in spite of the vanity that tugs at my heart to come aside and taste of the world's empty, deadly fruits.

I walk in confidence in light of this goal. In the end I know it will lead me into a relationship with God that will be marked by excellence and satisfaction. I will be able to come face to face with Him without fear. I will be able to meet Him as my friend.

I must keep this goal ever before me as I journey through this world. There is so much to discover about God, but if I can end up developing a sweet friendship with Him, I can be assured that there will be no discomfort in our meeting on the other side in glory.

Prayer: Lord, we only have now to establish a viable relationship with You. I do not want to just get by, I want to know You in an intimate way. This is the only way that I will experience any real satisfaction here. Amen.

August 31

"There is no soundness in my flesh because of thine anger, neither is there any rest in my bones because of sin" (Psalm 38:3).
When I am uneasy in my soul, I know it is spiritual but I must discern if Satan is causing it or if sin is present, affecting my attitude and mood.

It is not unusual to have to come face to face with the frailty of the flesh. Flesh is unpredictable, fickle, and moody. Even though it sees itself as sufficient and high-minded in its conclusions and ways, it proves to be unwise. Ultimately, it creates precarious situations that result in irritations, anger, and consequences. In fact, the flesh is subject to the dictates of sin.

Sin causes unrest in the soul, but the tendency is to somehow make it right in the mind. Even though sin has broken fellowship with God, people want to maintain their idea of innocence. Although there is an uneasiness in their souls, they do not want to believe they stand guilty.

I have learned that a guilty conscience can easily be cleansed by repentance. Repentance cleanses the spiritual environment of condemnation. It is liberating and refreshing but I must first face that which rages in my soul, slams against my silly excuses, and pricks my conscience.

Prayer: Lord, thank You for solving the problem of my restless soul due to sin. You have provided the way of forgiveness and cleansing. Have Your way Lord. Amen.

September

September 1

We can easily be blinded by the board in our eye that Jesus warned us of in *Matthew 7:1*. There are also other warnings we need to heed to remind ourselves that we need to examine where we are in our relationship with the Lord. Consider *Psalm 38:5, "My wounds stink and are corrupt because of my foolishness."*

When I look back at my life, I can't help but notice how the foolishness of my flesh, the tyranny of my selfishness, and the arrogance of my conceit affected my life. The traits of the old man in me set me up to be wounded by the sword of truth, the darts of indifference, the arrows of arrogance, and the spears of reality.

It was obvious that the weaponry contained within this earthly life had the means to knock me off my high horse, cause me to fall off my pinnacle of self-importance, and pull me down from my position as king of my particular molehill. Ultimately, these weapons are constantly being used to bring me down into the dust of failure, the cesspool of need, and the endless pit of ineptness.

I realize that what was wounded by the different weaponry of life was my pride. The smell of wounded pride is atrocious. It reveals how corrupt the ways and works of the flesh are. Only repentance, forgiveness, and reconciliation can wash away the stench left by the rotting decay of this sin.

Prayer: Lord, we are so used to the stench of our pride, we never detect it when it emits the smell that You will always resist when

You encounter it in our lives. You have my permission to reveal its exaltation, flattery, deception, "smell," and ways when it is taking center stage in my life. Amen.

September 2

Oh! How true it is that the "little things" can make a great impact on a person's mood, or emotional state. At least that's what happened to me yesterday—laundry day. I am beginning to believe that socks, especially new ones that are as rare as hen's teeth to find these days, just simply get up and walk off! All by themselves. It's like a conspiracy to drive me nuts. Yes, it's a little thing, of course, in the grand scheme of things, but big enough in my world to be very upsetting.

So, just like that I turned into a living replica of the woman in the parable of the lost silver coin who turned her house upside down, inside out searching for it. I would love to report that I found it and called all my friends and neighbors to rejoice with me, but that didn't happen.

But what did happen is it dawned on my frazzled mind and foul mood that while everybody occasionally loses things that they need, like, or use such as jewelry, keys, scissors, knives, screw drivers and other items, how many of us, who call ourselves Christians, truly go to any great lengths to diligently search for a lost soul to share the Gospel with, or rescue one of God's sheep who has gone astray? Perhaps we've forgotten what we're really here for.

Jesus asked, *"What man of you, having an hundred sheep, if he lose one of them, doth not leave the ninety and nine in the wilderness, and go after that which is lost, until he find it" (Luke 15:4)?* This verse always brings tears to my eyes, for many years ago I was a "lost sheep." But, praise God! The Good Shepherd found and rescued me in a mighty way.

Let's face it, things don't just "walk off" and get lost on their own, but people do. How about you? Are you a lost sheep today that the Good Shepherd is searching for? – J. Haley

Prayer: Lord, I remember what it was to be like a lost sheep. It was frightening to my mind, lonely to my spirit, and unbearable to my soul. But then, You found me and my life has never been the same, and yet am I aware, care about, and keep my ears open for the cries of the lost sheep. Lord, give me a heart and burden for the lost. Amen.

September 3

How many can relate to this Scripture, *"I am feeble and sore broken. I have roared by reason of the disquietness of my heart"* (Psalm 38:8). There are different battles raging. Whether within families, societies, nationally, or internationally we are living in times where the different seas of humanity are roaring with tumultuous waves.

There is so much conflict going on in the world. A great deal of this conflict never personally touches our lives, even though the ripple it sends through the oceans of the world often turn into angry waves of turmoil and destruction.

However, if such waves finally do intrude into our worlds, we begin to realize how feeble we are in the scheme of things. In such feebleness we can be broken by its impact because we come face to face with that greatest turmoil going on which is within our souls because we are not in control of anything.

How do we respond to the impact of such angry intrusion into our realities? We often roar against it because there is no peace in our hearts. The calm waters of self-sufficiency are no more, the serene shoreline of normalcy has ceased to be, and the rocks of worldly assurance are being consumed by the momentous onslaught of the waves.

As a believer, I have learned long ago that the only security I have is the Rock that stands in spite of the savage assault of the angry waves of the world. I can stand, cling, and hide in the cleft of this Rock, and know calmness and peace when the waves roar around it.

Prayer: Lord, the angry waves roaring around me can be frightening, but if I remember who You are, I will maintain the peace of my soul and the abiding confidence of my spirit. Amen.

September 4

One of the Scriptures I have mediated on is the one that declares the way of the transgressor is hard. However, it always amazes me that in our foolishness we shy away from, flee, or reject the hard, narrow way of the cross. Granted, the way of the cross is not pleasant to the flesh. It serves as repudiation to all selfishness, and is a complete affront against our pride, but it rids us of those things that make life hard for us in relationship to our Lord and Savior.

When a person goes the way of iniquity, he or she simply heaps great weights upon him or herself. Such individuals may flex their free-will to do as they please, but once they take the liberty to sin, they will begin to feel the oppression of it upon their souls. The hardness that it creates in life will suck the very breath out of the environment. It produces the cruelty of indifference and the hopeless pit of despair.

At such times I am reminded of *Psalm 38:17, "For I declare mine iniquity; I will be sorry for my sin."* As you can see, either way is hard, but the end results are different. I choose the narrow way of death and destruction by taking responsibility for my iniquity in

274

order to owe up to it. I choose to deny myself of that which serves as an avenue of the world that stands condemned. In essence, I choose the way of the cross in order to becomes identified with the work of redemption Jesus accomplished on the cross.

Prayer: Lord, I choose to glory in Your cross and embrace my personal cross. It may represent the hard way, a time of humility, repentance, and honest confession but in the end, it will prove to be the liberating way. Amen.

September 5

Enthusiasm may be the "wind in our sails" for a time, especially when we're young, healthy and energetic; however, more often than not, the boundless enthusiasm of youth when coupled with a spirit of competition can build enough momentum to catapult a person "up, over and out" of the realm of reality. I remember that fleeting, but intense time when I journeyed through the stressful mental and emotional mudflat of misdirected ambition.

The "vision of grandeur" of becoming "the world's greatest artist," coupled with a secondary goal of gaining financial security, was a bubble destined to pop into thin air. After a number of years of study and hard work, exhibits and art shows, my work began to gain attention from certain "movers and shakers," people who viewed art, not so much for its unique beauty, but rather as a potential money-making commodity. Bottom line, I was still naïve enough to believe that any talented, dedicated and committed person (in any field of endeavor) could make it "to the top."

At this point I'm not qualified to say it can't ever happen, but what I do know is that my career in the Western art world ended one night in a two-artist show in an art gallery when I said three little words. The person I said them to (now deceased) happened to be a very successful and famous artist for one of the world's biggest, well-known, household names on the planet. He highly complimented one of my paintings, made a personal gesture, and then told me what I'd have to do for him to "get me to the top."

My response was, "Not this girl!" He stated, "Then you'll never make it." All these years later, I have never regretted not compromising my soul for fame and riches. Jesus said, *"For what shall it profit a man, if he shall gain the whole world, and lose his own soul" (Mark 8:36).* After all, hell is forever. – J. Haley

Prayer: Lord, I know everything in this world is a temporary, fading glory that is here one moment then gone the next. It leaves nothing but emptiness, bitterness, and hopelessness in its wake. Lord, I may not see all the great things You have in mind for me when it comes to this world, but I believe the best is yet to come because I trust You and Your Word and as a result I live in expectation of what is eternal and glorious. Amen.

September 6

I so want to finish the course the Lord has set before me. We are told the days are evil and we need to redeem the time we have on this earth. I know this requires me to keep my eye on the Lord. For this reason, one of my prayers is found in *Psalm 39:4, "LORD, make me to know the end of my days, what it is; that I may know how frail I am."*

As I get older and grow in my knowledge of the Lord, I begin to realize how frail my flesh is. Yes, my flesh can override the right spirit, but I understand the battle and that the war has already been won on the cross but I must become identified to the great work of redemption.

My desire and goal are to secure wisdom from above by learning the lessons of life. Discerning my present decisions, attitudes, and actions will give me a sense of the direction I am heading. It will reveal the quality of my life, as well as my weaknesses.

The other aspect about wisdom from above is that it will allow me to discern the times in which I live. It will give me a sense of the lateness of the hour. If I properly discern the time, I will also be able to seek God's face as to how I must prepare. I must become aware of the end of a matter before I can prepare for it.

Today there is so much wishful thinking or fanciful notions present, but I do not see much preparation. We must be prepared to face the end of this dispensation, as well as the end to the life we know. We cannot live in denial about any of it. We must acknowledge the end to properly live today for that which is eternal so that we can face the future with abiding assurance.

Prayer: Lord, You are precious. You are our present hope and the focus of our future. We have nothing to fear except forgetting that You are our Provider and Way. You will provide as You lead the way to the finish line. Amen.

September 7

"He brought me up also out of an horrible pit, out of the miry clay, and set my feet upon a rock, and established my goings" (Psalm 40:2). How many times has the Lord brought you out of some miry pit and set you in a secure place in Him? Perhaps it was a pit of sin, despair, depression, hopelessness, and fear. The sin was too great, the despair too heavy, the depression too thick, the hopelessness overwhelming, and the fear too tormenting.

In the past I have groped in the darkness of uncertainty, slipped in the fog of confusion, fallen into the pit of despair, and felt buried by the rocks of hopelessness. No matter what I did, I could not get my footing. I needed a sure foundation to stand on, an anchor to maintain the course, and a standard or ensign to march to.

It was not until I met Christ that I discovered the Rock of ages, the abiding anchor of hope, and the immutable standard of righteousness. Upon receiving Jesus, I could stand firmly on the Rock when being shaken. I could withstand with the anchor when being affronted by the storms of life, and continue to stand under the shadow of the standard of heaven when all was being slammed against my resolve.

It is clear that there is nothing sure in this world but Christ. There is nothing so wonderful as the reality of His redemption, and there is nothing more excellent than the unveiling of His glory in my life. In essence, this is what it means for Christ to be all in all in me and to me.

Prayer: Lord, there is so much that can come against us in our Christian walk. Much of the terrain around us may change, but You will always remain the same. Praise Your holy Name. Amen.

September 8

Fear is a monkey on many people's back, but it need not be because of what *2 Timothy 1:7* tells us, *"For God hath not given us the spirit of fear; but of power, and of love, and of a sound mind."* The days we are living in are fearful and dreadful. The result is people are living in fear and some are even enslaved by paranoia.

Fear is an emotional, mental, and spiritual matter. It is emotional because you can feel fear that drives or paralyzes. It is mental because you can see the possible devastating results and it will cause one to faint in the mind. And, finally it is spiritual because fear can be a spirit that blankets our soul with grave oppression.

Most people don't know what to do with it because they can't discern it. When you come face to face with fear that is all you see, all you know, and it seems you have no other option but to bow down before it and give way to it, which is a form of worship. If you feel fear, you must step back from it, stand still and change focus from it to the Lord. If your mind is being affronted by fear you must consider Jesus and what He faced on His way to the cross and step over it. And, if it's spiritual, take authority over it, knowing it was defeated at the cross.

Fear's greatest affront comes down to a couple of things: First, it will expose how inept and incapable we are in dealing with the issue, and secondly, the inability to control the outcome because I can't trust anyone else to do it the way I think it should be done. Fear is unbelief.

Since we all will experience some type of threshold of fear in our lives, I have come to realize that I have the responsibility to decide what will serve as my greatest point of fear. Will I fear being found out by God's penetrating light, or will I fear not being exposed in the light so that I can properly address that which keeps me from enjoying the liberating truth of His light?

The first type of fear will end in delusion until the person faces God's light of fiery judgment. The second type of dread will cause a person to fear the prospect of the light never penetrating through his or her obstinate disposition to bring conviction of the Holy Spirit in regard to sin, repentance, reconciliation with God, and restoring a relationship with Him.

I must honestly examine what kind of fear I maintain when it comes to God's penetrating light exposing the darkness of my soul and ways.

Prayer: Lord, You have not given us a spirit of fear that prevents us from knowing Your overcoming power, Your abiding life, and clarity as to Your commitment to save us from that which causes fear. Thank You for Your abiding grace. Amen.

September 9

The paint sample from the hardware store began to give me second thoughts about the color we chose to repaint a bedroom. Granted, it was a much lighter color than the "muddy" hue that was there since we bought the house; but somehow, I began to regret making a hasty decision to go with it just because the paint was on sale. Finally, the dreaded day came, but I'm happy to report that when it was finished, much to my surprise and delight, it was perfect!

You know, sometimes in our walk with the Lord, we find ourselves making a decision based on an idea, or inspiration, and then before we're able to carry it out, we begin to have doubts about it and wonder if we've made a big mistake. Being human, it's easy to make mistakes, but the wonderful truth is, when we love the Lord, He directs our steps, and all ends well.

Psalm 37:23 says *"The steps of a good man are ordered by the LORD: and he delighteth in his way." –* J. Haley

Prayer: Lord, we are told that if we stand upright before You because of faith, we will discover that You are the One who clearly orders our steps. This proves that second guessing as to where we end up and what we end up with after declaring, "We will trust You," is a sign of wavering faith. However wavering faith finds its stability when it comes to rest on the Rock that never moves from what is true; therefore, it has no need to second guess the way of righteousness. I can and will trust You with every detail of my life. Amen.

September 10

"Blessed is that man that maketh the LORD his trust, and respecteth not the proud, nor such as turn aside to lies" (Psalm 40:4). It is not unusual for man to declare, "I will," about matters that he has no say or control over. Such claims are proud, foolish, and enslaving. After all, once such a claim is made, man must control his world or environment, to make sure the determination comes to fruition.

It does not matter how much I "will" something, I cannot make it so. I am not God and I cannot control my world or circumstances. Such notions speak of the proud heart and high-minded arrogance that will set me up to fall into the cesspool of failure.

There is only one determination I can rightfully make and that is, "I will trust the Lord." God does not have favorites among mankind, but He does have those who are faithful to put their confidence in Him when the lies and attractions of the world are bombarding them with false hope and vain promises.

Prayer: Lord, I praise Your blessed name. I ask You to help me wade through notions and wishful thinking and come to rest on what is true and eternal. Amen.

September 11

"But I am poor and needy; yet the Lord thinketh upon me: thou art my help and my deliverer; make no tarrying, O my God" (Psalm 40:17). The greatest type of liberty I have found in my spiritual journey is when I recognize and admit my present state of poverty.

It is in a state of spiritual poverty of requirements and lack, that I will be able to recognize how needy I am in my present situation and admit it. It is from such a state I am inspired to look up and seek the One who will meet me in such trying circumstances every time I call upon His precious name.

The arrogance of man causes him to operate in a state of self-sufficiency. He will not see his spiritual poverty and will not recognize his need. He will blindly walk in arrogance towards his utter fall and spiritual ruin. Such a man is full of self, blinded by his high opinion of self, and totally oblivious of His impending doom.

I discovered long ago my state of poverty and my need for heaven's intervention. I do not flatter myself about my abilities; rather, I seek heaven for help. I do not con myself about my importance in this world; rather, I cry out for God to deliver me from the traps of deception and blindness.

As a result, I discovered that there are great liberties to be found in such a humble position.

Prayer: Lord, I am poor and needy. I need You every hour. I choose to abide in the knowledge of Your blessed assurance when the vanity of this world begins to mock me with its emptiness. Amen.

September 12

"And as for me, thou upholdest me in mine integrity and settest me before thy face for ever" (Psalm 41:12). Integrity is an important virtue. As I have said before, integrity is not just given to us, it is forged into our character.

The truth of the matter is we all start with a base, vain character. In other words, we may be characters in how we think and what we do, but we do not possess any real character. Our tendency is to flatter ourselves about deviation when it comes to character instead of being honest that our ways are anything but excellent.

We prefer to twist the truth rather than embrace it because we might have to face how wrong we are in our prejudices and conclusions. We connive to get others to see it our way to feel we are not alone in our thinking rather than face the foolishness of our ways. It is a ridiculous game that many play with disastrous results.

According to the psalmist, the Lord can only uphold us in integrity. The truth must be our foundation, transparency our light, and present reality our gauge. Since we cannot hide anything, this allows the Lord to place us before His face to remember, consider, and uphold us in the ways of righteousness.

Prayer: Lord, thank You for Your faithfulness to remember, consider, and uphold me in the ways that bring life to my soul and glory to You. Have Your way, oh Lord. Amen.

September 13

"O send out thy light and thy truth: let them lead me; let them bring me unto thy holy hill, and to thy tabernacle" (Psalm 43:4). The psalmist's request in *Psalm 43:4* should be my request. He first asked the Lord to send out the light.

Light points to enlightenment and understanding. How can I know where to walk unless I first perceive where the path leads? I know that the light that was sent from heaven was Jesus. If I have received Jesus into my life, then I have the necessary light to show me the way through any darkness I may encounter--and there are various types of darkness. The greatest darkness is the spiritual darkness that wraps up man's soul into a stifling blanket of despair.

Another virtue that God must send forth is His truth. The world is wrapped up in lies, vain philosophies, false promises, and idle rhetoric. He must send forth the sharp sword of truth to cut through the dark web and entanglements of these false presentations so the light can come forth. However, the sword can cut, divide, offend, and wound.

I know that the truth is Jesus. Jesus was sent forth with the sharpness of truth to penetrate the darkness of man's soul. He has indeed penetrated my soul with His liberating truth of redemption.

Prayer: Lord, You have sent forth Your truth. It has shaken, cut, and torn away the nonsense in my life. I thank You for sending forth the light that will penetrate the grave darkness of the soul. Amen.

September 14

It happened before the days of car seatbelts, straps and buckles that kept your kid, cat and coffee cup snugly secure. In other words, it was the "good old days" and I was having a great time standing on the backseat of the car, while waving at the friendly people who waved back in the car behind us.

All was going well until Dad suddenly made a sharp left turn onto our street. In a flash I lost my balance, toppled against the car door handle, and rolled out onto the gravel. I can still hear my poor mother hysterically screaming for my dad to stop the car. No doubt my "guardian angel" had it all under control because, not only was I not run over by the back tire, but I didn't even have a scratch. However, I did have two very upset parents, and received one of the sternest lectures in the history of mankind about never standing on the car seat again!

This little incident reminds me of life in general. One minute you're innocently going along for the ride, being kind and somewhat entertaining to others, when life unexpectedly makes a sharp turn and you find yourself rolling on the ground, wondering what just happened. Whether the impact of an unforeseen change in your life is small and inconvenient, or large and heart-shattering, the only One who can lift you up, calm your fears and still your heart is the LORD Jesus Christ.

Through prayer, the Word and the power and presence of the Holy Spirit we will, as Job did, rise up to worship, serve and glorify our God until He calls us Home. *Isaiah 41:10* assures us, *"Fear thou not; for I am with thee: be not dismayed; for I am thy God: I will strengthen thee; yea, I will help thee; yea, I will uphold thee with the right hand of my righteousness."*– J. Haley

Prayer: Lord, You do watch out for the innocent, the vulnerable and the foolish. It will only be in eternity that we will see just how faithful You were to protect and keep us under Your abiding care. Thank You dear Lord for keeping a watchful eye on me at all times. Amen.

September 15

"As with a sword in my bones, mine enemies reproach me; while they say daily unto me, Where is thy God" (Psalm 42:10). Through the years I have tried to maintain a steady testimony of God, but when the circumstances of life shake my resolve and the trials of life mock my faith, it's not unusual for the enemies of God, of the cross of Christ, and of His servants to ask the question, "Where is your God?"

This question comes in from different angles in diverse situations, but behind it is unbelief. For example, when you have an ongoing illness, the question is, "What have you done wrong, for I don't see how God can be in this situation."

If you have suffered great loss, the question is, "Surely, your loving God would not allow such a thing to happen to such a person as you!"

When you have suffered a great tragedy, the question can be, "Where was your God then?" When the scoffing is done, each question implies that if there is a God, you surely do not know Him. At such times you must evaluate the person who is judging you and know they not only come from a limited perspective, but they do so with skepticism that is always void of faith.

Regardless of how right others may seem in their conclusions about the reason for your plight, you must choose the way of faith established by God's Word if you are to withstand the onslaught of unbelief of others. You need to remember that unbelief finds its way into the bones of a matter to tear down your resolve to stand on the Rock of truth. It is true that the penetration of cruel realities and accusations in vulnerable times can make you tremble, but this is when you must by faith declare what you do know about God. He will never leave or forsake you.

Prayer: Lord, unbelief will nip at our heels unless we stop trying to dodge the bullets of uncertainty and face its darkness of deception. We must choose to step over it and declare what we know about You. Thank You for giving me the measure of faith to overcome unbelief. Amen.

September 16

"For I will not trust in my bow, neither shall my sword save me" *(Psalm 43:6).* There are so many things we can choose to trust in. We can trust in our abilities, our knowledge, our shrewdness, our government, our programs, our churches, leaders, and families. However, the harsh reality is that none of these things can truly save any of us.

We often have a tendency to think that salvation is strictly associated with saving the soul. However, this is not true. God must save us from many things. He has to save us from our own devices because they lead to ruin. He must deliver us from the wicked tides of the world to ensure our testimony. He must preserve our sanity in the pit of hopelessness. The Lord must guide our steps down rocky, slippery slopes to ensure our very life.

Clearly, God is the essence of all salvation. To look to any other source for deliverance is foolish. Faith towards God is the choice of the will, trust is the preference of the wisdom of the intellect, and assurance is the place where all undisciplined emotions have landed on the path of righteousness.

Prayer: Lord, Your Word tells me that my faith must be towards You. To rely on any other source is a form of spiritual suicide. I choose to trust You. Amen.

September 17

"Arise for our help, and redeem us for thy mercies sake" (Psalm 43:26). God does not deliver us or save us just because He can. He must have the necessary grounds present before He can save us. This may seem strange, but salvation comes by way of redemption. This reality points to the legal aspect of salvation.

Salvation is a legal matter. The reason we need to be saved is because we are under a death sentence. As a righteous judge, the Lord cannot intervene or help me unless He has the grounds to do so. This means I must understand my plight in order to seek His intervention on my behalf. The truth is a righteous judge desires to show mercy where He can, but unless one sincerely seeks it, what is left for any righteous judge is to execute the sentence pronounced on the offender by the law.

As a Christian, I know that God sent His Son to establish the necessary grounds to redeem me. It is because of Christ that God is able to save me. However, I must humbly acknowledge that He does not save me for my sake; rather, He saves me for the sake of His precious Son who gave His life for me in order to satisfy the holy law.

Prayer: Lord, I realize all that has been done on my behalf was done because of You. Every time heaven graces my life, it is the means to honor You. Lord, it is for this reason I want my life to bring You the glory You deserve. Amen.

September 18

After replanting dill weed seeds in our garden this spring, I finally got a nice row of enough aromatic dill to make dill pickles. This may not seem too exciting to a lot of folks, but believe me, raising some of your own food, even though it can be time-consuming, backbreaking work is very rewarding. Besides, having my own dill saved me a trip to the grocery store six miles away where, last year, I had to special order it and make two trips to get it.

The only problem was, however, the cucumber plants. Two died, and the one that "sort of" managed to survive only produced one cucumber at a time. This meant having to purchase, from a local farm, enough pickle-size cucumbers to make the pickles. At least I had a nice supply of garlic a friend gave me. So, what's so important about cucumbers and dill to warrant writing about it?

Well, it's like this: after I stood back and admired the jars of pickles, it came to mind that the ancient Egyptians probably made dill pickles too! After all, the children of Israel murmured and complained in the wilderness, *"We remember the fish, which we did eat in Egypt freely; the cucumbers, and the melons, and the leeks, and the onions, and the garlic" (Numbers 11:5).*

Jesus mentioned dill in Matthew 23:23, and information on the Internet (Home Stratosphere) records, "Dill has been around for a long time. The first ever record of it being used comes from a petrified specimen that was found in the tomb of the Egyptian King, Amenhotep II. This plant dates back to around 1400 BC!"

You know, when Jesus calls and says, "Follow me," you have to count the cost, and if pickles happen to be part of that "cost" you're not willing to pay, then how will you leave behind your friends, family and lifestyle if need be? *"For which of you, intending to build a tower, sitteth not down first, and counteth the cost, whether he have sufficient to finish it? "So likewise, whosoever he be of you that forsaketh not all that he hath, he cannot be my disciple" (Luke 14:28, 33).* – J. Haley

Prayer: Lord, we have been conditioned to prefer the various tastes of the world, but if those tastes become our predominate preference, we will eventually fail to follow You. Lord, enable me to pay the price necessary to make You my complete focus and dependency when it comes to maintaining my life here. Amen.

September 19

"Thus saith the LORD; Cursed be the man that trusteth in man, and maketh flesh his arm, and whose heart departeth from the LORD" (Jeremiah 17:5). When I am wrestling with my faith towards God, it takes everything in me to not look towards my own understanding or the world. If I do, I will be putting my confidence in the arm of flesh. Granted, it may be an organization or governing body but man is still involved with man's strength, initiative, innovation, and agendas. These activities all point to the arm of the flesh.

It is clear that activities that originate, operate according to, and are maintained by the arm of the flesh stand cursed. There will be no life found in any of it. Controlled chaos may reign, but strife will prove to be the ripples beneath the façade of peace.

I am ever being reminded that eventually everything established by man will collapse in complete ruin. It will be judged by the Law of God, buried by the dust of vanity, lost in a maze of ineptness, marked by the ash of decay and death, and forgotten as the sands of time erase away all memory of its existence.

The Bible is clear that the things of the flesh stand condemned, and will be remembered no more in the world to come. Therefore, I choose to trust the hand of God and not in the arm of the flesh.

Prayer: Lord, the temptation is to look to the arm of the flesh for answers and solutions. However, You are the only true solution. Keep my focus steadfast towards You. Amen.

September 20

"Blessed is the man that trusteth in the LORD, and whose hope the LORD is" (Jeremiah 17:7). As I consider yesterday's meditation, I cannot help but grasp the necessity of realizing that I do choose who or what I will trust in. I will either trust the false seduction of the arm of pride that flexes its muscles in man, or I will choose to trust the Lord in all matters concerning life and godliness.

In *Jeremiah 17:7*, I am told, *"Blessed is the man that trusteth in the Lord."* "Blessed" points to one who is happy in attitude, content in soul, and settled in spirit. Such a man has no need because the Lord is his portion. He knows that all that is important is found in his relationship with God. After all, trust allows God to abide with us in sweet fellowship.

I am also told that this blessing is also present because of hope in the Lord. Hope in the Lord puts expectation in our walk of faith. It causes us to go forward towards God in expectation of what He is about to do and what He will do. Of course, He will do those things which are close to His heart, according to His will, and in line with His eternal plan. Therefore, the desires of my heart must be in line with His desires to ensure they come to fruition.

It is for this reason that the Lord causes me to seek to know what is in His heart. By having a sense of what is important to Him, I can be assured that an expectation wrought in such an environment will be realized in the end. This is what will confirm my faith towards the Lord.

Prayer: Lord, my goal should be to seek out and know what is in Your heart about the matters of life to ensure that my desires will cause You to delight in fulfilling them for Your glory. Line the desires of my heart up to Your heart. Amen.

September 21

"For he shall be as a tree planted by the waters, and that spreadeth out her roots by the river, and shall not see when heat cometh, but her leaf shall be green; and shall not be careful in the year of drought, neither shall cease from yielding fruit" (Jeremiah *17:8).* I love the picture that Jeremiah presented. If we are in Christ, we have indeed been planted by the river that brings life. Our roots in Him reach that precious river that revives the soul and refreshes the spirit, causing our lives to produce wondrous fruits.

We know that our lives produce some type of fruit. This fruit either contains the seeds of life or death. To partake of the fruit, will nourish, nullify, or poison us.

The fruits we produce depend on our root system and the water we partake of. In *Jeremiah 17:8* I am told that God's design for His people is to plant them as trees of righteousness alongside the river. Jesus tells us the river He wants to plant each of us by is the river of His Spirit.

As believers, we possess the life of Christ. As we grow into His life, the roots of His life will reach into the foundation of truth as they spread out to drink from the Living Water of heaven. The life these roots produce in each of us is eternal and glorious. I am indeed blessed to be given such a life and heavenly source that will feed those roots on a daily basis.

Prayer: Lord, You are the Vine of heaven. As a branch I have been taken from the earth and implanted in You through redemption. I desire Your life as the Living Water flows through my being with heavenly nutrients that will feed my soul and grow me up in You. Amen.

September 22

"And he shall be like a tree planted by the rivers of water, that bringeth forth his fruit in his season; his leaf also shall not wither; and whatsoever he doeth shall prosper" (Psalm 1:3). I cannot count the many times I have meditated on this Scripture. I am sure many volumes could be written about this one Scripture. When I think about believers being the trees of God, it is obvious that they will stand tall because of righteousness. The life of Christ in them will reach heavenward ensuring their right standing before God.

When I think of the rivers of water, I know the water points to the unending flow of the Spirit from the throne of God. He is that presence within the believer that flows upward, opening each of us up to the endless treasures of heaven. He is the presence around us that enfolds us into the protection and ways of God as He guides us to the treasures of truth. He is the presence that flows from above that connects with the water from within and emerges with the water around us, totally immersing us with and into a new, powerful, abundant, and fruitful life.

We next have the promise of the fruit. The fruit will reveal that we are indeed prospering. Even though there is a physical blessing involved with God's provision, the greatest fruit is that of eternal life. This life is not only ongoing, but it can reproduce itself in the barren, but humble, seeking heart.

The question is the same. What does my fruit tell about my root system?

Prayer: Lord, I am thankful for the position I have in You, along with the water that has been made available to my barren, thirsty soul. Make me that open-ended vessel that not only receives what You have for me, but will be used to pour it into others as well. Amen.

September 23

"And if it bear fruit, well: and if not, then after that thou shalt cut it down" (Luke 13:9). I had to once again meditate on this parable about the unproductive tree. The owner had waited for it to produce fruit for a couple of years, but it failed to produce. Granted, it was alive for leaves would make their appearance, but its purpose was to produce fruit.

The gardener had mercy on the tree and asked the owner to give him a year to nurture it. If it produced fruit, it would prove to be worth the investment. If it failed to produce fruit, then the owner would be justified in cutting it down.

As believers, we must produce fruit. In fact, if the life of Christ is in us and the Holy Spirit is freely moving through us, there is no way we cannot help but produce heavenly fruit. There is also no way that those who are hungry and thirsty would reject it.

However, if we fail to produce the fruit of heaven, we will be considered useless. We will have failed to reach our potential as we miss the mark set for us in the corridors of heaven. This is unacceptable because Jesus made the necessary investment to give us the opportunity to reach our high calling in Him. If there is a failure, it will not rest at the feet of the owner or the gardener, but at the feet of the one who lacked the vital connections to heaven.

Prayer: Lord, there will be no reason why we failed to produce heavenly fruit, except we chose to not believe, cutting off all connections to heaven. Forgive me for the weeds of unbelief. Help my roots of faith to reach deep and wide into the fertile ground of Your Spirit and truth. Amen.

September 24

"Thou lovest righteousness and hatest wickedness; therefore God, thy God, hath anointed thee with the oil of gladness above thy fellows" (Psalm 45:7). It is not unusual for people to strive to understand how to get God's attention and approval. They try doing good things, being decent, and curbing unpleasant ways, but the truth is none of these things will be anointed because they are not reckoned as righteousness.

To me the big challenge for people is to put aside all religious notions about piety and come to terms with how God considers matters. God is the One who reckons a matter to be righteous. He counts a matter as so on the basis of genuine faith.

To have right standing with God, I first must simply believe a matter concerning God before He can count my standing and attitude **for** righteousness. It is because of faith, God can reckon a matter as being acceptable which establishes us **in** righteousness before Him. Once that faith turns into actions of obedience, then He can count it **as** being righteous.

Notice God must reckon or count something as being righteous because man's best is as filthy rags and there is no good thing that can originate with the flesh. For man to think there is anything acceptable outside of God counting something for, in or as being righteous based on faith, is to frustrate God's grace.

Once man stands upright, is established in it, and acts upon what is right by faith, God can anoint the person with the approval of His Spirit upon it. This is why the Holy Spirit not only reproves the world of sin and judgment but of righteousness as well. His approval must be present to confirm righteousness and anoint the person and the action to ensure the right effect.

Prayer: Lord, Your Word is clear that man's best is filthy rags. It is for this reason You must count what we do out of faith as being righteous to You. Thank You for giving us the means in which we can have right standing in You and be considered right before You. Amen.

September 25

I rediscovered a beautiful truth the other day. On the back of a bookmark were these words, "The will of God will never lead you where the grace of God cannot keep you."

Due to our performance-oriented society, we have a hard time believing that we are not expected to conjure up some strength to accomplish a feat. The reality is we must submit what strength we have to the Holy Spirit and give way to His work. When each of us recognizes that all we have must be first submitted to the Spirit in order to realize the best God has for us, we begin to comprehend how God's grace works.

This is why the Apostle Paul made this statement, *"That according as it is written, He that glorieth, let him glory in the Lord"* *(1 Corinthians 1:31).* Everything accomplished in our life on behalf of the kingdom of God is a matter of His grace.

It is for this reason we will never be able to glory in what we do. All glory must go to God for He is the One who blesses us with the grace to see a matter through to the end.

It is with this in mind that I need to truly examine myself to see if I am touching God's glory by claiming it as my own, or am I giving it back to Him in a bouquet of acceptable service, sacrificial praise, and unadulterated worship?

Prayer: Lord, You constantly must show Your mercy to us because we are pitiful and You must give us favor because our best is as filthy rags before You. Thank You Lord that You do not regard me on the basis of who I am, but according to Your redemption. Amen.

September 26

"Wherefore by their fruits ye shall know them" (Matthew 7:20). How many are waiting around to see what kind of fruits are first produced before jumping on some bandwagon or getting caught up with the latest trend?

I ask this question because there is so much going on in the name of the Lord. You hear of this move here or that revival there, while watching the sheep running here and there to try to at least come away with a crumb which is better than dry, rotting bread from dead preaching and teaching or stagnant, poison water from corrupted cisterns. However, the Bible is clear that we are to test the spirit and wait to see the type of fruit something produces before running here or there, or jumping on some band wagon.

I was thinking of principles the other day. Principles have always fascinated me. The possible reason for this is because principles are what activates some law, determining the outcome in a situation. For example, if you start out on the wrong foot, you will most likely end up on the wrong footing. The reason for this is because there are laws in operation that call for order to ensure the proper execution of something. If you do not properly follow through, the end results, or fruits, will tell you that you set a matter in motion by your decision and conduct. Now you will either reap the benefits or the consequences of it.

I have to learn that I must consider my attitude and conduct in all matters. With each decision, I am setting some type of law in motion. Even though it might not be obvious up front, the fruit it produces down the line will tell on me.

Prayer: Lord, I have paid the consequences for wrong attitudes, decisions, and conduct in the past. In fact, I activated the law of sin and death, only to realize the vanity of my ways. Forgive me for being foolish in my attitudes and ways. Put leanness in my spirit to always come higher while avoiding chasing after what will be deemed as foolishness in the end. Amen.

September 27

"For the scripture saith unto Pharaoh, Even for this same purpose have I raised thee up, that I might shew my power in thee, and that my name might be declared throughout all the earth" *(Romans 9:17).* I have been thinking about God's providence, His divine guidance upon my life. I realize that I cannot imagine in what ways God has guided my steps, but I know He has because the outcome has been beneficial and glorious.

It often amazes me that I have the tendency to take the reins from Him, thinking I know best when it comes to my life. I cannot begin to tell you of the trouble I have caused for myself because of taking the wrong steps. Instead of my actions proving to be beneficial to anyone including myself, they have proved to be unproductive and sometimes destructive.

I have discovered that the hardest test of faith is to trust, accept, and embrace God's providence. Another name for His providence is "Sovereignty." So many times, I think I know best when in reality, I know nothing. I am limited by the dying flesh, worldly knowledge, selfish attitudes, and indifferent, rude ways.

It is for this reason that I must humble myself and simply say, "Have Your way, oh Lord!"

Prayer: Lord, You have contended with me in so many ways. I praise Your holy name because You not only have the power to enable me to finish the course, You are committed to seeing me through to the end. Amen.

September 28

"And because iniquity shall abound, the love of many shall wax cold" (Matthew 24:12). The Bible tells us in the last days, man's love will grow cold What would make love shrivel and die? Obviously, there was no real life in it in the first place. However, we still must be aware of what will cause our love to cease.

Truth: The truth will set a person free from being swallowed up by that which would cause the heart to become glossed over with indifference. In order to ensure that the truth properly cuts, circumcises, and exposes any hardness of heart or indifference of attitude, we must love it and prefer it over any other reality.

Fear: Perfect love casts out fear, but in the environment where love becomes lifeless, fear will reign with a stifling vengeance. It will swallow up a person into a state of despair.

Unbelief: The next element that causes love to wax cold is unbelief. Unbelief will harden a person's heart against the reality that is present. Instead of truth penetrating the person, it will only hit a hard outer shell of unbelief.

Hopelessness: In a state where love has waxed cold, hopelessness enfolds a person. Such a person cannot see around fear or through unbelief to have any glimmer of hope. All appears lost, and the despair is so enslaving the person cannot look up to see the real source of their hope.

As a believer, I must choose to love truth and follow after righteousness in order to direct my affection towards the Lord. This is the only way to keep my love fresh towards my Lord and Savior.

Prayer: Lord, I do know that my heart must remain committed to You to make sure it remains tender towards You. Help me to keep my vision straight as an arrow towards You. Amen.

September 29

There's just something about fish calmly swimming in an big outdoor aquarium, fish tank, or glass bowl that holds a certain fascination for me. For many years of my young life, way back when nature provided more educational entertainment, pure enjoyment and clean humor than any soulless technology can provide today, my mother always had a big goldfish pond. Thanks to the goldfish, our mountain trips on old two-lane highways would turn into a rock-hunting adventure for just the right shape and size of rocks to take home to place around the edge of the pond, and to build a "bridge" in the water so the fish had a shady place in which to hide.

Beautiful white and pink pond lilies were situated in those wonderful fish ponds, along with other green water plants that fish like. Later, wherever I lived I always had a big glass bowl with a variety of pretty goldfish. It was fun putting things my colorful little friends liked into their small world. Did you know that it's been proven that fish recognize faces? I knew that long ago, because the fish I had would swim to the surface when they saw me, but quickly zip under something in order to hide from strangers.

Eventually the time came when the little guys in the bowl needed to be set free from their small world so they could join the bigger goldfish in the outdoor pool. Goldfish only grow in proportion to the amount of water they live in, so fish in a bowl never outgrow it and neither do they procreate. Before setting them free, we were careful to slowly adjust the temperature of the water in their bowl to the water in the pond so they wouldn't go into shock and die. Then we carefully partially submerged their bowl, tipped it so they could venture out of it into a whole new world. With a great deal of caution, they slowly moved out of their former home, and nervously surveyed their strange, new environment—an environment in which they began to "grow up" in both size and experience.

You know, maybe this can be an illustration of how some in the church are today—they think they are all-knowing "big fish" in a "little pond" (their church) when in reality they are merely little fish in a very big pond (the World). And the "god of this world," Satan, knows his time is short, and his wrath is very great. It's a sad thing to think that sometimes it's easier for a curious little goldfish to "wake up" and discover the "bigger reality" of things than it is to get an unteachable, hard-headed, religious, self-righteous person to wake up to the true state of this present world, and the lateness of the hour!

"The harvest is past, the summer is ended, and we are not saved" (Jeremiah 8:20). "I must work the works of him that sent me, while it is day: the night cometh, when no man can work" (John 9:4). "And knew not until the flood came, and took them all away; so shall also the coming of the Son of man be." (Matthew 24:39).

Are you awake yet to the bigger picture, or are you content to ignorantly remain the same in your little "goldfish bowl world"? – J. Haley

Prayer: Lord, the hour to work in the harvest field is coming to an end because the darkness is encroaching on us. Cause us to realize that we are in the murky pond of the world and that we can point people to the flowing, unending Waters of Your life and salvation. Amen.

September 30

My journals remind me that heaven keep the books on our words and activities. *Matthew 12:36-37* warns us about idle words. Idle words reveal that a person's activities most likely are going to be considered vain in the end. If my activities are simply a matter of worldly busyness, they will end up fading with the rest of the world's glitter.

I have often meditated on the empty pages of our lives. There are many things we can fill our lives with, but how many activities have the power to write upon our hearts concerning the things of eternity that truly possess lasting substance and hope? In our finite state we rarely consider how we are filling the vacuum of our souls.

These souls are vulnerable because they have experienced broken fellowship with God. In such brokenness our souls remain empty, broken, and unable to contain the things of heaven. We do not realize how much we are driven or try to fill our lives with false promises, temporary glory, and vain activities. It is because of the emptiness of such attempts that I have continually discovered one eternal truth, only Christ can fill our longing, empty souls.

We as believers need to quit looking at the world, government, and personal strengths and abilities, and realize if heaven's touch is not upon a matter, that it will be found to be vain in the end.

Prayer: Dear Lord, there is success in Your ways, victory in Your strength, and confidence in Your wisdom. Thank You for being our all in all. Amen.

October

October 1

"But I say unto you, That every idle word that men shall speak, they shall give account thereof in the day of judgment" (Matthew 12:36). The other day I went through my journals and found something very disturbing. I found empty pages. They were stuck together and I had overlooked them. Here I had thought that I had filled all the pages of the journal in order to ensure that none were wasted.

This may sound silly, but I hate to waste anything. I use the back side of sheets of paper that are only printed on one side to write notes, Bible Studies, messages, etc., before putting the final draft on the computer. To me a blank paper represents an opportunity to express thoughts, conclusions, and discoveries. I cannot imagine letting such an opportunity go to waste. In the back of my mind, I conclude that surely, there must be something that can be used to utilize the blank space on the paper.

At the same time, I don't want to be idle in my presentations. There is enough propaganda, rhetoric, and foolish ramblings being purported in the world without me adding to them. However, as a Christian I have much to write about when it comes to my Lord. Every facet of His character, work, and way is eternal. Therefore, how could I let any good piece of paper go to waste when my source and information is inspirational, true, and everlasting?

I rejoice in the fact that I will be discovering truths about Him for ages to come. But, meanwhile, if inspired to do so, it is my goal to silence empty paper with the beautiful declarations of heaven.

Prayer: Lord there is so much we can declare about You. There is so much we have yet to discover about You. I am excited about filling empty sheets of paper with the glorious reality of Who You are and what You have done for me. Amen.

October 2

"For by thy words thou shalt be justified, and by thy words thou shalt be condemned" (Matthew 12:37). Words fill my breath. In a sense they are an intricate part of my life. I think about them, ponder their use, and strive to enlarge my vocabulary.

I want to challenge minds, encourage hearts, and edify souls with them. I want my words to count as being true and trustworthy, inspired by the Spirit and filled with life. I want them to be laced with grace, salted by truth, dipped in the sweetness of heavenly wisdom, and anointed by the oil of heaven.

Jesus brings out the importance of our words. It is clear in this Scripture that words will justify us or they will condemn us. It is not that our words have power to change reality, but that they have power to destroy or edify a person. They can speak the words of truth or weave a deadly web of destruction. In the end, they will reveal the attitude of our heart towards God, life, and others. It is for this reason our words will be held against us, or they will justify what is already known by heaven on that great Day of Judgment.

Regardless of how I have used words in the past, I must consider my present words to determine my life before the Lord. They will tell much about my hidden life in Christ.

Prayer: Lord, I know what my words must be, but I must be willing to listen to see what they are saying about my heart condition. Am I being true or false? Am I being clear or hypocritical? Lord, reveal the ways of my heart to shore up my words. Amen.

October 3

"For there shall arise false Christs, and false prophets, and shall shew great signs and wonders; insomuch that, if it were possible, they shall deceive the very elect" (Matthew 24:24). Jesus' warning for those who are living in the end days that there will be much deception in the world needs to be greatly heeded to by His Church. There will be many who will present another Jesus besides the One who was clearly unveiled as the great mystery of the ages by the Written Word.

These imposters can actually transform themselves in such a way that unsuspecting people can receive them as being genuine. Once people open themselves up to a false leader, the leader can begin to condition them to be indoctrinated into deception. The people who follow these leaders will find themselves falling into the same ditch of error, judgment, and condemnation.

It is vital that we know the real Jesus in order to properly discern a counterfeit Jesus. Jesus has a way, a touch, a particular sound to His voice, and an order in which matters of His kingdom are carried out.

It is for this reason that His followers will only walk in the one true way because they know His touch, hear His voice, and understand His perfect order. I desire to continue learning of Christ so that I will know or recognize His mark upon a matter. By recognizing Him in a situation, I will be able to follow Him in the path of righteousness and into the green pastures of God's will and rest.

Prayer: Lord, You did not leave us in ignorance. Your Word has warned, exhorted, and instructed us according to the way in which we must walk. Thank You for providing the light that will lead me home. Amen.

October 4

"Having a form of godliness, but denying the power thereof: from such turn away" (2 Timothy 3:5). It is important to recognize those who are trying to counterfeit Jesus, especially those who are influential among God's people. Granted, it can prove to be hard to discern such individuals. In many ways they have devised a craft to seduce people into their deceptive reality.

In a sense, these people have fine-tuned an art that enables them to sound like a Christian, give the appearance of a believer, and be an intricate part of the work of the kingdom of God. Such individuals have an outward form of godliness, but when you get beneath the religious cloak, they are void of power.

The power they are void of is the power of the Holy Spirit. They have no identifying mark that they have been born again of the Spirit of God and truly possess an eternal inheritance that identifies them to a spiritual legacy that will be fully realized in glory.

I desire the power that gives credence to my life and testimony. May people see the godliness of Christ in this age as the power of the Spirit that comes down from heaven to convict, change, and anoint for service. Such power will be illuminated by the unchangeable truth of who Jesus is and what He has done for each of us.

Prayer: Lord, people need to see You in my life. I so want to reflect Your disposition and attitude. Forge my character, shape my attitude, and mold my ways to reflect Your glory. Amen.

October 5

"For such are false apostles, deceitful workers, transforming themselves into the apostles of Christ" (2 Corinthians 11:13). When we think about the false leadership in the church, we must realize that some of these heretical individuals will come across as actual apostles of Christ, sent by Him to declare the truth and power of His message.

These counterfeits will even have a light, but it will be a false light because they do not know or possess the real light of the world, the Lord Jesus Christ. Due to the false light these individuals emit, they can be easily received by unsuspecting sheep as being legitimate because the sheep do not know how to properly discern the messenger and the message.

How do you discern false apostles and deceitful workers who come across as the real deal? It comes down to how such people handle Jesus. Those who are the counterfeits of religion possess a counterfeit Jesus. A counterfeit Jesus simply means that the real Jesus has been perverted concerning His nature, adjusted as to His examples, watered-down as to His instructions and message, and minimized as to how important it is to understand and possess Him in relationship to His true glory.

Through the years I have met a lot of imposters. It is the truth of Jesus that causes me to rebuke the imposter when given a chance, and flee his or her presence and influence in my life when there is no response of repentance on his or her part.

Prayer: Lord, You have given us the sword to use against the wolf, the rod to use against the hireling, and the Spirit to expose their wicked agendas. Help me to learn how to use Your arsenal in the fight against all that affront Your truth. Amen.

October 6

One of the things that I've finally learned (I'm a slow learner, by the way) is that dogs, like people, are all different in their likes, dislikes, responses and personalities. While dogs are dogs, and people are people, we cannot force our ideas, ways, opinions and expectations on any of them.

To expect our new fur baby to do the same cute things, or behave like a formerly beloved dog isn't fair, or realistic; and the same applies to people. God created each one of his creatures and people to be unique and special for His glory.

This sometimes requires a great deal of patience, understanding and love on our part to simply appreciate others, whether they be animals or humans, for what they are, and leave it up to the Author and Finisher of our faith to carry out His will in their lives. (See *Hebrews 12:2*.) - J. Haley

Prayer: Lord, in our attempt to fill a vacuum left by some loss, we want to replace it with the same thing we lost, but it is not possible. Our heart is big enough to embrace what is different about others in order to enjoy the surprises that often comes by way of Your unexpected blessings. Amen.

October 7

"Be still and know that I am God; I will be exalted among the heathen, I will be exalted in the earth" (Psalm 46:10). This Scripture has always caught my attention and in a sense brought the awe back into my attitude towards God. Admittedly, I have a tendency to wrestle before the Lord about matters that are disheartening to me. I take a matter to His throne to cast at His feet only to find myself wrestling with wanting to take it back. After

all, I want the situation to turn out a certain way because I think I know best.

Hence, enters the wrestling match within the arena of the soul. I perceive myself as wrestling with God, but the reality is I am wrestling with whether I will give way to His Spirit and entrust Him with working the matter out for His glory or give way to my selfish disposition that has not been properly crucified that day.

I hate to admit that I want my way and I want to see a matter according to my idea instead of trusting in the Lord. I am trying to justify it through the logic of the flesh, knowing underneath that if I do not choose soon to take hold of my Scriptural convictions, I will give in to the temptation that is now looming in front of me.

The Lord often waits for me to finally let go of personal agendas and let Him be God. It is when the wrestling ceases that I can stand still and know that God is God and I can trust Him with the outcome.

Prayer: Lord, I have striven to not be stiff-necked when it comes to my way of thinking and doing. The truth is I must so often be taken down on the mat of misery and failure before I concede to Your perfect ways. Forgive me for trying to maintain my foolish ways. Amen.

October 8

"God is our refuge and strength, a very present help in trouble" *(Psalm 46:1).* Life brings challenges our way, but how we handle such tests reveal the inner working of our person. Once again, such inner working points to character.

I have striven to develop strong character. I desire the inner strength more than I do the outer strength. Inner strength points to the courage or means to stand, while outer strength implies abilities to accomplish certain feats in the physical arena.

However, such strength has its limitations and in time its weaknesses are exposed.

Although strength points to endurance, I would rather see a personal test through to the end, than a physical feat. The reason for this is because the personal test will point to the source of my real strength.

For me, I know God is the source of my strength. He is the One I hide in, the One who serves as my strength and helper in the time of trouble. He is the One who ultimately ensures the integrity of my character and enables me to endure to the end.

Prayer: Lord, I discovered long ago that You are my only real source of strength and hope. I am so thankful You do not move from the foundation of truth and the throne of justice and majesty. Praise Your Holy Name for all that You are and all that You do. Amen.

October 9

As my fingers roamed around the potato sack searching for a few medium-sized ones, the one thing you never want to bump into I bumped into. Oh yuk! A wet, stinky, half rotten potato! As soon as I pulled it out of its hiding place, I saw them—a mass of tiny, wriggling maggots. How disgusting!

I rushed the gross mess outside to the garbage can before dumping the few remaining potatoes in the sink in order to wash and carefully examine them. One of the potatoes seemed to be perfectly normal on the outside, but once I began to peel it, then cut into it, I discovered that it was rotting from the inside out.

"Just like sin," I thought to myself. It begins on the "inside" and then works its way out for all the world to see and smell. No matter how polished, perfumed and "spiffed up" we may appear outwardly, God sees what's going on deep inside of us. A simple truth, to be sure, but one that should keep us daily aware of how the LORD sees us, and what He desires to find in the hidden places of our hearts. *Psalm 51:6* says, *"Behold, thou desirest truth in the inward parts: and in the hidden part thou shalt make me to know wisdom."*

Proverbs 15:11 says, *"Hell and destruction are before the LORD: how much more then the hearts of the children of men?"*

I'm sure that you don't want to be a stinky "rotten potato" in your life before God any more than I do. *"For the wages of sin is death; but the gift of God is eternal life through Jesus Christ our Lord." (Romans 6:23.)* Praise God for His gift! – J. Haley

Prayer: Lord, we hate to work with "rotten potatoes," but they remind me that You took my decaying, stinky life and made me into a new creation. Thank You Lord for not throwing me away. Amen.

October 10

"Therefore, I take pleasure in infirmities, in reproaches, in necessities, in persecutions, in distresses for Christ's sake: for when I am weak, then am I strong" (2 Corinthians 12:10). When I think about my personal strength, I must keep it in perspective. I do this by remembering that everything in this world is backwards. Even though we may perceive ourselves to be strong, in the light of the forces and power of nature, we are the weakest of all creatures.

The reality is we have no strength outside of God. The strength we have will ultimately prove to be our weakness in the end. It will reveal our limitations and downfalls and that we are incompetent to see a matter through to completion. We are not in control of our lives, nor do we have the means to control circumstances that confront our lives.

It is only when I realistically face how weak I am that I have been able to discover just how strong God is. It is in weakness that I will fling myself on His mercy, cry out for help, and wait on Him to show me grace so He can intercede on my behalf out of pity because I am so weak and helpless.

In this pitiful state, I have learned much about God's strength. Weakness always allows Him to be God, the only solution to all challenges and problems.

Prayer: Lord, You are the strength that covers my weakness. In fact, my weakness allows You to show me grace. I am so glad that Your hand covers my weakness to work the strength of Your life in my character and walk. Amen.

October 11

"The mighty God, even the LORD, hath spoken, and called the earth from the rising of the sun unto the going down thereof" *(Psalm 50:1).* We often minimize the power of our eternal God. We allow that which exerts its power on us in this present age to affect our reality. However, we are told that the Lord has spoken things into being, mainly creation. Can you begin to imagine the power that God possesses? To speak creation into being gives us a slight glimpse into God's power.

As believers, we must remember that our Lord is almighty and that all things are under His control. He is the one who calls for the sun to rise in the east and to set in the west. He directs the stars in a symphony, as the moon highlights the artistry of His abilities to produce beauty even in the darkness.

This beauty may be hidden by darkness, but in time the dark curtain will be pulled back to reveal how that which proved priceless was first conceived and formed in darkness. This is also true for every Christian. Our life in Christ is conceived in darkness and formed in obscurity, but once the light is turned on the handiwork of God will be revealed.

Prayer: Lord, so much of my life in You is shrouded by that which remains unseen. However, I know You are doing a deep work and one day the light will come forth to reveal the glory of Your work in my life. All I can say is, "Have Your way." Amen.

October 12

Psalm 39:1 states, *"I said I will take heed to my ways that I sin not with my tongue: I will keep my mouth with a bridle while the wicked is before me."* What does it mean to take heed to my way? I can tell you what it does not mean and that is taking heed of the way of others so we can throw the light away from our questionable ways and put it on others.

The Bible is clear that the flesh is at war with the Spirit of God. This is why the soul becomes a battleground. The reason the soul finds itself in conflict has to do with the ways of righteousness. It is our natural tendency to give way to the flesh. It is our preference to express whatever is in our deceitful heart.

This is why Jesus stated that what comes out of the mouth comes from the heart. I have learned I cannot properly discipline my words until my heart is right before God. Without being under the control of the Holy Spirit my tongue allows disruptive flows of foolishness, vanity, and ridiculousness. As a result, my philosophy is the tongue will give a person away as to his or her character. In fact, it has a way of highlighting a person's attitude, emphasis, and desires.

It is for this reason I must cease looking around to point out the flaws of others and learn to listen to what I am speaking to discern the spirit that is motivating me.

Prayer: Lord, I know the tongue is the most undisciplined member of the body. Lasso it with Your love, bind it to Your grace, and chain it with Your mercy so that what I speak will honor You. Amen.

October 13

Back in the 1940's and 50's most of the television heroes we kids watched rode horses across the wild west, carried guns, and fought the bad guys. I liked them all (especially because of their horses) but the one who captured my heart the most was Zorro played by Guy Williams.

Granted, I knew nothing about Guy Williams, but Zorro and his black horse, Tornado, was always my favorite. I remember when the Zorro series played on black and white TV, the Seattle neighborhood I grew up in suddenly sprouted the painted letter "Z" almost everywhere.

A few years ago, before this Zorro series was archived, I enjoyed watching it again. I had to ask myself why I was always so attracted to Zorro and it came down to the fact that he was always a moral, brave, clean, neat, gracious, respectable gentleman! Of course, that opened the door to comparing the decadent culture we live in nowadays to a time long ago when there were actually a greater percentage of real "Ladies" and real "Gentlemen" with real manners, real respect, real etiquette, real charm, real grace, and real morality.

Now we live in a corrupt and lewd world where ugly fashions, skimpy modes of dress, slovenly appearances, paganism, satanism, occultism, hatred and disrespect for anything clean, moral or decent is mocked and despised, evil is called good, and good is called evil and by even saying the words "Ladies" or "Gentlemen" you might bring down the wrath of the wicked upon your head.

As believers, we may sometimes long for the return of strong, brave, yet gentle, hero "gentlemen," but remember, we do have the Holy Spirit of promise who is ever a Gentleman, never forcing us against our will, but always faithfully pointing us to the One who has all power in heaven and earth, the LORD Jesus Christ, our soon returning LORD and Savior who promised, *"And, behold, I come quickly; and my reward is with me to give every man according as his work shall be" (Revelation 22:12).* – J. Haley

Prayer: Lord, the more I deal in this lewd world, the more I long for You and heaven. The more I taste the purity of Your glory, encounter Your righteous ways, and taste Your goodness, the more I glory in my heavenly citizenship, knowing that Your Spirit gives me glimpses into that which is heavenly even now. Thank You. Amen.

October 14

Enemies of righteousness seem to abound. The cry of the prophet Micah summarizes the battle, *"Rejoice not against me O mine enemy: when I fall, I shall arise; when I sit in darkness, the LORD shall be a light unto me" (Micah 7:8).*

When people allow justice to be perverted with a bribe, they will prove to be enemies of God, His righteousness, and His servants. Clearly this Scripture in Micah is applicable for today when you consider that our greatest enemies are our own despotic leaders who have sold their souls. As a result, they are ready to rob, kill, and destroy anything that would dare oppose them in their wicked agendas.

The Apostle Paul stated that we do not fight against flesh and blood, but against unseen powers of darkness. Sadly, wicked people make themselves available to the kingdom of darkness to gain power. Satan will gladly use them to do his wicked, deceitful bidding.

In *Micah 7:8* the enemies of righteousness are warned not to rejoice over their "so-called" victories over the righteous or during times when the righteous appear defeated because in due time God will raise up His people. Even though great darkness is beginning to enfold us, we have the promise that God will be our light in such times.

As believers, there is nothing to fear but giving in to the lies of fear. We must choose the way of faith, knowing that the life of Christ in us will light our way.

Prayer: Lord, You are the eternal light of heaven. No darkness can prevent Your light from shining into the dark night of the soul. Praise Your holy name. Amen.

October 15

"For he seeth that wise men die, likewise the fool and the brutish person perish, and leave their wealth to others" (Psalm 49:10). I have struggled to understand the purpose for life. In the end all must die to the life that we now know. This means all foolish hopes, silly dreams, worldly ambitions, and accomplishments go into the grave to be forever silenced by the vanity of what was a temporary existence here.

When I consider life according to the end of the existence I now know, all that once seemed important now seems foolish, silly, and useless. With such a conclusion, I could very well adopt the attitude, "What is the use! In the end it will not matter how I live."

As a believer, I know such a conclusion is foolish. I must determine to live life not in light of this world, but in light of the glory that is yet to come. The darkness of vanity and death may rule the present world, but the light of hope and life rules the next. Therefore, let this body waste away with death, but meanwhile, I will live in the promise of an eternal inheritance to make sure that all I do here is not in vain, knowing that the mark of the Holy Spirit and eternity must be upon it.

Prayer: Lord, You have many precious promises that will be realized in the next world. I thank You for that eternal inheritance and look forward to experiencing the fullness of it in the resurrection to come. Amen.

October 16

The Bible forever speaks of the vanity of this present world. Its glory is fading, its treasures temporary, its promises fleeting, and its end that of death. This brings us to the shortsightedness of those who put their hope in this present world.

Psalm 49:11 reminds us of a sad truth that, *"Their inward thought is that their houses shall continue for ever, and their dwelling places to all generations; they call their lands after their own names."* People who put their hope in the present age value the temporary riches of the world. They strive for mansions that speak of illusive successes and happiness. They seek to make a legacy that will be passed down to following generations as a memorial to their so-called "greatness" They perceive that if their name is on some institution, street, or building that those who follow will take note that they once existed. The truth is, these people may leave some small token of history behind, but eventually the winds of time and the storms of life will wipe out all knowledge of them.

It is for this reason that I choose to be part of the eternal legacy established by the redemption of Christ. Granted, this legacy may be hidden from this world, but I know with confidence that I will enjoy the inheritance that comes in the world to come.

Prayer: Lord, the pride in us wants a personal legacy that will be admired by those who follow us. However, the life of Christ in me reminds me that I am to leave a witness of You. In fact, my life will be consumed by a cloud of witnesses that will only speak of that which is lovely and eternal. So be it. Amen.

October 17

It is people's tendency to think that since God is love, He is tolerant towards sin, easy on compromise with the world, and understanding about moral deviation. After all, He wants us to be "happy" because He is "so fond of us." However, *Psalm 50:3* tells us, *"Our God shall not keep silent when it comes to offenses against Him: a fire shall devour before him, and it shall be very tempestuous round about him"*

Any casual presentation of God is close to being blasphemous. It is not only wrong, but it shows utter contempt towards the holy character of God and the unchangeable truth of His righteous ways. God never moves from who He is to come into agreement with our perverted, limited understanding of Him. He will not wink at the sin of ignorance towards Him; rather, he calls people to repent. In fact, He is long-suffering towards people in sin to give them ample time to repent before they perish in their sin.

God hates sin and does not love the wicked in spite of the psycho-babble nonsense that has been adopted by a lukewarm, worldly-minded church. God is who He is. In His holiness, He is a consuming fire that will consume in judgment all that is contrary to His nature and Word.

Prayer: Lord, I hate this psycho-babble that throws all common sense out the door in order to adopt a nonsensical attitude towards You. Thank You for Your truth that penetrates and divides the ridiculous presentations of this world in order to shake the shifting sands of deception to wake people up as to the faulty foundation they are building on when they come into agreement with such foolishness. Amen.

October 18

"And the heavens shall declare his righteousness: for God is judge himself. Selah" (Psalm 50:6). This Scripture reminds me that in the end we will all face a type of judgment. All matters must be weighed in some type of balance. The reason for this procedure is because God is just.

In His exertion of justice, His righteousness will be declared and upheld. There will be no debate as to why one receives the type of judgment he or she is allotted. The sentence of the Law, that of death, will be carried out for those who rejected God's provision of salvation, and according to *1 Corinthians 3:12-15* fire will be put to the works of believers to determine the quality of their spirit, attitude, and conduct.

For some believers, their works will be burned up, but they will be saved. Sadly, they will hang their head in shame as the dust of their works lies at their feet, for they will have nothing of substance to offer to their King, their Lord, their God. For others, their works will come forth as valuable gems that will reflect the glory of heaven.

I, for one, want my works to reflect the glory of God. Therefore, I give God permission to put the fire to my character and faith. May my life take on His life and glory!

Prayer: Lord, You have heard my heart cry. I want to offer You those gems that reflect Your fire, Your light, Your life, and Your glory. In order to have the passion of fire, fire must be put to my faith. In order to reflect Your light, I must walk in it. For Your glory to come forth, You must be unveiled in my life. Thank You Lord, for You will answer my prayers. Amen.

October 19

"Ohhhh! Look at the little yellow flower!" I exclaimed in surprise as I bent over to gain a closer view of the tiny blossom next to my shoe. Granted, fall-blooming weeds, golden ferns, wild grasses and all sorts of plant life are spread out for many acres on both sides of the winding old dirt country road we walk our dog on, but never had I seen another little flower there just like that yellow one.

Granted, it was very small and seemingly insignificant, but it's upturned "face" seemed to be smiling up at me as if to say, "God sees you too," and in that moment, I felt as if God's smile was coming down on me from above. This may all seem silly to you, but it touched my heart because just this morning I chose to wear the one solid yellow top I have because it might help me feel "sunny" on this cloudy day. And the LORD knows I needed a "happy" color after the recent final rejection, false accusation, and betrayal from someone dear to my heart.

I love the intimate and little personal ways the LORD reminds us that He sees it all, He knows it all, He understands it all, and that He is the Judge of all. *"For his eyes are upon the ways of man, and he seeth all his goings" (Job 34:21). "For the eyes of the Lord are over the righteous, and his ears are open unto their prayers: but the face of the Lord is against them that do evil"* (1 Peter 3:12). Hallelujah! – J. Haley

Prayer: Lord, those of the world will scorn, hate, and reject us no matter what kind of relationship we have had with them, but You never reject us; rather, You will lift us up. Thank You for being that perfect parent, family member, and friend. Amen.

October 20

"For the time is come that judgment must begin at the house of God: and if it first begin at us, what shall the end be of them that obey not the gospel of God?" (1 Peter 4:17). It is easy to take Christianity for granted. We can make it into a religion, box God in with our notions or ideas about Him, or wrap our understanding about Him into a nice neat package called "theology."

We can become casual about what Christ did for us as we lose a sense of who He is. We can forget that all He has done was/is a matter of grace. After all, it was in His very character, calling, and mission to redeem us from the tyranny of sin, and it had nothing to do with any value or worth in us. The truth is there is nothing redeemable in us.

It is because of our life in Christ and His life in us that we are saved. However, it is because of our position and relationship with the Lord, that judgment will begin in His house. We are the ones who stand first before His throne; therefore, we will be the first who must stand in light of His righteous judgment.

Since we are in Christ, our lives are deemed righteous, but our place or position in the kingdom of God will be determined by the quality of our works. Granted, all works that are refined in the fires will be laid at the feet of Jesus because they came from Him, but the works that find their origin in the flesh and the world will be consumed by the fire. Whether we possess ashes or priceless gems will determine what we did with those treasures that Jesus entrusted to us.

As a believer, I do all I can to prepare my life to stand before the Lord. I want to be able to offer something back that will speak of His abiding life and commitment towards me and my love and commitment towards Him.

Prayer: Lord, I know that judgment will begin with Your people. I want to be prepared to stand without shame before You, withstand with that which has been made precious by You in my life, and to continue to stand because there is no reproach to be found in my testimony of You. Praise Your Name for providing me with Your precious life and Spirit. Amen.

October 21

"And he said unto them, Take heed, and beware of covetousness: for a man's life consisteth not in the abundance of the things which he possesseth" (Luke 12:15). A. W. Tozer made this profound statement, "Of all the calamities that have visited upon the world and its inhabitants, the willing surrender of the human spirit to materialistic values is the worst!" There is nothing that will bring out our base, wretched self more than coveting the material things of this age. How many people have sold their souls to possess the useless vanity associated with this temporary world? Granted, the world equates happiness with possessing things, but it is a lie.

Everything about this world points to fading glory, decaying morals, rusty values, and useless junk. When you consider the tons of debris from the Japanese earthquake and tsunami floating on the ocean landing on our shores, the foolishness of materialism becomes quite defined. We cannot hold onto anything of this present world, for it will all be washed away by some force.

Those who pursue after the gods of materialism are miserable. After all, they serve an indifferent idol in a tyrannical environment that is void of hope, life, and purpose. As Christians, we must keep such vain pursuits in perspective. As the Scripture states in *Luke 12:15*, our lives do not consist of the things that we possess.

Prayer: Lord, in our attempt to survive in this world, we often find ourselves becoming a victim of it. Please help me to separate the vain activities from that which would ensure my future with You. Help me to discern foolishness from necessity, and the good from the bad, the better from the best, and the excellent from that which has a false or temporary glory. Amen.

October 22

"For I know this, that after my departing shall grievous wolves enter in among you, not sparing the flock. Also of your own selves shall men arise, speaking perverse things to draw away disciples after them" (Acts 20:29). Through the years I have noticed an important pattern occurring in God's Church. Jesus will always call His people to follow Him, and when He turns His back to lead His sheep, the wolves will come in to attack, devouring and taking away vulnerable sheep.

It is hard for God's people to realize that when it is time for them to follow Jesus, they are the most vulnerable. If they linger behind or stop to graze on bits of worldly "grass," they will find themselves falling prey to wolves.

Jesus is clear that all disciples must first deny themselves of the luxury to linger a bit longer, crucify the tendency to graze on that which has no substance or purpose, and become serious in following Him up the path of righteousness, in spite of the loss of this present world.

In my years of ministry, I had to learn the hard way about heeding the voice of Jesus. After all, the voice of a wolf may be perverse, but it can be enticing and destructive. To keep my spiritual edge, I must remain within hearing distance of my Lord.

Prayer: Lord, You have given us the staff of Your Spirit and the rod of Your Word to deal with the wolves, but we must be following You to avoid becoming their victims. Enable us to stand in Your Spirit and take our sword to the wolves in order to expose and run them off. Amen.

October 23

"But thou, O God, shalt bring them down into the pit of destruction: bloody and deceitful men shall not live out half their days, but I will trust in thee" (Psalm 55:23). Our days are numbered. Only the Lord knows the length of our lives. However, I remember what George Whitefield said about the lives of the saints, that they are immortal until their work is done for the kingdom of God.

Even though my days are numbered, I know as long as I serve the Lord, my life will be complete, my mission fulfilled, and my calling satisfied. I also know that regardless of how much hell flexes its muscles against me, I am immortal.

However, this is not true for the wicked. According to the Scripture, their days will be cut in half. They will never see the fruition of anything in their lives. The most they can hope for is that a few loved ones might feel sad about their departure, but at worst their very name will be spit out by others like a byword who knew the bitterness of their wicked ways.

In most cases, such people are quickly forgotten. The impression they leave behind is not worth considering or it causes such distress that it is buried as deep as it can be in the recesses of people's minds to be remembered no more.

Prayer: Lord, Your justice will win out. The wicked will not live to declare any substantial victory. They will be cut off to be remembered no more. Lord, I am thankful that I am on Your side.

It places me on the side of eternity that guarantees me of my eternal inheritance. Praise Your Holy Name. Amen.

October 24

There's just no doubt in my mind that God made animals to have a way of teaching us humans a lot of things. Take our new fur baby for example. The other day he demonstrated how to truly enjoy yourself this time of the year by running and jumping through mounds of gold and orange leaves that lay at the base of one of the trees. There was no way we could watch him without laughing at his big grin and silly antics.

Watching such sheer joy and listening to the rustle of the leaves took me back to a special fall day when I was a very young child, gleefully kicking my way through mountains of colorful leaves that lay along a tree-lined street in Seattle. The question is, what makes us happy?

People nowadays often mention their "happy place," but just what is a "happy place"? I suppose the answer to that depends on the individual as to what constitutes the perfect "happy place," but in the long run, anything short of the presence of the Lord Jesus Christ will only give temporary satisfaction at best because the world cannot truly offer real happiness that lasts for eternity. One thing our dog has shown us about "happy places" is that, as long as his "pack" is around, he's happy wherever he is, and in whatever he's doing.

The Bible doesn't tell us to go search for our "happy place," but instead to be joyful and rejoice in the Lord always. If Jesus is your Lord, then He is your "happy place." *Philippians 4:4* says, "*Rejoice in the Lord always: and again I say, Rejoice.*"

In *Psalm 16:11* we read "Who" and "where": "*Thou will shew me the path of life: In thy presence is fulness of joy; at thy right hand there are pleasures for evermore.*"

Jeremiah 15:16 tells us this about joy: *"Thy words were found, and I did eat them; and thy word was unto me the joy and rejoicing of mine heart: for I am called by thy name, O LORD God of hosts."* – J. Haley

Prayer: Lord, people are looking for some "happy place" in the wrong place. You are our only "happy place." Since You are the way, there is no other avenue to find this place. As the truth, there is no liberating place that denotes happiness outside of You, and since You are the life, there is no happy place without true life to enjoy and experience it. Thank You for being my "happy place." Amen.

October 25

"But unto the wicked God saith, What hast thou to do to declare my statutes, or that thou shouldest take my covenant in thy mouth? Seeing thou hatest instruction, and castest my words behind thee" (Psalm 50:16-17). When we think of the wicked, we sometimes think of the worst individual we have encountered. However, the wicked can prove to come in various forms, from those who wear religious cloaks to the ones who wear a veneer of decency.

To summarize in one word, the fruit of a wicked person is quite simple. He or she is an utter "fool." These individuals can use the right terminology, but they hate instruction that would expose their heart attitude towards life and God. They can come across as declaring the ways of God, but behind closed doors they cast such ways aside in disdain and mockery revealing the utter hypocrisy of their religious pose.

The true test of character is how a person handles the Word of God. If God's Word is honored, adhered to, and obeyed, such an individual will be counted as righteous, but the person who casts aside His words must be considered wicked. For me, I not only want to honor God's words, but tremble before them.

Prayer: Lord, it is easy to discern the imposter. It all comes down to how Your Word is handled. Lord, give me the discernment to see around the cloaks and through the veneers so that I can righteously judge the spirit of a person to discern if I have any spiritual agreement with them. Amen.

October 26

"A man that is an heretick after the first and second admonition reject; Knowing that he that is such is subverted, and sinneth, being condemned of himself" (Titus 3:10-11). In the end days, the number of heretics running around with their own form of poisonous doctrines and theologies will be great. Their vision is self-serving. They are looking for an audience that will adore them and support their heretical advancements.

The Bible is clear that you must admonish or warn a heretic twice, but if he or she does not repent, there must be a complete separation between the truth and heresy, light and darkness. This can be hard for some individuals because being wrong is not an option, admitting they were duped by one who has gone apostate, and having their present foundation destroyed would be unbearable. Where would they start from and who could they trust because even Scriptures have been perverted. Yet, we are told the truth can set us free even from such wicked entanglements and indoctrination, but we must choose to love it and look to the One who is the essence of all truth, Jesus Christ.

In this Scripture, we are told what heretics do with the truth. They subvert it. In other words, they want to overturn it or reverse its intent or judgments. In a way, they are trying to start their own revolution as to what people should believe. We are told such a person is sinning and if he or she continues to insist on his or her reality, that such an individual already stands condemned.

It is a serious offense towards God to subvert His truth. Such an individual can only stand condemned because truth will never cease to be the eternal standard of heaven.

Prayer: Lord, Your truth is eternal. We have nothing to worry about as long as we stand on it, withstand with it, and continue to stand in it. Thank You Lord for Your eternal truth that never changes with the times, seasons, and fads. Amen.

October 27

"As also in all his epistles, speaking in them of these things; in which are some things hard to be understood, which they that are unlearned and unstable wrest, as they do also the other scriptures, unto their own destruction" (2 Peter 3:16). There are so many wannabe leaders in the kingdom of God. Whether they desire the notoriety, the money, or the title, they prove to be imposters because they have no heart towards the sheep. These individuals have their own agenda and their own way of doing. They may even have zeal, but they are ignorant of God.

In this Scripture in Peter, we are told that these ignorant people will take Scriptures that are hard to understand and wrest them to their own destruction. In fact, they will use them to build their own cultist platform to lead many people down the dark path of delusion and destruction.

This brings us to the simple reality that those who wrest Scripture are unstable. They are unstable because they do not know God. They are, in essence, barren in their knowledge of Jesus Christ.

Jesus is the way to establishing stability for He is the foundation of our spiritual lives. He is the truth that stands as a true cornerstone to all that we must line up to in instruction, example, and conduct. He is the anchor in life that keeps us steady in the waters of the world. It is for this reason my desire has always been to seek out and know Jesus Christ.

Prayer: Lord, You are everything I have need of to be saved and to grow up in You. Help me to remember my spiritual journey is about discovering and possessing more and more of You. Amen.

October 28

Today people contend with a lot of problems. They have bad hips, stiff knees, aching joints, troublesome backs and so forth. These are physical problems, but we have like problems in the spiritual realm. We can have dull hearing when it comes to truth, eye problems when it comes to Satan's traps, as well as knee and shoulder challenges when it comes to true worship, that will affect our life in Christ. However, *Deuteronomy 10:16* summarizes the source and the solution to such problems, *"Circumcise therefore the foreskin of your heart, and be no more stiffnecked."*

In considering my personal take on matters, I realize that the truth is I cannot be sure of what is going on in my world until I take the time to honestly exercise my "neck muscles," as well as examine the attitude of my heart. So many times, my neck is so stiff towards maintaining my particular take on reality that I often miss that which has the potential of destroying me.

It is for this reason that the Lord condemned those who proved to be stiff-necked because they have not allowed that which is destructive to the soul to be circumcised by His sharp sword of His Word. Such individuals are unreceptive towards His instructions and warnings even though it is obvious there is something wrong with their hearing, eyes, and worship.

To be able to exercise my "neck muscles" correctly, I must get rid of the obstinate arrogance of demanding my own way by ignoring unpleasant reality. This is the only way I can avoid being slammed by the waves of destruction and judgment that are upon me. It is only by allowing my heart to be circumcised daily and being shut in the Ark of God's truth, Jesus Christ, that I can be ready to face the tidal waves that are rushing toward the shores of my life and to avoid being spiritually blindsided and destroyed by them.

Prayer: Lord, my neck will either be broken by judgment or bowed in an attitude of worship towards You. I choose to bow my neck under the circumcision of Your Spirit and Word. Make my heart tender before You so that my neck will naturally bow in awe and worship of You. Amen.

October 29

The two hardest challenges for man to admit to is 1) there is nothing salvageable in his old man or the old way, and 2) that in spite of how much a person may consider a matter according to personal understanding, it leads to death and destruction. Although *Proverbs 14:12* states the truth, *"There is a way which seemeth right unto a man, but the end thereof are the ways of death,"* even the religious man has a hard time accepting such an evaluation.

In our society we are promoting an amoral philosophy of "Political Correctness" and "Tolerance" towards that which is morally deviant. It is clear that people perceive according to their own take on life what will be right in their own eyes, regardless of the destruction left in its wake. In such an amoral reality, the decisive lines between good and evil are done away with as people conclude there is no sure truth, moral boundaries, or consequences to be paid for moral indiscretion. For a person to advocate that there is a clear standard of righteousness and goodness in such a wicked environment, such a stand will most likely guarantee that he or she will be labeled as being evil and unloving.

Such a philosophy allows deluded individuals to believe that the ends will justify whatever means they need to take to bring about their particular take on a situation. This means that they can lie, cheat, murder, and sacrifice anyone who gets in their way. Clearly, it is not a matter of what is right in these peoples' minds; rather, it comes down to the humanistic philosophy that in the end the fittest will ultimately survive. In their arrogant delusion, these deluded souls assume that they will naturally survive. However, my Bible states differently. Such humanistic ways will lead to death and destruction, and in the end, it will be the meek who will actually inherit the earth *(Proverbs 16:25; Matthew 5:5).*

Prayer: Lord, we live in precarious times, but You are still in control. One day Your holy standard will be lifted up, silencing all of the reprobate fools who have refused to acknowledge You as the true God of heaven. It will be the meek who will inherit all of Your glorious promises. Amen.

October 30

"Whoso offered praise glorifieth me: and to him that ordereth his conversation aright will I shew the salvation of God (Psalm 50:23). The big question is, "What must I do to be saved?" this is indeed the most important question that must be answered before the door of eternity is unlocked by the key of physical death. However, the next important question is, "How can I know for sure that I am saved?"

The Bible is clear that there are works that accompany salvation. We may not be saved by good works, but we are saved unto good works. They will be a natural extension of the life of Christ in us. After all, if we love Jesus, we will obey Him.

in *Psalm 50:23* we are given insight into one such work that will manifest salvation and that is our conversation (walk) will be disciplined and ordered according to righteousness. Uprightness in our standing, attitude, and walk will confirm that salvation is present.

The other manifestation of salvation is praise. If one is saved, he or she cannot help but to offer the sweet sacrifice of praise. For me, when I finally sensed my great depravity in light of God's incredible holiness, I was broken. I got a glimpse of how great the gap that my precious Lord and Savior had to close with His sacrifice, and out of utter brokenness, praise was sent forth on the wings of gratitude. "Praise" offered from a sincere heart of gratitude will glorify the Lord.

To avoid being a bona-fide hypocrite, I so want to ensure that my lips of praise are upheld by a life that truly glorifies the Lord.

Prayer: Lord, You deserve to be glorified. If I fail to glorify You by my life, I will know that I am falling short of the mark of excellence You have set for me. Help me to not settle for the decaying crumbs left behind in my life. Amen.

October 31

I was about 16, and it was a dark, Halloween night. Since it was a late hour most of the younger neighborhood "trick or treaters" were off the streets and home overindulging on sugary treats. My mother had turned off all the lights in the house, and we decided to sit for a while in the darkened living room when it happened.

Seemingly out of nowhere two teenage boys dressed in all black and clutching bars of soap ran towards our big picture window with the worst of intentions, but before they were able to make a single mark, I jumped up and stepped towards the window. Suddenly the closest figure let out a scream as his soap went flying into the air over his shoulder, and took off running after his terrified partner who was beating a hasty retreat down the sidewalk.

My mother and I were amazed at what happened, but then, after looking at my appearance, she began to laugh. "You scared them off," she said, still laughing. "Your shiny white bathrobe, and all that white stuff on your face, and curlers in your hair scared them off! They thought you were a ghost!"

The simplicity of it makes me think of all the times God's people were in a terrible fix with enemies all around, such as in the story of Gideon when God, instead of providing swords and shields to the small band of 300 unarmed men, used trumpets, and empty pitchers with a lamp within each one. *"And they stood every man in his place round about the camp: and all the host ran, and cried, and fled" (Judges 7:21).*

It's good to know that our God is a God of battles in these perilous times, and He will fight for us if we put our trust in Him, and in His marvelous ways. *"The Lord shall fight for you, and ye shall hold your peace" (Exodus 14:14). "Who is like unto thee, O LORD, among the gods? who is like thee, glorious in holiness, fearful in praises, doing wonders?" (Exodus 15:11).* – J. Haley

Prayer: Lord there are a lot of frightening things in this world, but I know the greatest dread would be meeting You outside of Christ and His redemption. I am so thankful You reached out to me in love so I would not have to tremble before You as the ultimate Judge of all. Amen.

November

November 1

"Have mercy upon me, O God, according to thy lovingkindness; according unto the multitudes of thy tender mercies blot out my transgression" (Psalm 51:1). Occasionally, I have pondered God's mercy. I have assumed much about this virtue. I always thought it was available for the sinner. However, this is not true. A sinner who loves sin does not seek mercy. He or she sees no need for it. Therefore, who seeks mercy?

The humble seek mercy. They recognize they have need for it. They know their plight and will seek the Lord to intervene on their behalf.

The broken in spirit will seek mercy. They realize they must be made whole and restored if they are to continue in their lives. After all, they have no spirit in them to seek anything that can revive the inner man from the pit of despair and hopelessness.

The righteous will seek mercy. These individuals understand that without God, there is no hope. They need God every day. They know that they must continually seek mercy before they can obtain God's grace or favor in a matter.

I know I have need of God's mercy. I am poor and needy when it comes to life. Without His intervention, I am a sitting duck ready to be struck down on the rotating, grinding belt of the world.

Prayer: Lord, thank You for Your mercy. I know out of love, it is a type of hand You have extend to each of us to help us to wade through the endless maze of our flesh, the cesspool of our selfishness, the foolishness of the world, and the traps of Satan. It is what clothes us with assurance of overcoming because of what You have done on our behalf. Thank You for providing it, blotting out my sins, enabling me in my weakness, and helping me overcome in my despair. Amen.

November 2

"But the mercy of the LORD is from everlasting to everlasting upon them that fear him, and his righteousness unto children's children" (Psalm 103:17). It is easy to assume much about the matters of heaven. I have bumped along in my spiritual journey. As I hit one obstacle, I am moved from the path, only to hit another hindrance. At times I feel that life can be compared to being in one of those bumper cars. It seems that the ways of the world around me constantly take aim at me to see how hard they can hit me to move me from my spiritual destination.

I realize that I have often felt jerked around, but I have always known that anytime life has affronted me, God has shown me mercy. There are times that He has even shown compassion to me by entering into my plight to encourage me and direct me around the maze of immovable walls and out of the endless dead-ends.

It is for this reason that I am glad that the Lord's mercies are not only from everlasting to everlasting, but they are new every day. After all, the mercies from yesterday will never be able to address the present challenges. Therefore, it is clear that the Lord's mercies continually flow from His throne to forever meet the challenges of the present.

Prayer: Lord, I have a tendency to take Your mercies for granted. Thank You for allowing them to flow from Your throne room, making them available to meet me when I come back to You in great need, repentance, humility, and brokenness. Amen.

November 3

"Cast thy burdens upon the LORD, and he shall sustain thee: he shall never suffer the righteous to be moved" (Psalm 55:22). It is easy to collect burdens as you walk through this world. It is quite natural to acquire burdens throughout the daily demands of life, but it is also inevitable that people, responsibilities, and challenges will put burdens on you as well. The truth of the matter is, we humans have not been formed to bear such burdens, and as a result we find ourselves oppressed by them.

The other challenge we have when it comes to burdens is that we feel obliged to bear them until they are resolved in some way. We feel a certain loyalty to bear them as a badge of courage to show our love, character and our resolution to be responsible and honorable to see a matter through to the end.

The Bible tells us to cast our burdens on the Lord and He will sustain us. The truth is burdens bury us. In time our emotions become raw because of them, our resolve weary, and our mind becomes confused. Even though burdens bury us, our soul becomes like a hopeless leaf ready to be blown into the ocean of complete despair.

I realized a long time ago that in order to survive the "waves" created by the world's "oceans", that by faith I must cast my burdens on the Lord, knowing that the righteous will never be moved from the Rock of glory.

Prayer: Lord, we have so many winds and waves that affront us in this world. Please establish me firmly on You. I know that I will never be completely driven to destruction by the elements of this present age. Amen.

November 4

"Cast me not away from thy presence; and take not thy holy Spirit from me" (Psalm 51:11) It is easy for Christians to assume that their association with God will suffice any discrepancy in their attitude and conduct. Because of the assumption, some have even made presumptions. The presumption is that what they have in God can never be lost. Sadly, such presumption can cause these individuals to put God to a foolish test.

King David was a man after God's heart. He had great revelations concerning God's faithfulness and abiding care on his life. However, there was a time when the king flung all spiritual realities to the wind. He transgressed the Law, and in so doing, showed utter contempt for the Lord's Word.

When the sharp sword of conviction penetrated David's conscience and heart, it stripped away the cloak that hid his sin. At that time, it dawned on him as to the seriousness of his actions. He realized that he could lose everything he had in the Lord. God would be justified if He cast him away from His presence, as well as take the presence of His Spirit away from him. After all, holiness cannot remain where the profane exists.

I personally do not want to take my life in Christ for granted. God can only entrust and assure His people with His presence when His righteousness is present.

Prayer: Lord, I know how deluded I can become when the lies of sin begin to take my mind captive. Keep my mind clear and my ways pure before You. I so want to have a right environment in which Your presence can freely reside. Amen.

November 5

"Hide thy face from my sins, and blot out all mine iniquities" (Psalm 51:9). I once heard a wolf in the pulpit claim that God did not hide His face from sin. In a sense, this heretic implied that God was not all that concerned about sin. Since God is love, He would not turn His face away from sin.

The difference between King David and the imposter is that King David knew God. He knew His holy character, understood His attitude towards sin, and was aware that God would not tolerate sin in His presence. In fact, for God to look on sin would require Him to judge it in order to put it far from His holy presence.

The king asked the Lord to hide His face from his sins. He then went on to request that He blot out all of His iniquities. As believers, we understand that God addressed our sins at the cross. He did not just cover sins to hide them from His eyes, but He actually took them away.

However, man must also address sin by bringing it to the cross of Christ where he can lay it down at the foot of this altar. There the Lord Jesus Christ can blot them out forever with His blood.

I, for one, am glad that the altar of God once and for all addressed my past sin through justification, continues to address my present sin through forgiveness, and will meet my future sin through the ongoing provision of His mercy and grace, allotted to us through His Son, Jesus Christ.

Prayer: Lord, we have been given so much through You. However, we cannot take such things for granted and put You to a foolish test. Help me to keep You in a right perspective. Amen.

November 6

If you love dogs, then you know how quickly you can make an acquaintance with a perfect stranger who also loves dogs. This can take place anywhere—on the street, in a parking lot, a walking trail, park, or in any other setting. Suddenly you find yourself engaged in an open, heartfelt communication that overflows with understanding, empathy, humor, and good will that few can barely find in the average family gathering these days.

Dogs do so much for us (volumes could, and have been, written on that) and there is no doubt in my mind that God knew we needed such faithful, loving companions on this earth. Dogs don't care what we look like, have no political preference, are thankful, forgiving, and want to always be with us even when they think we're being stupid (and you can tell by the look on their face sometimes that they do think that.)

Just turn the word "dog" around and you have "God." We know that God wants us to love one another with the same openness, transparency, genuine compassion, caring and understanding that our dogs give us, and we, hopefully, give our dogs. Therefore, with the LORD as our "common ground" shouldn't we all have agreement in the Spirit? One might think so, but sadly, this is not always the case. Perhaps the key word to think about is "trust."

Like our canine friends, we normally feel free to open up to people we believe we can trust; but how much more should we trust God, (who sent His only begotten Son to die for our sins) with our very lives and innermost thoughts? *Proverbs 3:5, 6* tells us who to trust: *"Trust in the LORD with all thine heart; and lean not unto thine own understanding. In all thy ways acknowledge him, and he shall direct thy paths."*

We can trust Him, for as *1 Peter 5:7* says *"Casting all your care upon him; for he careth for you."* – J. Haley

Prayer: Lord, as Christians we hear all the wonderful promises about Your great care, but do we choose to believe them in order to trust You with our lives and circumstances. Lord, I choose to believe, knowing that I can trust You with everything. Amen.

November 7

"Then will I teach transgressors thy ways; and sinners shall be converted unto them" (Psalm 51:13). In a world of political correctness and the woke insanity, the greatest affront to this quasi-state of nonsense is truth itself. Truth cuts through the rhetoric of such foolishness, strips away its false light of deception, and exposes it for the fallacy it really is. The key is to be able to teach transgressors the ways of God in order to bring contrast by upholding them in purity, while the sinner will have the opportunity to hear the truth, be saved and converted to the Lord.

As a believer, it is my responsibility to bring such a contrast to people in my teaching and preaching. I want them to be converted to the Lord. This means they will be converted to His ways of righteousness.

When King David wrote this part of the song, it was in relationship to his great sins of adultery and murder. The Law called for his very life to be taken. The only case he could pose to the Lord was if he was forgiven and spared, that he would indeed learn his lesson, giving him the opportunity, in turn, to teach others about God's righteous, perfect ways. This would allow repentant sinners to be converted to what is right before the Lord.

I have become aware that there is no real reason to keep me around unless I am doing God's bidding. I must be quick to give away or share His truths with others. This is the only way my life will make any sense in this insane world with its onslaught of absurd philosophies of fools.

Prayer: Lord, I want my life to make sense and it will not if my ways and actions do not count for Your kingdom in some way. Guide my steps down the path that will ensure the quality of my walk and the integrity of my relationship with You. Amen.

November 8

"Behold, thou desirest truth in the inward parts: in the hidden part thou shalt make me to know wisdom" (Psalm 51:6). When the Bible talks about truth in the inward parts, it is making reference to integrity. Integrity is character that will uphold the inner person. It is the abiding wisdom that is established by right choices that will enable one to stand on godly conviction, withstand with truth, and continue to stand because not to would be a betrayal of a person's commitment to God, righteous convictions, and inner man.

One of my goals is to always maintain my spiritual edge with the sharp sword of truth. I not only desire its sharpness in my life to keep me spiritually awake in the darkness, but I have made a commitment to cling to it as my only means of sanity.

We are told that when truth is in the hidden parts of our being, it will actually ensure a right attitude towards God and His Word. It will also ensure how we approach and receive instruction, reproof, and correction concerning the matters of heaven.

I desire the truth of heaven more than any of man's inept knowledge, the world's base philosophies, and the foolish, ecstasy produced by the crude self of the old man and the different temporary stimulus the world provides.

Prayer: Lord, lies abound in this world through the foolish, vain imaginations and conclusions of man. Save me from the onslaught of the ridiculous, caused by the insipid delusion of darkness. Keep me free from the seductive voice of heresy and false promises. Amen.

November 9

"And with all deceivableness of unrighteousness in them that perish, because they received not the love of the truth, that they might be saved" (2 Thessalonians 2:10). How does unrighteousness express itself? First of all, those who walk in unrighteousness operate in deception. These people's view on life is contrary to what God deems as righteousness. In a sense, they are blinded by the false light of wickedness that they are walking according to.

The harsh reality is that they are perishing in their present reality of sin and death. They are walking towards the abyss without any awareness of the destruction that lies before them.

This verse tells us that these people fail to receive an inclination to love the truth. It takes the Spirit of God to put within our hearts a desire to love the truth. In fact, love is shed abroad in our hearts by the Spirit. He always leads us to the essence of truth. And, who is the truth? Jesus Christ. To love the truth means to love the Jesus of the Bible.

I have learned that the more I love the Word, (read, study, meditate on it), the more I love the Living Word and Expression of God, Jesus Christ. Such love is also inclined to be attracted to the complete truth about Him.

Prayer: Lord, give me a love for Your truth. Cause anything that is not of Your truth to become repulsive in my mouth, ineffective to my mind, and unacceptable to my spirit. Amen.

November 10

"And for this cause God shall send them strong delusion, that they should believe a lie" (2 Thessalonians 2:11). One of the warnings that brings sobriety to me is this scripture found in *2 Thessalonians*. We are warned that if we do not receive a love for the truth, God will send us a strong delusion.

It is important to recognize that delusion is simply the means by which God will test people's hearts. I realize that for God to send a delusion it will probably be very religious, have the necessary terminology, and possesses a veneer of what appears to be Christian, but it will be void of the right Spirit and missing the truth.

Those who have no inclination towards the truth will choose to believe the lie. Sadly, they will be turned over to it, giving way for their mind to become reprobate. Such a mind in the end will not retain any real knowledge of the true God.

It is a fearful reality to think that God will turn people over to their preferred reality, even if it is a delusion that will test their love for the truth, while it will also become their judgment. It is for this reason that I desire to tremble before the Word as I establish a real preference towards the truth.

Prayer: Lord, give me a love for the truth by giving me love for who You are. In such a state, it will not be so easy to walk away from what is true and fall into a cesspool of indifference. Keep my love sharp towards You so I can rightfully discern where I am in You. Amen.

November 11

"That they all might be damned who believed not the truth, but had pleasure in unrighteousness" (2 Thessalonians 2:12). As I study

each verse in *1 Thessalonians 2:10-12*, the Lord is leveling an indictment against those who prefer a lie to the truth. In the end, there will be no debate as to why they find themselves damned.

In *2 Thessalonians 2:12*, we gain insight into why these people prefer a lie. They take pleasure in unrighteousness. Clearly these people are marked among those who prefer darkness because their works are wicked.

I realized long ago that my flesh prefers the pleasures of unrighteousness, but my status as a child of God will not tolerate such pleasures. In fact, it will cause me to flee from such temptations and choose to follow after righteousness. The more I become repulsed and restless with the vain and wicked ways of the world, the more I become aware of how far removed from the mark of holiness the world really is.

Prayer: Lord, it is obvious that there can never be agreement between the spirit of the world and Your Spirit. Help me to flee the influence of the world and flee to the place of safety in You. Thank You for being my High Tower that lifts me above the present world to consider, see, and know Your glory. Amen.

November 12

Standing tall and bright-eyed, with his topknot proudly bobbing, the "sentinel" quail watches for any danger that might threaten his little flock as they happily scratch and peck for food. They all trust his ability to faithfully warn them if they need to scurry for cover, and their care and concern for their young inspires one's soul to look upward in awe and gratitude to the Creator of all.

It also serves as a reminder to us that as Christians we must be alert, wise, and discerning as to the encroaching danger of cult leaders posing as Christians. What are some of the "danger signs" we should be aware of?

Volumes could be written about this subject, but here is a simple "check list" that may prove to be helpful to you: CULT – "C" stands for control, critical and cruel; "U" stands for unbiblical, unloving and ungodly; "L" stands for legalistic, love of money, lust (for anything); and "T" stands for truth bashing, temper, and tyrannical.

Such predators in the pulpits "spare not the flock" but instead leave behind a trail of hurt, wounded, confused, broken and bruised sheep. *"Woe be unto the pastors that destroy and scatter the sheep of my pasture! saith the LORD" (Jeremiah 23:1).*

Remember what Jesus told us, *"My sheep hear my voice, and I know them, and they follow me." (John 10:27). "...he goeth before them, and the sheep follow him: for they know his voice. And a stranger will they not follow, but will flee from him: for they know not the voice of strangers" (John 10:4b, 5).*

Therefore, just as the little quail know the voice of the sentinel, let us listen always for the voice of our Savior and follow Him, fleeing from the voice of hirelings just as the little quail heed warning calls and quickly flee from danger, seeking shelter under the wings of the Almighty. – J. Haley

Prayer: Lord, You offer us the shelter of Your wings that will cover us, but we must flee the predator and run into You. Thank You for always being there. Amen.

November 13

One of the one-liners in Scripture I love to consider is Hebrews 11:6a, *"But now they desire a better country, that is, an heavenly (one)." (*Parenthesis added.) When you are an heir of righteousness, you have a better country to look towards. However, according to the many examples of those who walked by faith, steps of obedience advance you towards the better destination, and the attitude of godly fear keeps your focus clear and decisive. We see this in the case of Noah. He believed God, and obeyed Him because he dreaded disappointing Him in any way. Therefore, Noah experienced the reality of grace by being made an heir of righteousness.

To be an heir of righteousness means you will inherit the promises attached to righteousness. There are many promises in the Bible, but most of them have conditions. These conditions ensure that an environment of righteousness will be present so that God can honor His promises. Because Noah built an ark, God was able to get him through the judgment that was about to be poured out upon the whole world.

Noah's example teaches us that we must be baptized in some way to pass through judgment and come out on the other side of it. Sadly, our tendency is to remain on the side of judgment where the wrath of God will be unleashed rather than entering the place of safety to be ushered through the midst of judgment to embrace a new life.

Prayer: Lord, I do not want to be content with residing on the wrong side of Jordan. I do not want to experience Your wrath, but my desire is to taste the blessed fulfillment of Your promises. Lord, put the necessary reins on me that will keep me close to You. Amen.

November 14

"For we can do nothing against the truth, but for the truth" (2 *Corinthians 13:8).* Have you meditated on this Scripture? Why is it that mere man thinks he can change his reality by defining his own concept of truth without ending in delusion? It does not matter how he or she proclaims a matter to try to control what is, wishes a matter to be a certain way, or rages like a spoiled angry child

against what is contrary to their reality, truth will remain standing and unmoved from what is so.

When it comes to the truth of God, there are just a few things we must remember about it.

1) Truth is eternal. When all other beliefs, philosophies, and theologies lie in utter judgment and ruin, truth will remain standing. In fact, it will judge all other realities that prove to be contrary to it as being fallacies.

2) Truth is trustworthy. Granted, it may be sharp for it is meant to circumcise the heart. It is blunt for it is meant to awaken our spirits, and it is like a hammer that will shatter what is faulty in order to nail down what is right.

3) The truth is also a fire that purges, cleanses, and liberates a person's soul from bondage. But in the end, it will prove to be the only trustworthy stake or standard that one can trust.

4) Finally, truth is simple. It is summarized in two words: Jesus Christ. Truth is not an intellectual notion, a religious stance, or a philosophy; rather, it is a person. Jesus is God in the flesh. As a result, nothing can silence or do away with the truth. All one can do is stand on it, stand for it, and withstand with it.

Prayer; Lord, we are so thankful for Your unchangeable truth. We so love You because You will never be moved from who You are. You are the eternal, unchanging manifestation of truth. Amen.

November 15

"Let them praise the name of the LORD, for he commanded, and they were created" (Psalm 148:5). It is interesting to consider the ways of life. Everything in creation speaks of life. The trees speak of the beauty of life, the river the constant flow of life, the flowers

the grace that sustains life, and the wildlife the order that maintains life.

Each aspect of creation has its own heartbeat that pulsates through its very fiber. Creation also reminds us of the cycles and seasons of change. Change must come to test, refine, define, and advance life.

Seasons remind us nothing is meant to remain the same. There will either be progression in a matter or it will regress in the functions that point to life. Life declares that one must march ahead with change or he or she will be left behind to succumb to the elements of decay and death.

In a sense this is true for our spiritual life. Faith is meant to advance us forward. If we fail to go forward, we will be left in a state of spiritual stagnation and hopelessness.

Prayer: Lord, faith is active. It leads us to places of praise and worship. It enables us to see and finish the course before us because it rests in the immovable Rock of heaven. Praise Your Holy Name. Amen.

November 16

"And why take ye thought for raiment? Consider the lilies of the field, how they grow; they toil not, neither do they spin" *(Matthew 6:28).* Creation provides us with an array of examples. We must consider these examples to keep in perspective the simplicity of Jesus. The reality of God is that He is practical in how He meets needs and challenges.

There is no greater display of creation's declarations than in the fall. For this reason, months such as March, June, September, and December represent months that signal change is coming. In Spring there is a crisp clarity in the air, in the summer the temperature gauge is rising, in September, the air has a nip to it, the hornets are more active, and the water traffic on rivers dwindles, and in December life seems to be taking a special rest.

I must admit fall is one of my favorite seasons. Whether I look forward to it or back at it, I can't help but take note of how God uses a paintbrush to reflect His beauty in the stunning array of colors that change the countryside. I marvel at how creation adjusts to and reflects God's working and order.

We used to live by a river and it reflected each season in a special way. In the spring, fog often served as a curtain that, when it parted, revealed the vibrant countryside with new life. In the summer it was alive with human activities, in the fall the colors were so magnificent that you could not imagine anything to be more beautiful, except heaven. In the winter, the water would recede, the ice would form on the outer edges of the river banks, but the river never ceased to reflect the light of the moon at night or caused the snow to sparkle like diamonds.

What does each season say about our Creator's abilities and power? I know for me that regardless of the season, I still stand in awe of His greatness and rejoice in His power.

Prayer: Lord, Your creation reveals so much about You. Give me the eyesight to see You in it, the ears to hear it praise You, the smells that speak of Your heavenly fragrance, the touch to feel Your presence, and the means to taste Your goodness. Amen.

November 17

"Not by works of righteousness which we have done, but according to his mercy he saved us, by the washing of regeneration, and renewing of the Holy Ghost" (Titus 3:5). Spring has its own special time because it reminds us of regeneration, new life, and resurrection of a new life where that which was old and dormant used to rest in the cold earth.

Every season involves a changing of the guard when it comes to creation. It reminds me that the current of life brings constant change to revive and renew the earth. Without such changes life would never be reproduced and perpetuated. This change is part of the cycle of life.

As Christians, we must take time to consider how our lives are reflecting the perpetual change that will come as the life of Christ is established in us. There should be a change of guard as to the type of service that should be occurring. Are we reflecting the glorious array of the character of Christ's life and attitude in greater ways, or are we manifesting the ways of the world? The glory of the world will fade, but the glory of Christ will become more evident in each flow of current that brings revival and renewal to our souls.

Prayer: Lord, we cannot save or change ourselves. We can only decide what type of current we plan to get into to ensure a particular type of life. I want to get into the flow of Your Spirit. Amen.

November 18

It can be a bit confusing, but for the most part the nation of Israel and the spiritual kingdom of God, the church, have the same election to be a nation of priests and kings with a holy calling, as well as having a unique purpose in the world. For example, compare Deuteronomy 14:2, *"For thou art an holy people unto the LORD thy God, and the LORD hath chosen thee to be a peculiar people unto himself, above all the nations that are upon the earth,"* with *1 Peter 2:9*.

As I consider our high calling, I wonder if, as a church, we are standing so distinct that our light is actually shining through the darkness, or if our candlestick is void of light because it is being hidden or becoming dim due to compromise with the world. I ponder this because certain Scriptures that have caught my attention many times are found in *Leviticus 18:28-29, "That the land spew not you out also, when ye defile it, as it spewed out the nations that were before you. For whosoever shall commit any of these abominations, even the souls that commit them shall be cut off from among their people."*

Have you ever thought about the moral repulsion that would result in the land actually spewing the people out of it? In spite of the various attempts of environmentalists and animal activists, the greatest threat and destruction in regard to the land has to do with the abominations of immoral practices *(Proverbs 15:8-9)*.

When you go down the list of what God considers immoral, you cannot help but notice these practices are not only flaunted in this nation by a minority, but they are being systematically taught to our children, shoved down our throats as being acceptable by the different mediums, and legalized as a means of calling them good.

Ironically, people are worshipping the earth, and trying to save it while polluting the land by sacrificing the unborn, (and in some cases babies and children), promoting abominable lifestyles that are revolting to any with a moral conscience, and robbing the innocence of our children and young people through various perversions *(Romans 1:24-32)*. Obviously, wickedness grows when the standard of righteousness is not present.

God's people were set apart to be a moral compass in the midst of abominable practices. They were to bring the contrast between the holy and the profane. Today, it appears as if some of God's people are sliding into the pit of immorality and coming into agreement with the abominable. Such agreement shows utter contempt towards God; therefore, we must clearly avoid coming into agreement with the profane.

Prayer: Lord, You are holy and will not ignore iniquity. We must as Your people accept the calling for separation from the unholy to ensure that we strive for excellence in all that we do. Amen.

November 19

"I have …finished the course" (2 Timothy 4:7b). How does one ensure the integrity of change? We can change for the better or change for the worse. The matter is always determined by what we allow to influence us the most.

I used to enjoy watching the changes taking place in regard to the river that flowed by our former residence. I don't know what influences its flow or the height of its water, but I do know the weather greatly influences what it reflects.

As believers, we must consider what is influencing our lives. There are so many matters we must consider, but what we must realize is, like the river, we can only travel in one direction. The river has only one purpose and that is to travel the terrain according to the path that has been carved by its own flow.

As Christians, we have an ordained path that we must walk. If we take detours, we will never finish our destination. If we try to carve another path, we will be stopped by the boulders of destruction. If we refuse to flow according to the terrain, we will become a dry river bed. We must walk the path if we are to complete course.

Prayer: Lord, I avoided getting into the flow of Your Spirit in the past. As a result, I have taken defeating detours, been stopped dead in my tracks by ineptness, and found myself drying up from hopelessness. Keep the lessons ever before me so I can fear missing not only my destination, but discovering what You have for me. Amen.

November 20

Even though I tried hard to calmly ignore the sweet, upturned "flower faces" as I uprooted them from their pots, I still had to suppress ripples of colliding emotions. "You can't go there," I told myself as a gray mist of depression and regret temporarily swamped feelings of relief and accomplishment. I knew full well what was going to happen when the forecasted major cold front thrust itself into our area. Nevertheless, the happily blooming annuals seemed to exude an innocent confidence in themselves that made it hard for me to say a final "goodbye."

Life! Even plants and flowers show forth the mystery of life. Sometimes I ponder how every living thing in nature has within it the desire to live because our Creator God put it there, although man is often the exception, choosing death instead of life. And, it seems that all too often the innocent, the young and the righteous are "taken away," leaving us with numb minds that cannot grasp "why;" oceans of uncontrollable emotions that fail to find peace, and shattered hearts that seem broken beyond repair. There is only one place to turn, and that is to the One who knows the depths and secret places in each heart.

There is only one place to go when you feel like a lost, lonely cork bobbing on an endless sea of turmoil, and that is straight to the throne of God in prayer and His Word. *"Trust in him at all times; ye people, pour out your heart before him: God is a refuge for us"* (Psalm 62:8).

Psalm 147:3 says *"He healeth the broken in heart, and bindeth up their wounds."*

Finally, take comfort in *Isaiah 57:1* which tells us, *"The righteous perisheth, and no man layeth it to heart: and merciful men are taken away, none considering that the righteous is taken away from the evil to come."*

We serve a merciful and mighty God! – J. Haley

Prayer: Lord we can't control the currents of life, but we can hide in You, knowing that You oversee all matters. You know how to meet us, heal us, and keep us. Thank You for being all in all. Amen.

November 21

"He that believeth on me, as the scripture hath said, out of his belly shall flow rivers of living water" (John 7:38). Yesterday, I was pondering the flow of the Spirit. In the Living Water resides the life from heaven. We know that life to be the life of Christ. His life must be flowing in, through, and from us. However, the life of Christ in us can only flow one way. Granted, there may be tributaries along the way, but the flow of the water does not travel through the tributaries, rather the tributaries feed the river and its water blends with the current of the river.

Like tributaries, there is much in life that can take our attention, but we must realize that we determine the current we are in. As believers, we must be aware of not only what we allow to influence us, but we must recognize that such influence will determine what our lives will eventually merge with in this present age.

There is the flow of water that comes from the throne of God, or the dirty waters that come from the world. Ultimately, we will take on the disposition and reflection of that which we ultimately expose ourselves to.

Prayer: Lord, we think we are so clever trying to keep one toe in the Living Water while bathing in the waters of the world. We then wonder why the bitter taste of vanity is welling up in our mouths and we come out smelling of the filth of the world. We cannot serve two masters or walk in two directions. I want to be in Your flow going in the direction of righteousness. Amen.

November 22

"And being assembled together with them, commanded them that they should not depart from Jerusalem, but wait for the promise of the Father, which, saith he, ye have heard of me" (Acts 1:4). I appreciated the time I lived by Priest River. Granted, I did not always take the time to enjoy it, but there was nothing more satisfying to my inner being during that time than sitting out on the deck and observing the life that was pulsating in conjunction with the river.

When I took the time to enjoy the beauty of the river, I recognized how it affected my soul. It could inspire many pleasant emotions in me. Its serenity would calm my raging soul. Its colors had the capacity of bringing peace to my restless, undisciplined mind. Its beauty brought comfort, its ripples a sense of life, its reflections encouragement, and its shadows a sense of awareness of the depth that is necessary for contrast and growth.

As I have studied the work of the Spirit of God, I have begun to see how He does indeed change the inner environment of the soul. He is the promise of the Father. In the flow of His work are life, love, joy, and peace. As a result, the Spirit is the only One who brings that wondrous satisfaction to the spirit of man, while He lifts the soul above this world to soar in the heights of hope and expectation.

Prayer: Lord, You have given us the promise and gift of Your Spirit. Make me an open vessel in which Your Spirit has the liberty to flow into, through, and out to others. Amen.

November 23

"Behold, the ark of the covenant of the Lord of all the earth passeth over before you into Jordan" (Joshua 3:11). The beauty about

water is that it can be easily parted by the very hand of God. This is good because the Lord is always parting the waters for me. Whether they are too deep, too wide, too rough, or too stormy, He must take the controls and cause the waters to be pushed aside for me to pass through.

I was also reminded of how the waters can be parted when something flows within its currents. When I was living by the river, one day I watched a lone boat make its way down the placid river. It appeared as if there was only one person rowing the boat. The boat's speed was slow but steady as its bow gently parted the surface of the water. It was then that I noticed that someone stood up in the boat. I was surprised to see that another person was in the boat.

We are all in the current of life. Each life represents a boat that must make its way through the different channels of the world. Each boat will have its own speed, but the key is who is rowing or standing at the helm of the boat? This will determine what kind of ride each person will have in this world.

Jesus must be the one who directs the boat or mans the helm. He is the One who must be seen, while we must be hidden in His glorious shadow.

Prayer: Lord, I so appreciate Your shadow. There is no end to it when it comes to the cover, shade, or even coolness it provides to the thirsty soul. Thank You for providing the incredible shadow of heaven. Amen.

November 24

"And when they were come into the ship, the wind ceased" *(Matthew 14:32).* Yesterday I spoke of the lone boat that was making its way down the river. I perceived that there was only one

person in the boat, but it turned out that there were two individuals. One was hidden in the shadow of the other person.

As stated yesterday, the currents of life will determine the type of ride we will experience. For example, there are people who fling themselves into the different currents of the world to experience the thrills, which prove to be bumpy and dangerous. There are some who want to experience the high speed of sensationalism; therefore, they push the throttles to their capacity, always edging their way towards disaster.

There are those who like to ride, but have no intention of rowing. They prove to be lazy and want life handed to them. If they don't get their way, they tend to rock the boat, risking the possibility of sinking it.

Then there are those who know that it is only by having the right type of person at the helm that a successful ride can be assured. Jesus must be the one who determines the direction and speed of the boat. He is the only One who can assure the quality of our lives in the different boats of the world.

I must ask myself if Jesus controls the boat of my life.

Prayer: Lord, the uncertainty of life tosses me back and forth. I trust You to control the intensity of the storms and the direction and length of my life. Amen.

November 25

For just a brief moment it was as if I had stepped through an invisible doorway into the peace, love and joy of heaven. It happened one chilly, but calm, morning when I went out to hang two birdfeeders.

My custom is to always call out "Hi birdies" as best as I can with my Spasmodic Dysphonia "voice." Then, from among the treetops, come the joyful, melodious chirps, tweets and songs of each feathered friend. These sweet little "miracles from a wee egg" always lift my thoughts to our Great Creator God who has fashioned each and every creature, great or small, visible or invisible with marvelous and amazing intricacy and care.

It amazes me how the Lord can use the seemingly small, ordinary and insignificant things in our daily lives to unexpectedly overwhelm us with a "touch from heaven" in such a way that we gain a greater inner "knowing" and revelation of the glory that is to come that will fill the whole earth in the day of the Lord Jesus Christ.

Any out-of-the-ordinary experience of true love, joy and peace we may momentarily experience in this chaotic world is but a foretaste of the world to come, *"For the earth shall be filled with the knowledge of the glory of the LORD, as the waters cover the sea" (Habakkuk 2:14).* O glorious day! – J. Haley

Prayer: Lord, all of Your creation speaks or sings of You. Oh, to be as Your creation. It is my heart to praise You and my inspiration to sing to You, to be part of the chorus about me that brings glory to You, for You alone are worthy. Amen.

November 26

"It is of the LORD's mercies that we are not consumed, because his compassions fail not. They are new every morning: great is thy faithfulness" (Lamentations 3:22-23). These two Scriptures are those I love to meditate on that remind me of God's faithfulness. He is everywhere I go and it does not matter if it is on land or sea, in storms and extreme elements, He is always there.

I have lived in many different places. In deserts, valleys, and mountains, the distinction of each place can be clearly defined by the air. For example, in the deserts the air can be dry, stifling, and unbearable. In the valleys, the air can be heavy, weighed down by stale, lifeless air. However, in the mountains, especially in the morning, I was greeted by crisp air.

Crisp air brings a stillness that is clear and calm to the atmosphere. It is not weighed down by the residues of stifling heat and the polluted air of the valleys; rather, the air is fresh. It reminds me of the fresh wind of the Holy Spirit who brings forth the new supply of God's mercies and compassions every day. It is because of such mercies and compassion that we are not consumed by the daily challenges of life.

Therefore, mountain air reminds me of the glorious work of the Holy Spirit. Every day we need the crisp air to refresh our souls and bring quietness to our spirits.

Prayer: Lord, thank You for Your Spirit. I need His dew to fall upon the dry areas of my soul, the water to flow through the desert places of my spirit, and fresh wind to blow through the different chambers of my mind to keep it free from that which brings decay. Amen.

November 27

"And this word, Yet once more signifieth the removing of those things that are shaken, as of things that are made, that those things which cannot be shaken may remain" (Hebrews 12:27). Everything in and of this world that can be shaken will be shaken. Such action will bring about change. Any real change can prove to be hard to face. Seasons of change are expected, but what happens when unexpected change looms on the horizon? Does one prepare for it, brace against it, or fight it?

In my lifetime I have experienced many changes. Some changes have been expected, others proved to be quite pleasant and needed, and some brought great dread with them.

How do you handle change that shakes every area of your life and leaves you in the wake of overwhelming dread? Obviously, such changes will radically redefine the landscape of your life. How do each of us face changes that will change the terrain of our very world in an uncomfortable fashion? We must initially face them while being prepared to accept them for what they are.

I have learned that Jesus is the only place of protection. In Him I can accept changes as well as be prepared to face the shaking of the times, brace against the destruction of that which is unpleasant, and stand ready to fight the onslaught of despair that comes when changes leave devastation in their wake.

Prayer: Lord, we have an unrealistic view of the Christian life. The Christian life does not spare us from the winds of the world, it simply prepares us to walk through them with You in glorious victory. Amen.

November 28

"And the LORD said, Behold there is a place by me, and thou shalt stand upon a rock. And it shall come to pass, while my glory passeth by, that I will put thee in a cleft of the rock, and will cover thee with my hand while I pass by" (Exodus 33:21-22). It is hard for people to accept unpleasant changes. The uncertainty that it brings with them requires us to fling ourselves on the Rock of ages. In other words, it calls for us to activate faith towards God.

The promise of God is that in spite of the changes, He will hide us in the cleft of the Rock. But before He can hide us in the cleft of the Rock, He must first firmly stand us upon the Rock. Once we learn to stand, we can learn how to hide in its cleft. Both actions require faith on our part. We must trust that the Lord is the Rock and that He will also become the cleft as He covers us with His hand.

We like to think we have great faith, but we do not know what faith we do have until change rocks our personal world with uncertainty. It is then that we discover the level of maturity of our faith by whether we quickly seek God as our refuge and trust Him to cover us with His hand, or whether we seek elsewhere.

Prayer: Lord, our faith is forever being challenged to remember who establishes us on the immovable foundation of heaven, while being hid in the cleft of the Rock. Thank you for hiding me in that safe place of comfort, peace, and communion and placing me on that which is true and eternal. Amen.

November 29

Sass, stomp, slam and spanking. That pretty well sums it up as far as my childhood expressions went. I'm sure there are a few who can relate to this predictable procedure, at least up to the spanking part.

Thank God, I grew up in a day and age when applying "the board of correction to the seat of knowledge" wasn't considered "child abuse." I'd love to be able to confirm that all those spankings did a thorough job of changing my natural impulse to voice my opinions before putting my brain into action, —well, maybe they helped a lot but certainly not completely!

As for the stomping part, I have knee problems, and it's not seemly for old ladies to jump up and down in disgust over life's insanity. But, the slamming part, well now, there have been occasions when doors have been a handy means of expression. Not that I'm proud of that or anything. I remember my mother making me "practice" opening and closing a door quietly so I'd get the point. And, when it comes to spanking, there is no Father on earth who can "spank" like our faithful heavenly Father!

All of this may be somewhat amusing in the physical realm, but when it comes to the door of our hearts, that is another matter. We all know that Jesus stands at the door of our heart and knocks, and we all know that if the door is shut it's probably been slammed shut in God's face because of unbelief, anger, resentment, fear, or rebellion.

All communion with God is lost until we open the door to Him. However, as I recently discovered, sometimes when our hearts are broken and overwhelmed with sorrow we can close the door of our heart so slowly, and so very softly that we're not even aware of it ourselves until the Holy Spirit shows us. It's not that we're rejecting Jesus, or falling into unbelief—on the contrary, we mentally know we need Him more than ever, but it can seem that He has distanced Himself from us when we need Him the most, so we wrap ourselves up in a blanket of gray despair until we finally cry out to Jesus to "touch us again". And, what does He do? He shows us by His Spirit exactly where we are and why we're there, behind a closed door that we never realized we had shut.

Jesus, in His grace, mercy and love patiently waits for us to reopen the door and cry out for Him to come in to stay. Maybe this is where you are today. Remember, *"He healeth the broken in heart, and bindeth up their wounds" (Psalm 147:3).* – J. Haley

Prayer: Lord, we often work ourselves up into a dither because we can't feel, sense, or believe You are there in challenging times. However, our faith can take hold of expectation because You are the essence of our Hope that no matter what is going on, You are waiting for us to land on You, the immovable Rock of Ages. Amen.

November 30

"For they speak not peace, but they devise deceitful matters against them that are quiet in the land" (Psalm 35:20). Most

people just want to live their lives in peace. Their concept is "You don't bother me, and I won't bother you." However, there are those who are not content to let alone what appears to be normal or mediocre. They must stir up the pot with their despotic ways. They must take the nominal and enslave it. They must seize the mediocre and oppress it. The reason for such tyranny is because such tyrants are not at peace within themselves.

These individuals are tormented by their own lifeless, lawless ways. They despise nominal because it appears to have no clarity or purpose. They hate mediocrity because there appears to be no life or meaning in it. Such an environment seems inferior and unacceptable to their way of thinking. After all, they possess what they perceive to be grandiose ideas that will transform, use, and redistribute the aimlessness of the masses.

When it comes to the Christian life, Jesus is not impressed with a lukewarm environment either. Lacking real fervor for what is right allows the despots of the world to take center stage. To be lukewarm is deemed inferior to what is righteous and excellent, and it will leave people in a dull, vulnerable state to be swept away by any wave that rushes onto the shoreline that is able to create excitement.

As a believer, I must become sober and vigilant when it comes to my life and attitude towards God and the matters of His kingdom.

Prayer: Lord, You were not lukewarm in Your commitment towards us. You came from the glories of heaven so You could die on a cross for me. How can we, as Your followers, be content in being lukewarm in our commitment towards You? Forgive us for our casual attitude. Amen.

December

December 1

Who wants to drink muddy water? No one does. Just the thought of it can make a person's stomach churn. But this is the situation I found myself in, decades ago, on a daily basis for four years when I lived in western Washington. Granted, the surrounding countryside was beautiful with its thick forests, green pastures, rivers and streams. However, for many people in my particular county, the old wood water conduit was not only undependable, but grossly outdated.

I figured the original pioneers had somehow managed to put it together and that is what we were all stuck with. Back in that day no sly, greedy bright brain had come along yet and figured out that by bottling a God-given, free resource such as water, they could become filthy rich overnight. I have to admit, though, that I would've appreciated clean drinking water no matter who was behind it! (Note: Any bottled water except steam distilled water is still not "pure.") So, there I was, holding up a glass of water and wondering what all the "stuff" was in it that seemed to have a life of its own. (Which much of it did.)

As Christians, we know that Jesus is the "Living Water," and that whosoever drinks of the water He gives (Himself) shall never spiritually thirst again. The water that Jesus offers is pure, holy, undefiled, life-giving, and satisfying. When we drink of His Word by believing it, loving it, and obeying it our souls are refreshed and our spirits edified.

So, why are so many religious leaders and churches these days handing out "muddy water" for the people to drink? Woe to them that fear not God, but rather fear losing their positions, pensions, and popularity!

The day is coming when all liars, thieves, fornicators, hireling shepherds, heretics, wolves, swine, and goats will be separated from God's sheep whom Jesus is calling to "come out and be separate" from. Don't drink muddy water! – J. Haley

Prayer: Lord many of us don't even realize we are thirsty for your water because we are used to muddy waters. Even though such waters contaminate our understanding and life in You, we fail to realize that it is dulling us down to our need for Your living water. Lord, give me a thirst for Your water by causing me to thirst after Your righteousness. Amen.

December 2

One of the things I meditate on when it comes to action is inaction. Our first parents' inaction of failing to eat of the Tree of life, ended with them eating of the wrong tree. I have discovered that inaction is a reflexive action. It may seem indifferent in one arena, but can be easily stirred up to pursue the opposition once the right environment is present. It is for this reason the Bible is clear, INACTION is a sin. It is referred to as the sin of omission because what is not upheld by active faith is sin, and failure to do right in light of knowing what is right is sin (*Romans 14:23; James 4:17*).

Inaction when it comes to doing what is right reveals much about the person. It shows that they have a self-serving attitude that weighs matters according to personal preferences, pursuits, and desires and not based on what has been established as being righteous. They are operating in unbelief because they have not chosen to take God and His Word seriously, which ends in them despising or showing contempt towards His truth when challenged to deny self and go against the grain of their own personal pursuits and agendas in order to uphold and obey it.

Inaction also proves to be the great act of treason because instead of standing for what is right, it will give way to what is wrong, which reveals a divided heart and a fickle devotion making the person unfaithful as a servant in the Lord's household, a deserter as far as being a reliable soldier in the battle, and ultimately an enemy of God and His kingdom and people.

It is clear that in inaction the person prefers to do it their way, on their terms, and when they decide to do it—that is, if they ever decide to get serious and real about what has been set forth by God, they will do it according to their fancy. In the past my inaction has caused me to miss valuable opportunities to be a witness, fail to stand on the truth so I could advance forward in my walk of faith, discover priceless treasures, or gain spiritual blessings that would enrich my life. It is for this reason I continue to press forward in my Christian life to avoid looking for a way to somehow justify any laziness, complacency, or inaction towards the matters of God.

Prayer: Lord, I know how selfish the old man is and how weak the flesh is because it has no inclination towards You, as it prefers the ways of the world over Your perfect ways. I know that when I fail to stand on what is right in order to do what is right before You, I leave a trail of regrets, defeats, and despair behind me. Therefore, I gladly stand on what is so, and am determined to march forward in obedience as I press through this dark age while trusting Your commitment to preserve me, Your Spirit's ability to enable me, and the truth of Your Word to keep me on the right path. Amen.

December 3

One of the hard realities for me is found in *2 Corinthians 4:3, "But if our gospel be hid, it is hid to them that are lost."* We are all born in a blind state towards the matters of God. The idea that some will not see the light of God's love and the Gospel because they are lost is very sobering for me. My question is simple, "Are such people unwilling to see or do they love and prefer darkness to such an extent they refuse to see and remain comfortable in their blind state?

Some of the greatest times of illumination come when the spiritual darkness is the most intense upon our souls. It is in such times that we have reason to open up the eyes of our hearts by faith to really see what is true and real. If we are truly seeking to know God, we will find the real essence of hope that He has provided in Jesus Christ. Although great darkness is coming upon this world, we must not fear it; rather, we must fear not seeing the penetrating light of Jesus. Most people suffer from spiritual blindness that prevents them from seeing His light.

The Apostle Paul stated that if the Gospel is hidden, it is hidden to them that are lost. The minds of such people have been blinded to the glorious light of the Gospel, Jesus Christ, by the god of this world, Satan. Clearly, the greatest type of blindness is not what we cannot see in the light in regard to this present world, but what we fail to see in regard to the darkness that is upon us.

Light allows us to distinguish the darkness, but darkness will prevent us from seeing the light. I must consider if I am spiritually groping in the darkness created by Satan or walking in the light of Jesus Christ.

Prayer: Lord, I desire to walk in Your precious light. I want to see my sin, examine the way that I am walking in, and be assured of seeing You when all is said and done. Amen.

December 4

"Enter ye in at the strait gate: for wide is the gate, and broad is the way, that leadeth to destruction, and many there be which go in thereat" (Matthew 7:13). Living with a professional artist has made me aware of how shadows bring depth to a painting or scenery. Of course, shadows are cast by the light being deflected or made obscure by objects and clouds. I have been able to appreciate this very fact by watching how the shadows affected the river that ran freely by our former residence.

Depending on the light and the movements of the water it appeared at times that the water was actually parting. However, it was a mirage. As the light hit the sides of the river from a certain angle, the objects on the banks of the river, such as trees, cast a shadow on both sides of the river. This caused the middle of the river to appear as if it is parting. In fact, it looked like a regular pathway in which you would be able to trek.

The Bible also casts shadows to define the way of salvation. The light came into the world to reveal that there is only one way in which man can enter to secure salvation. Because of the shadow that was cast by the light upon the cross, the narrow way to heaven has been revealed. It points to Christ and His redemptive work that took place on the cross.

Prayer: Lord the way to heaven has been highlighted in Your Word and through Your sacrifice on the cross. You are the narrow way, the only way to salvation. Thank You for illuminating the way to me. Amen.

December 5

Everyone who has ever been to Seattle knows that most of the city is either uphill or downhill, and that's what made the street in front of our house so great when it snowed. Back then, we got some real doozy snowstorms, and all of us neighborhood kids were beside ourselves with joy.

On went the warm jackets, hats, scarves, gloves and boots and out came the sleds. I was proud of my Flyer and couldn't wait to fly down the hill with the rest of the kids, but the neighborhood bully who lived at the top of the hill positioned himself about halfway down the hill behind a telephone pole and proceeded to mercilessly pelt snowballs at the kids as they slid past him.

His fortified position was directly across the street from our driveway, and it unnerved me to know what I'd be hit with if I tried to get on my sled. So, I did what any kid like myself would do—I went and told my parents, and they did what good parents are supposed to do and followed me out to the end of the driveway to watch what was taking place.

By this time some of the kids had been knocked off their sleds, some were sidelined and the bully was in full swing--and I got mad! I clearly remember forming a missile of a snowball and heaving it straight at that telephone pole just as the bully stuck his face out to see what was happening, and, you guessed it…SPLAT! That snowball hit him square in the face, leaving him so shocked and stunned that he pulled himself together and ran home.

Now, the moral to the story is this: We have an adversary bully to stand against: his name is Satan. He is always watching for ways to bring distress, disturbances, and destruction to God's children. He bullies us by roaring like a lion, prowling about to cause fear, while falsely accusing us with his lies and slander. But as God's children, we have the power in the mighty Name of Jesus, the truth in the two-edged sword of the Word of God, and the anointing of the Holy Spirit to gain the victory.

Jesus said, *"Behold, I give unto you power to tread on serpents and scorpions, and over all the power of the enemy: and nothing shall by any means hurt you" (Luke 10:19)* When the devil uses others against us, remember *Psalm 118:6, "The LORD is on my side; I will not fear: what can man do unto me?"* – J. Haley

Prayer: Lord, You are the Victor who fights the battles. All I need to do is stand in Your authority, lift the sword up, and be confident You will ensure that I hit the mark, causing the enemy to flee. He is a defeated foe before You. Amen.

December 6

I have mentioned the need to bear our own burdens when it comes to our life and ministry in the Lord. The Lord carries the heavy end of the yoke, and sometimes when we become weary, He sends others to help us as well. This brings us to *Galatians 6:2, "Bear ye one another's burdens, and so fulfill the law of Christ"*

We are called to bear the burdens of others, and I must be open and willing to be prepared to bear or carry the burdens of brothers and sisters in the Lord, whether it be in prayer, easing the burden if possible, or entering in when the opportunity presents itself. I must never be weary in well-doing when it comes to other believers. However, if the love of God is not present, such burdens will bury you.

Godly love forms a yoke that will be easy to come under making the burden light. As I have already pointed out, the beauty about the yoke of love is that the Lord carries the heavier end of the burden.

His love is what inspires or compels people to be passionate in their devotion and sacrificial in their commitment to ensure the integrity of their attitude and actions in regard to others. In fact, love's main desire is to honor that person in every possible way. Such honor prefers the benefactor over the well-being of self. It is for this reason that in the end the love of God proves to be a light burden.

Prayer: Lord, it is easy to design our own yoke, but pride will dictate that it must be immense, self will call for it to bring distinction to us, and the world will require it to be ornate with the things of the present age. In the end, it will simply bury me. Lord, replace Your yoke for my yoke. Amen.

December 7

One of the hard realities for me is found in *2 Corinthians 4:3, "But if our gospel be hid, it is hid to them that are lost."* We are all born in a blind state towards the matters of God. The idea that some will not see the light of God's love and the Gospel because they are lost is very sobering for me. My question is simple, "Are such people unwilling to see or do they love and prefer darkness to such an extent they refuse to see and remain comfortable in their blind state?

Some of the greatest times of illumination come when the spiritual darkness is the most intense upon our souls. It is in such times that we have reason to open up the eyes of our hearts by faith to really see what is true and real. If we are truly seeking to know God, we will find the real essence of hope that He has provided in Jesus Christ. Although great darkness is coming upon this world, we must not fear it; rather, we must fear not seeing the penetrating light of Jesus. Most people suffer from spiritual blindness that prevents them from seeing His light.

The Apostle Paul stated that if the Gospel is hidden, it is hidden to them that are lost. The minds of such people have been blinded to the glorious light of the Gospel, Jesus Christ, by the god of this world, Satan. Clearly, the greatest type of blindness is not what we cannot see in the light in regard to this present world, but what we fail to see in regard to the darkness that is upon us.

Light will extinguish the darkness, but darkness will prevent us from seeing the light. I must consider if I am spiritually groping in the darkness created by Satan or walking in the light of Jesus Christ.

Prayer: Lord, I desire to walk in Your precious light. I want to see my sin, examine the way that I am walking in, and be assured of seeing You when all is said and done. Amen.

December 8

"And Moses stretched out his hand over the sea; and the LORD caused the sea to go back by a strong east wind all that night, and made the sea dry land, and the waters were divided" (Exodus 14:21). Once again, I am remembering the shadows on the river that gave the impression that there was a path or that it was parting. I know that the angle of the sun was creating such an impression. It reminded me of the parting of the Red Sea.

God stepped on the scene in the wilderness on behalf of the people of Israel. On their behalf, He drove back the waters of the Red Sea to make the path dry for them to pass over from the old bondage of slavery to embark on a new life.

It is vital for believers to realize that faith towards God is what allows Him to part the waters. Even though at first the situation looks impossible, or that it is an illusion of wishful thinking, God is able to part the waters according to the measure of faith allotted to His people.

The question is, what measure of faith have I been given that will allow Him to part the waters for me regarding a matter?

Prayer: Lord, You will always have to part the waters for me, but I know You will enable me to pass through the challenges of life on dry ground. Thank You for Your faithfulness. Amen.

December 9

Fall harvest brings back colorful memories of bountiful supplies of fresh produce and happier times. Many years ago, I lived near a broad, fertile river valley that supported large farms and ranches. After harvesting their crops, some of the farmers opened up their fields for gleaners to come in and take all the free food they could gather to help feed their families. I remember how some of us, who had grave concerns for the needy, were so thankful to be able to inform poor families of this opportunity to gather fresh, healthy food.

Imagine, then, my surprise when I was later informed that many of the poorest turned down this great opportunity because they didn't want to do the work of gathering food from the fields—potatoes for example—because then they would have to clean, store, and prepare them! It was a disheartening learning experience for me to realize that some of the poorest were poor because they were basically ungrateful, lazy, and self-centered enough to assume others should do all the hard work for them.

This brings to mind the incredible spiritually anemic condition of so many self-serving, professing Christians today who are lean in spirit, lacking in knowledge, poor in character, morally bankrupt and incredibly inept when it comes to the deeper Christian life of self-sacrifice and sacrificial giving (both financially and physically.) Such people want to be entertained rather than challenged; "hand-fed" rather than study the Scriptures for themselves; offered "junk food" rather than "meat" and cutting-edge truth; and pampered with flattery rather than exhorted by God's Word.

May the LORD help us to beware of laziness, and instead let us be watchful and diligent. *"Study to shew thyself approved unto God, a workman that needeth not to be ashamed, rightly dividing the word of truth" (2 Timothy 2:15).*

For when for the time ye ought to be teachers, ye have need that one teach you again which be the first principles of the oracles of God; and are become such as have need of milk, and not of strong meat. For every one that useth milk is unskilful in the word of righteousness; for he is a babe. But strong meat belongeth to them that are of full age, even those who by reason of use have their senses exercised to discern both good and evil (Hebrews 5:12-14).

"Therefore, my beloved brethren, be ye stedfast, unmoveable, always abounding in the work of the Lord, forasmuch as ye know that your labour is not in vain in the Lord" (1 Corinthians 5:58). – J. Haley

Prayer: Lord nothing is wasted when it comes to Your kingdom but we must partake of it for it to benefit our life, and learn to walk according to the spiritual growth taking place. Amen.

December 10

"For which cause we faint not; but though our outward man perish, yet the inward man is renewed day by day" (2 Corinthians 4:16). I realize that I had the incredible blessing of living along the path of an extraordinary river. Rivers are fed by a source as they flow into some other source of water. The river I used to live beside is fed by one of the largest lakes in the Northwest. This river then flows into a larger river.

When I first moved to this area, the river had been swollen from the snow runoff. Within the view of our former residence, it appeared as if it was a miniature lake. However, when fall came, it seemed that a dam was opened or closed. The water began to recede revealing a whole new side to its makeup. At its widest point a sandbar began to emerge. The river simply forged around it.

As I considered the lesson of the sandbar, I realize that the water often hides that which affects its flow. This is true for us. People may be inclined to settle for what they see, but there is much more to each of us. The current of life that flows through us is being greatly influenced by that which lies beneath its surface.

As a Christian, I must allow the different spiritual seasons to expose the terrain of my character. I must make sure that the current of life is allowed to forge ahead as it pushes aside any deviance in my character to make that which was, new and fresh.

Prayer: Lord, there is so much about my physical life that is digressing, but I can be assured that my inner man is being made forever young while maturing by the work of Your Spirit. Amen.

December 11

"Then brought he me out of the way of the gate northward, and led me about the way without unto the utter gate by the way that looketh eastward; and behold, there ran out waters on the right side" (Ezekiel 47:2). The power of water always amazes me. Yesterday I spoke of a sandbar that changed the flow of the river I had the privilege to observe for three years. This sandbar served as a popular place for the geese to rest. However, I had to consider how it actually impedes the flow of the river, especially in the summer time.

During the summer the speed of the river seems to be moving at a crawl. It allows for much traffic on the river from small boats to those who float it. You can swim across it because there are no waves or real currents that hinder you.

However, as the sandbar became more exposed, it became obvious that the river has somewhere along the way gained momentum. This momentum allows the river to forge its way around the sandbar. Its flow seems freer as it rushes to its destination. Since its flow has escalated, it becomes clear in appearance and loud in its descent.

I realize we humans spend much of our time confused and floundering. It seems that there is so much that hinders us. Granted, it is hidden, but nevertheless it is there slowing down or stopping altogether our spiritual progress.

For this reason, we desperately need such obstacles exposed in our character. Once it is exposed the Holy Spirit can use the life of Christ to cleanse us of debris, as well as forge around such obstacles to ensure clarity and victory.

Prayer: Lord, I thank You for the free-flowing work of the Spirit in my life. Keep all the channels open in my life so that God can have His way. Amen.

December 12

"And the Word was made flesh, and dwelt among us..." (John 1:14a). Redemption is a simple word, but when it comes to God it is profound. I have sought to understand the word in a way that it will cause even more awe in me when I consider the work Jesus wrought on the cross on my behalf.

I have written different exhortations about it, but the depths of its meaning will not be reached by me in this lifetime. Herbert Lockyer brought more understanding to me about "redemption" in his book, *All The Messianic Prophecies of the Bible.* Lockyer points out that one could not redeem someone unless he or she was related.

Although I knew that only a kinsman could redeem or buy back that which was allotted to his inheritance, this simple understanding was brought more into focus concerning the Lord.

As Lockyer pointed out, "…Jesus became one of our race in order to have the right to redeem. Incarnation was imperative for redemption."

Today there are many who refuse to believe the incarnation of Jesus. Yet, this was the only way God could satisfy His holy Law and save us from the consequences of sin. I am thankful that I can simply believe that God became flesh. Childlike faith silences logic, puts reason on hold, and allows us to securely land on the work and promises of God.

Prayer: Lord, You even give us the measure of faith to believe what Your Word says, but we would rather pride ourselves in our unbelief than receive life-changing truths from heaven. Thank You for the faith You give me to experience Your promises. Amen.

December 13

Rats! Being an only child, and "all ears," meant that I overheard much of what was being said from "day one," so at around two years old I knew that rats lived under Miss Merrithew's front porch. And, Miss Merrithew lived in the house right next door.

Since I was my mother's shadow, I was within earshot one day when she was trying to style her thick brunette hair, and suddenly blurted out, "I need a new rat!" Ever wanting to please her, I set out to solve the problem.

I do remember how dark and dirty it was as I crawled around under Miss Merrithew's front porch looking for a rat. Suddenly, I saw some adult shoes outside the small opening under the porch, and heard voices calling me to come out of there. Apparently, Miss Merrithew had called my mother and told her that I was crawling around under her front porch. "Jeannette! What on earth are you doing under there?" To which I answered, "I'm looking for a rat for Mommie's hair!"

We can all laugh at that, but it can also serve to remind us of a greater darkness: that is, if we fail to understand the Word of God, comparing Scripture with Scripture, it's easy to end up misunderstanding and missing the principles and meanings behind a word, verse, or portion of Scripture taken out of context. Many cults, aberrant movements, and false doctrines are the result of a lack of knowledge, understanding, study, and meditation on the whole Word of God. *"Then spake Jesus again unto them, saying, I am the light of the world: he that followeth me shall not walk in darkness, but shall have the light of life" (John 8:12).* – J. Haley

Prayer: Lord, it's easy to end up misunderstanding Your Word because we have our own take on different subjects. Give me a pure heart to hear Your Word so I can properly see You in the right light. Amen.

December 14

"Be careful for nothing; but in every thing by prayer and supplication with thanksgiving let your requests be made known to God" (Philippians 4:6). There was much wildlife where we used to live. The lonely yipping of the coyotes in the night, the signs of a bear in our driveway, the intrusion of fawns bouncing through our yard, and the flight of the eagles and osprey as they search for fish are constant reminders that God's creation is in full operation around us.

The first autumn we lived there I had to add another life form to the already growing record of the creatures that we share our space with, and that was wild turkeys. On our walk we noticed two wild turkeys at the residence of a neighbor. One turkey was frantic, while the other one was totally stressed. The frantic turkey accidentally walked through an open gate and found itself caged in a narrow space between the gate and the house. The other turkey was running on the outside completely stressed because it didn't have any solution.

I watched that turkey run back and forth a few steps at a time to try to find a way out of the small space, always stopping short of reaching the entrance it had walked through. It appeared that it was stuck in an imaginary rut.

I know that I have been like that turkey in the past. I have been stuck in a rut that has no power over me except that it is all I could see in my frantic time. My initial logic was since I got myself into the situation, I should be able to get myself out of it, but I was helpless to find my way out.

Even though I may know Christ is the answer, at times I become stuck in some rut, mentally, emotionally, and spiritually, preventing me from seeing Him. Even though Jesus was with His disciples in the boat that was being tossed about, like them all I can do is feel anxious, overwhelmed, and trapped. Occasionally I even hear Jesus words, "Oh you of little faith." At such a time I know I'm looking at the obstacle and not looking to Him. It is Jesus who brings rest to our troubled souls.

Prayer: Lord, I have been trapped by various things in my life, but the bars often prove ineffective, the chains imaginary, and the panic a waste of time. The greatest bondage occurs when the bars of fear grip my mind with the narrow perspective of my understanding. Enlarge my understanding so that I can see the way out You always provide. Amen.

December 15

"There hath no temptation taken you but such as is common to man: but God is faithful, who will not suffer you to be tempted above that ye are able; but will with the temptation also make a

way to escape, that ye may be able to bear it" *(1 Corinthians 10:13)*. Yesterday I wrote about a turkey that thought he was trapped. It fascinated me because it so much reminded me of my past moments of hysteria. I cannot count the many times I have found myself in ensnaring situations. I had become so entrenched in the rut of my own imagination that I failed to see the way out that God had provided.

As I became more embedded in my imaginary entrapment, I began to panic. As fear gripped me, hopelessness began to nip at my heels as my vision became increasingly limited by my plight.

Through the years I have learned that in such situations, I need to stop running back and forth in my imaginations and take stock. God promised that He will provide a way out and I need to take Him at His Word. In essence, I needed to look up before I would be able to look around me to see the way out of the situation.

I have discovered that the real temptation in such times is to become more frantic as unbelief takes me captive instead of first looking up to gain His perspective. Once I get His perspective, I have discovered that the way out is located just a few steps of faith away from me.

Prayer: Lord, forgive us for our doubt. We cease to consider You and look at the circumstances that display hopelessness and destruction. Thank You for being who You are. Amen.

December 16

"Submit yourselves therefore to God. Resist the devil, and he will flee from you" *(James 4:7)*. Through the years I had to be honest about my spiritual life in relationship to my enemies. Is my battle pose an act where I take some type of warrior stance that seems comical to others or do I pose a real threat to my enemies? Am I chasing that which poses no threat or am I standing against that

which is ready to destroy me? Am I putting on an imaginary armor, or am I wearing the armor that has been allotted to the saints of the Most High?

The enemies are real, the battles rage, and the war has yet to be won. Like all battles and wars, they are a matter of life and death. It is not comical, imaginary, or a sentimental notion, it is real and souls are on the line.

The Bible is clear that we have the means to overcome the world, defeat the self-life, and cause Satan to flee. However, I must become crucified to the world by mortifying the self-life, while drawing near to God to ensure that Satan flees before Him. In times of great conflict, God is our great refuge that I must always flee to, to ensure victory.

Prayer: Lord, thank You for providing me with all I need to stand, withstand, and continue to stand. I know that what I speak of is repetitious, but as a soldier of Your cross, I must remember it. Amen.

December 17

"Be merciful unto me, O God: for man would swallow me up; he fighting daily oppresseth me" (Psalm 56:1). Wicked people become vessels in the hands of Satan. Satan's goal is to rob people of their faith, kill their testimony, and destroy their life in God.

It is clear that wickedness is a cesspool, a quagmire of vanity and ruin. Those who walk in it desire to swallow up the vulnerable and oppress those who are strong. They do all they can to entice them into this cesspool. After all, they hate anyone that possesses spiritual liberty. They want to defile that which is pure and taint that which is true.

Since such people are out to do Satan's bidding, God's people need to rely and trust God to show them mercy at an appropriate time. They need to realize that only God can hide them and protect them from Satan's advancements.

I am so thankful that I can hide in my Lord. I know He will fight the battle for me and will ultimately deliver me out the oppressive clutches of these wicked people.

Prayer: Lord, You are my deliverer. I sometimes forget that until my back is up against the wall of destruction. Thank You for knowing how to not only deliver me but hide me in such times. Amen.

December 18

As most of my friends know, I recently did something that's a first in my entire life. And, no it wasn't a super sin, but it was definitely what I call "super stupid."

When I plan to make a nice dinner, I try to focus and get all of my "ducks in a row" so everything is prepared and seasoned satisfactorily, and ready to serve at the same time. So, imagine my surprise when I went to check a small pork roast for doneness, and found it still sitting on the counter! The oven was going for an hour with nothing in it.

Now, here's the thing. Some people are really, really good at having an excuse for everything and I'm one of them. So, here's my excuse for this flub—it was John Wayne's fault! I kid you not—it was such a great movie, all in color too, with beautiful scenery and horses—right up my alley.

The two ladies who make up my small "family" were kind and gracious, but to be honest with you, I don't think they blamed John Wayne. Thankfully, they ate the meager leftovers I quickly retrieved from the fridge without complaint.

While we can laugh at ourselves over silly mistakes, one thing that has never been funny, isn't funny, and never will be funny is SIN. No matter how much a person tries to justify his or her sin, whether it's great or small, sin is still sin in God's eyes. *And "the wages of sin is death" (Romans 6:23).*

Therefore, instead of thinking up creative excuses for sin, remember the three important "If's" in *1 John 1:8-10, "If we say that we have no sin, we deceive ourselves, and the truth is not in us. If we confess our sins, he is faithful and just to forgive us our sins, and to cleanse us from all unrighteousness, If we say that we have not sinned, we make him a liar, and his word is not in us."* – J. Haley

Prayer: Lord, being human can prove to be comical, being wrong is humbling, being realistic is sobering, but when it comes to sin, it is a serious matter of life and death. Lord, give me the right attitude towards the matters that will count for eternity. Amen.

December 19

"Every day they wrest my words: All their thoughts are against me for evil" (Psalm 56:5). The biggest attack against righteousness comes by way of gossip and slander. Such ways are cursed; however, the wicked can do nothing more than their father, Satan. They cannot help but lie. Their goal is to kill decency and destroy any real testimony of righteousness. This destruction comes in a subtle way.

Innuendos dropped in the imaginations of the vulnerable, hurtful impressions left to create a mire of suspicion in the weak, a flow of tears of self-pity to start a wave of sentimental nonsense with the emotional, and so-called "noble gestures" to cover up the hate and wickedness from the masses. However, to God such attempts are profane. Regardless of the reality that is created by these people, it is void of truth. It is self-serving and destructive. It ultimately leads nowhere.

Once again, as believers we must keep in mind that these people can do nothing outside of the low ways of Satan. He also accuses the saints on a daily basis. How he must weary the courts of heaven with his onslaught of lies.

Prayer: Lord, You know the ways of the enemy. However, You gave us the belt of truth to discern Him, the sword to put him on the defense, and the game plan to defeat him. Amen.

December 20

"For they that are after the flesh do mind the things of the flesh; but they that are after the Spirit the things of the Spirit" (Romans 8:5). Through the years the biggest challenge I have encountered along the way has been with my mind. I can actually become paralyzed by what I think or conclude. Remembering that which is holy, pure, and simple allows me to come to a place where my mind can be changed and transformed in its way of thinking.

We all start out with a carnal mind. Such a mind can only care about, or pay attention, to the things of the flesh. A carnal mind is worldly in its thinking and fleshly in its ways. It displays a selfish attitude and gives surface presentations of beauty, goodness, and decency.

The carnal mind surely prefers the world. It is tainted by its philosophies, perverted by indoctrination, and defiled by its practices. Its preference is driven by the lusts of the flesh, is being perpetually consumed by selfishness, and is made mad by the indifference and cruelty of pride.

As a Christian, I have striven to consider what I am minding when it comes to the things of God. How much do I value my life in the Lord and how much do I set my affections on the virtues and ways of heaven. I must take on the mind of Christ if I am going to be prepared to take on His future glory.

Prayer: Lord, my mind can become a real problem depending on what I am minding. Lord, make me aware of Your business and cause me to become sharp towards Your ways. Amen.

December 21

"For to be carnally minded is death; but to be spiritually minded is life and peace" (Romans 8:6). The mind is an interesting instrument. It has such potential to dream the impossible, to scale the heights of great possibilities, and to explore beyond this present world. However, there is one problem with the mind, it is in a fallen state.

The mind may be able to dream, but it has no power to bring a matter about. It may scale heights in its imagination, but it still is subject to the lowlands of vanity. It might want to explore new worlds, but it has no means of getting launched from its pinnacle of overinflated arrogance. After all, it perceives itself as always reaching the ultimate heights of its understanding.

The reality of the mind is that it must be transformed. Until it is transformed it has a tendency to think in a counterclockwise way. In other words, it is incapable of operating according to the flow of truth and righteousness. It will think in a contrary fashion as it begins with the end of a matter in light of selfishness, while trying to move against the current of righteousness, clearly missing the starting point of truth.

In such a mind, thinking will always be off, conclusions backwards, and understanding missing the mark of reality. It will cause the individual to look foolish, untrustworthy, and ridiculous.

Prayer: Lord, I have operated with such a mind in the past. Thank You for saving me in spite of my insane conclusions about You and life. Amen.

December 22

The binding is loose and the fragile pages yellowed with age, but the precious Children's Bible that was passed down to me from many generations on my mother's side of the family is a treasure to me. It is over a hundred years old and replete with beautiful etchings of biblical events and people of renown.

Everything about it from the carefully engraved covers to the artistic lettering, along with the poignant and powerful etchings, emphasized to my young mind, the holiness, majesty, and reality of God and His Word. It brought reverence, love and awe for God into my innermost being.

I have to admit, I'm so thankful that my early impressions of the Lord Jesus Christ and biblical characters was beautiful, honest, majestic, truthful, tasteful, and realistic in, not only this big children's Bible, but church bulletins and Sunday school papers as well, instead of the ridiculous, cartoonish, silly and often downright ugly illustrative depictions of Jesus and the great men and women of the Bible that we find in today's ludicrous illustrations for impressionable minds and hearts. (And that includes the near-blasphemous Veggie Tales.)

When will Christians wake up to the fact that what children see (and hear) makes a lasting impression on their young minds and hearts, and that the church has willingly gone along with Satan's wiles? When will the church wake up to the dumbing down of, not only the youth, but adults as well, with corrupt Bible "versions," stupid "biblical" illustrations, and downright satanic music?

God have mercy on us! *"And unto man he said, Behold, the fear of the Lord, that is wisdom; and to depart from evil is understanding" (Job 28:28.) "Let all the earth fear the LORD: let all the inhabitants of the world stand in awe of him. (Psalm 33:8.) "The fear of the LORD is a fountain of life, to depart from the snares of death" (Proverbs 14:27) "And his mercy is on them that fear him from generation to generation" (Luke 1:30).* – J. Haley

Prayer: Lord, we were born with innocence to see Your beauty, the simplicity to understand Your great wisdom, and wonderment that would cause us to stand in awe of Your ways. Lord, we need to cease being a child in foolish ways, but we must remain a child in disposition so we will walk in a trusting faith of Your Word and ways. Amen.

December 23

"Unto the pure all things are pure, but unto them that are defiled and unbelieving is nothing pure, but even their mind and conscience is defiled" (Titus 1:16). I have witnessed the complete toll perversion takes on people. Perversion actually creates another reality that is void of any sense of purity. It can only consider everything from a warped sense of morality.

In a way, morality becomes a surreal state where nothing is real, legitimate, or trustworthy. Therefore, if anything serves the person's fleshly preference at the moment, any form of morality can be offered up on the altar of personal happiness or sensationalism.

When you consider where perversion has the greatest affect, it is on the mind and conscience. The mind is clouded by a twisted reality and the conscience has been seared by a hot iron of indifference. The only sense such people have is of the fleshly lusts of self. They have no consideration or concern of what they are doing to others. If something makes them happy, that is all that matters. After all, their world is okay.

Prayer: Lord, our perception about life is not trustworthy. Our minds must be changed by the power of Your Spirit. We need to take on Your disposition and attitude to develop a right mind towards the matters of life and Your kingdom. Amen.

December 24

It is Christmas Eve day. What do we need to consider to change what has pagan origins and has become so commercialized that people taste misery and not celebration? We know Christ came into this world because of a miraculous conception that involved Him being fashioned as man in the womb of a virgin. This is the reality that, as a believer, I should be pondering.

He came to become the Lamb of God to take my place on a cross so that life could be imparted in me. The Bible is clear that His death had to take place so I could have life. *"Verily, verily, I say unto you, Except a corn of wheat fall into the ground and die, it abideth alone: but if it die, it bringeth forth much fruit"* (John 12:24).

I continued to ponder the reality of the life in me, knowing another miracle is that it is Jesus' life in me. Even though the body will reflect the life within me, it is still a thin veneer. One day this thin veneer will part like a curtain and fall to the wayside as another law takes hold of my spirit and soul. I will be ushered into a different existence.

As I think of my outer shell, I cannot help but think that Jesus took on this veneer when He became man. For Jesus, the Living Word of heaven, to take on something that was surface, temporary, representative of the vainglory of the world, and would have to eventually be put aside is incredible to me.

There is nothing temporary about the eternal Son of God, yet He would take on the temporary. There is nothing vain in His glory, yet He would be exposed to that which proved to be empty, contrary, and hateful in its attitude towards Him.

Jesus taking on a body reminds me that I am responsible to manifest the gift of life. As I consider the life I have been given, I must examine if I am properly living out this life in the body that has been given to me, ensuring that I bring glory to Him.

.

Prayer: Lord, my prayer is that the curtain of my body will be parted by Your life to reveal Your glory to the lost, dying world. Amen.

December 25

It is Christmas today. I can imagine how excited the children are. They have waited in great expectation for this day and now they can open their presents and see what surprises await them.

As I consider Christmas, I have always sensed a special feeling of expectation. But, what expectation do I possess? When Jesus came the first time, people expected Him, but *John 1:11* lays out the reception He ultimately received, *"He came unto his own, and his own received him not."* The truth is they chose not to recognize Him. My question must be, what am I now expecting since I possess the greatest gift of all?

Jesus came into the world by way of a manger. His goal was to bring life, and I can honestly say I possess this life. I have been born again with the very eternal life of Christ. I already experienced the first advent with my new birth. But what am I expecting now?

In the past, I expected to have a certain feeling arise in me during the holiday season. It was a feeling of warmth towards God's gift, a feeling of goodness because of what God has done for me, a feeling of well-being because of who the Lord is in my life, and a sense of hope because of God's intrusion into the world, specifically into my life.

However, Christmas causes me to consider if I want to be sentimental towards Jesus or live in expectation of the blessed hope of His second coming. The sentimental notion calls for my flesh to be stirred up, while the second one requires my spirit to become active towards the hope, and my soul to be constantly made ready for such a time so that I can receive His blessing.

I pray that the latter is always true of me. It is time to leave the fleshly sentimental notions behind and go on to that which is greater and more satisfying in my life when it comes to my faith.

Prayer: Lord, You are always calling us to advance forward in faith toward that which is higher and more excellent. Steer me away from foolish sentiment and establish me in sobriety that will keep me grounded in You. Amen.

December 26

Christmas is for children, but it was not meant to create an ungrateful, covetous attitude produced by commercialism; rather, it was to produce a certain awe in them towards the greatest gift humanity has been offered through Jesus Christ. Paul stated, *"When I was a child, I spake as a child, I understood as a child, I thought as a child: but when I became a man, I put away childish things" (1 Corinthians 13:11).*

On the 26th day of December I often I take down all outdoor and indoor Christmas decorations unless weather or some other situation causes me to put it off. I remember when I was a child, I wanted to keep the Christmas decorations up as long as possible. My family usually didn't take them down until after New Year's. Emotionally I didn't want to let go of the holiday season, I wanted to hold on to it in some way.

As I grew older, I realized that I no longer hold to such a notion. You must let go of the past before you can embrace the present. Time will march on regardless of where I am in my personal journey.

After Christmas is over with, it is time to move on. Granted, I hate to see it go because it marks the passing of time and facing the unknown in regard to the future. However, each new year also represents an open door to possibilities of exploration and growth. It is obvious that I must quit thinking as a child of yesterday and embrace the challenges of personal growth like a mature adult.

I must go on if I am to finish this journey. Holding on to what could be or looking back to what was, would only create a stiff neck of unbelief and rebellion in me. I do not want to be compared to Lot's wife.

Prayer: Lord, I do not want to look back like Lot's wife to what was and will be no more. I want to always advance forward to what will be according to Your plan. Amen.

December 27

Paul stated, *"But I fear, lest by any means, as the serpent beguiled Eve through his subtilty, so your minds should be corrupted from the simplicity that is in Christ (2 Corinthians 11:3).* After all the hoopla surrounding the Christmas holiday, I have a tendency to think about much of the vanity that surrounds our celebration of Christmas. I know it is quite pagan.

We can console ourselves that it is a time of giving, but for many it is a nightmare where demands, traditions, and expectations can literally bury a person. It often reminds them of what they do not have, and the oppressive demands of those around them to keep up with the expectations of Christmas. As a result, it is not a time of rejoicing, but one of depression. After all, where is the homey Norman Rockwell setting portrayed in his paintings of the American experience? What does giving produce in people who know more about abundance and abuses than leanness and lack? Does it encourage a sense of appreciation and joy, or one of greater selfishness and ingratitude?

In all honesty, the Christian idea of Christmas has been overrun by pagan emphasis. Each year the mask is taken away to reveal that the happenings around Christmas is all a ploy of commercialism in its most pagan form. The eternal Christ has been substituted by an all-seeing, all-knowing Santa Clause. The gift of God has been replaced with a bombardment of advertisement as to what will make people happy on that day. Even though such happiness is temporary at best and illusive at worst, people are conditioned by a selfish emphasis to pursue after the promise of such ecstasy with great expectation.

As I consider each Christmas, I realize that the more pagan it becomes, the less sentiment I will have towards it. At such times I realize that I must come back to the simplicity of Christ as God taking on flesh to come into the world as a baby in order to become the Lamb of God to once again remember the reason that we believers have set this time apart.

Prayer: Lord, sentiments do not constitute good ground for the Christian life to be established upon. In fact, they represent shifting sand. Help me to truly be established on You. Amen.

December 28

While meditating on the happenings surrounding the holiday rush, I had to admit that it is humanistic in every way. It truly has become man-centered regardless of the Christmas songs, the nativity scene, and religious emphasis. It often creates greed, jealousy, and depression. It becomes a platform for the social gospel of

Socialism to take center stage as many go about doing good things for the less fortunate to level the playing field between the rich and the poor.

Don't get me wrong, I am for being charitable, but the motive behind such giving is not love and the attitude is not benevolent. It is all about making self feel better about self. As a result of such actions, goodness and decency takes on a militant pose that becomes critical towards those who simply possess something. It's as if it is a crime or a point of shame that any person would have a cup when there are those who have no cup. Therefore, the cup must be taken away from the one who has it to make the world fair. Even though the person who had the cup is without a cup the other person will now know what it feels like to possess a cup.

Such a philosophy makes all people poor, oppressed, and vulnerable to the tyranny of evil hearts and wicked Communistic agendas. The thing I love the most is that the cross of Christ makes all people equal. However, the cross also divides, revealing the heart condition of people.

Prayer: Lord, humanism allows for thievery from those with very little in order to oppress those who are even poorer. In the end, the very rich get richer, while those who have something are robbed of it and made paupers. Lord, thank You for being fair in all You do. Amen.

December 29

Each Christmas seems to mark a milestone in my spiritual life. A milestone can only be established by something that brings distinction to something. For example, the mileposts alongside the highways mark a particular mile. They help to identify the location for the traveler or police in case of trouble.

The reason Christmas marks such a milestone is because it is easy to take much time to prepare for the celebration. To me it allots the opportunity to mark the progression of the life of Christ in me.

The Apostle Paul reminds me of this in *Colossians 1:27, To whom God would make known what is the riches of the glory of this mystery among the Gentiles; which is Christ in you, the hope of glory."* I try to examine myself as to accomplishments in relationship with the Lord and His kingdom work. In fact, I try to double my activities to finish projects before the year is out.

In my mind if I finish my projects, I will be able to celebrate the season in a special way. I will offer such projects as a gift back to the Lord for His use and glory. Once a project is completed, I can advance forward in other areas.

Christ must always mark the dividing point in our lives. We must take note of where we have come from, take stock as to where we are, and take inventory as to of whether we are prepared to go forward. It is this type of examination that allows me to face the New Year. I can be confident that I am on the right track going into the next year.

Prayer: Lord, keep me from taking detours in my life in the coming year. Help me keep focus on You as I follow You into uncertain times. Amen.

December 30

We used to live by Priest River. I have often wondered what determines the change in the river. One day, a long-time resident, informed me that there are various dams located at its sources, as well as some of its tributaries that affect its flow.

Jesus stated, *"But whosoever drinketh of the water that I shall give him shall never thirst; but the water that I shall give him shall be in him a well of water springing up into everlasting life" (John 4:14).* The Holy Spirit is the Rivers of Living Water that not only flows down from heaven, but needs to freely flow through our inner beings. After all, being born again points to Jesus uncapping that inner flow in your innermost being.

Through the years I have been aware of the various dams in my life that have hindered the flow of the Spirit. It is true that I have adjusted to these dams, and I continue to figure out ways around them. However, the reality is that when the flow of the Spirit is hindered, the quality of my life will be taken down several notches. I will not experience rest, victory, and peace. There will always be a restlessness that must flow around any obstacles, which causes me to lose a sense of my rest, purpose, and destiny.

It is for this reason that as I move into a new year, I want the dams removed so that the Spirit of my life can flow throughout the corridors of my soul into the depths of my spirit. I also so want to be in the flow of the Spirit and not allowing any dam hindering my advancement in any way so that I can be effective for the Lord's kingdom.

Prayer: Lord, there are so many hindrances that can exist in the soul. You have my permission to knock each one of them down so that the flow of Your Spirit will not be hindered in any way. Amen.

December 31

What are you looking forward to? Today marks the last day of the year. It is a time of looking back as well as looking forward. Looking back allows us to examine what we did with the gift of our life and looking forward allows us to consider how to advance forward. For some, this time marks despair and sorrow because the past was dark and the future bleak.

The Apostle Paul was facing his physical death when he wrote this, *"Henceforth there is laid up for me a crown of righteousness, which the Lord, the righteous judge, shall give me at that day: and not to me only, but unto all them also that love his appearing (2 Timothy 4:8).* For believers, the future holds great expectation for us, not bleakness.

Even though every year brings us to uncertainty in this present world, we can walk in blessed hope knowing each year brings us closer to Jesus' Second Advent. His blessed return is the only thing we can be sure of in this present world. It will be then that we will realize the fullness of our redemption.

As I face the New Year, there are some special events that could mark beneficial possibilities in the midst of what appears to be an all-consuming darkness. However, I know that hope in anything of the world will prove to be disillusionment at best and destruction at worst.

It is for this reason that I must choose to make the subject of my hope and expectation Jesus Christ. I cannot imagine going into the New Year without the expectation of Christ coming again. Each year simply reminds me that my opportunity to gain more of Christ is before me as I strive to make Him my all in all.

Prayer: Lord, I can never be assured of tomorrow in this world, but I can be confident that one day the clouds will part and You will come in the clouds to fulfill all of Your promises. Even so, come quickly. Amen.

About the Authors

Rayola Kelley and Jeannette Haley are ordained ministers of the Gospel. Rayola was born-again and saved out of a cult in 1976 while serving in the U.S. Navy. Her spiritual journey continued through extensive discipleship, before following the Lord's call upon her life into full-time ministry 30 years ago, when, with Jeannette Haley, she founded Gentle Shepherd Ministries in 1989.

Jeannette was born in Seattle, and is a gifted artist and teacher that has used her various talents to faithfully, and at times, boldly share her faith. She has written Bible studies, Christian fiction and books for children that contain a strong Gospel message.

Through the years, both ladies' gift of teaching the Word has opened many doors for them to teach adult Sunday school, oversee a fellowship for many years, hold evangelistic meetings in churches, conduct seminars, and speak at retreats. They have served in jail ministry, and are well known for gifts of spiritual insight, encouragement, and counseling. Upon being called to be missionaries in America, Rayola and Jeannette established different fellowships where intense Bible Studies and discipleship training were conducted to equip believers for the ministry. These different mission fields in America entailed working in various churches as well as working with other cultures such as the Korean and Hispanic nationalities.

Rayola and Jeannette began sending out a monthly newsletter containing articles for the Body of Christ in 1997 which continues to grow. Ms. Kelley has authored over 55 books, and numerous Bible Studies including an advanced Discipleship Course (available in both English and Spanish) that is being used in countries such as Africa, Bulgaria, Israel, Ireland, India, Cuba, and Pakistan. Among her many books is *"Hidden Manna"* which deals with destructive cycles in people and relationships, and *"Battle for the Soul"* which presents a clear picture of the battle that rages in the soul. She has written seven in-depth devotional books, including both the Old Testament and New Testament devotional study which takes the reader through the entire Bible in one year. All of her books are hard-hitting, bottom-line spiritual food for the hungry and thirsty soul to "chew" upon in order to *"grow strong in the Lord, and in the power of His might."*

Both Rayola and Jeannette currently reside in Northern Idaho where they continue to fulfill Christ's commission to make disciples through teaching, spiritual counseling, and through the internet and publications.

Please visit Gentle Shepherd Ministries Web Site at: www.gentleshepherd.com for further information, and to access Rayola's challenging and informative audio sermons.

Other books by Rayola Kelley:

Hidden Manna (Original)
Battle for the Soul
Stories of the Heart
Transforming Love & Beyond
The Great Debate
Post to Post: (1) Establishing the Way
Post to Post: (2) Walking in the Way

Volume One: Establishing Our Life in Christ

My Words are Spirit and Life
The Anatomy of Sin
The Principles of the Abundant Life
The Place of Covenant
Unmasking the Cult Mentality

Volume Two: Putting on the Life of Christ

He Actually Thought it Not Robbery
Revelation of the Cross
In Search of Real Faith
Think on These Things
Follow the Pattern

Volume Three: Developing a Godly Environment

Godly Discipline
Prayer and Worship
Don't Touch That Dial
Face of Thankfulness
ABC's of Christianity

Volume Four: Issues of the Heart

Hidden Manna (Revised)
Bring Down the Sacred Cows
The Manual for the Single Christian Life
Parents are People Too

Volume Five: Challenging the Christian Life

The Issues of Life
Presentation of the Gospel
For the Purpose of Edification
Whatever Happened to the Church?
Women's Place in the Kingdom of God

Volume Six: Developing Our Christian Life

The Many Faces of Christianity
Possessing Our Souls
Experiencing the Christian Life
The Power of Our Testimonies
The Victorious Journey

Volume Seven: Discovering True Ministry
From Prisons and Dots to Christianity
So You Want To Be In Ministry

Devotions
Devotions of the Heart: Books One and Two
Daily Food for the Soul: Books One and Two

Gentle Shepherd Ministries Devotion Series:
Being a Child of God
Disciplining the Strength of our Youth
Coming to Full Age

Nugget Books:
Nuggets From Heaven
More Nuggets From Heaven
Heavenly Gems
More Heavenly Gems
Heavenly Treasures

Gentle Shepherd Ministries Series:

The Christian Life Series
What Matter Is This?
The Challenge of It
The Reality of It
The Leadership Series
Overcoming
A Matter of Authority and Power
The Dynamics of True Leadership

Other Books By:
Jeannette Haley
Books co-authored with Rayola Kelley:
Hidden Manna (original)
The Many Faces of Christianity (Volume 6)
Discovering True Ministry: Volume 7

Other Books:
The Pig and I
Reflections of Wonder (Devotional)

Children's Books:
Little Stories for Little People
Traveler's Tales
The Adventures of Zack and Mira
The Adventures of Paul and Dana
(A House on the Beach)
The Monster of Mystery Valley

www.ingramcontent.com/pod-product-compliance
Lightning Source LLC
Chambersburg PA
CBHW060237100426
42742CB00011B/1559